Whoso Findeth a Wife

by

William Le Queux

Whoso Findeth a Wife
by William Le Queux

Copyright © 2023

All Rights reserved.

ISBN: 978-93-59955-12-4

Published by

DOUBLE 9 BOOKS
2/13-B, Ansari Road
Daryaganj, New Delhi – 110002
info@double9books.com
www.double9books.com
Tel. 011-40042856

ABOUT THE AUTHOR

Anglo-French journalist and author William Tufnell Le Queux was born on July 2, 1864, and died on October 13, 1927. He was also a diplomat (honorary consul for San Marino), a traveler (in Europe, the Balkans, and North Africa), a fan of flying (he presided over the first British air meeting at Doncaster in 1909), and a wireless pioneer who played music on his own station long before radio was widely available. However, he often exaggerated his own skills and accomplishments. The Great War in England in 1897 (1894), a fantasy about an invasion by France and Russia, and The Invasion of 1910 (1906), a fantasy about an invasion by Germany, are his best-known works. Le Queux was born in the city. The man who raised him was English, and his father was French. He went to school in Europe and learned art in Paris from Ignazio (or Ignace) Spiridon. As a young man, he walked across Europe and then made a living by writing for French newspapers. He moved back to London in the late 1880s and managed the magazines Gossip and Piccadilly. In 1891, he became a parliamentary reporter for The Globe. He stopped working as a reporter in 1893 to focus on writing and traveling.

CONTENTS

Chapter One
A State Secret

"Whoso findeth a wife findeth a good thing, and obtaineth favour of the Lord." —Proverbs xviii, 22.

"Have those urgent dispatches come in from Berlin, Deedes?"

"Captain Hammerton has not yet arrived," I answered.

"Eleven o'clock! Tut, tut! Every moment's delay means greater risk," and the Earl of Warnham, Her Majesty's Principal Secretary of State for Foreign Affairs, strode up and down his private room, with his hat still on, impatiently snapping his bony fingers in agitation quite unusual to him.

"Hammerton wired from Berlin yesterday, when on the point of leaving," I observed, taking a telegram from the table before me.

"In cipher?"

"Yes."

"No accident is reported in the papers, I suppose?"

"Nothing in the *Times*," I replied.

"Strange, very strange, that he should be so long overdue," the Earl said, at last casting himself into his padded chair, and lounging back, his hands thrust deep into his pockets as he stared thoughtfully into space.

I resumed my writing, puzzled at the cause of the chief's excited demeanour, but a few moments later sharp footsteps sounded outside in the corridor, followed by a loud rapping, and there entered the messenger, clad in his heavy fur-lined travelling coat, although a July morning, and carrying a well-worn leather dispatch-box, which he placed upon my table.

"Late, Hammerton. Very late," snapped the Earl, glancing at his watch.

"There's a dense fog in the Channel, your Lordship, and we were compelled to come across dead slow the whole distance. I've driven straight from the station," the Captain answered good-humouredly, looking so spruce and well-groomed that few would credit he had been travelling for nearly twenty-four hours.

"Go and rest. You must return to-night," his Lordship said testily.

"At seven-thirty?"

"Yes, at my house in Berkeley Square."

Then, taking up the receipt I had signed for the dispatch-box, the messenger, to whom a journey to Constantinople or St Petersburg was about as fatiguing as a ride on the Underground Railway is to ordinary persons, walked jauntily out, wishing us both good-day.

When the door had closed, Lord Warnham quickly opened the outer case with his key, and drew forth a second box, covered with red morocco, and securely sealed. This he also opened, and, after rummaging for some moments among a quantity of papers, exclaimed, in a tone of satisfaction, —

"Ah! Here it is. Good! Seals not tampered with."

Withdrawing from the box a large official envelope, doubly secured with the seal of the British Embassy at Berlin, and endorsed by Sir Philip Emden, our Ambassador, he walked hastily to one of the long windows overlooking the paved courtyard of the Foreign Office, and for some moments closely scrutinised both seals and signature.

"Did you fear that the papers might have been examined in transit?" I inquired of my grave-faced chief in surprise.

"No, Deedes, no. Not at all," he answered, returning to his table, cutting open the envelope, and giving a rapid glance at its contents to assure himself that it was the same document he had sent to the German capital a week before. "Hammerton is trustworthy, and while dispatches are in his care I have no fear. The only apprehension I had was that an attempt might possibly have been made to ascertain the nature of this treaty," the great statesman added, indicating the document beneath his hand.

"The result would be detrimental?" I hazarded.

"Detrimental!" he cried. "If the clauses of this secret defensive alliance became known to our enemies war would be inevitable. Russia and France would combine, and the whole of the Powers would become embroiled within a week. Exposure of these secret negotiations would be absolutely disastrous. It would, I verily believe, mean irretrievable ruin to England's prestige and perhaps to her power."

He uttered the ominous words slowly and distinctly, then carefully refolding the precious document, with its string of sprawly signatures, he placed it in another envelope, sealing it with his own private seal.

The great statesman, the greatest Foreign Minister of his time, upon whose tact, judgment and forethought the peace and prosperity of England mainly depended, was tall and thin, with scanty, white hair, a pale, refined face, slightly wizened by age, deep-sunken, steely eyes, shaggy brows, a sharp, straight nose, and a breadth of forehead indicating indomitable perseverance and an iron will. His reputation as brilliant orator and shrewd and skilful diplomat was a household word throughout the civilised world, whilst in our own land confidence always increased when he was at the head of Foreign Affairs. As his confidential private secretary, I, Geoffrey Deedes, had daily opportunities of observing how conscientiously he served his Sovereign and his country, and how amazing was his capacity for work. With him, duty was always of paramount consideration; he worked night and day to sustain England's honour and welfare, for times without number I had gone to his great gloomy house in Berkeley Square in the middle of the night and roused him from his bed to attend to urgent dispatches.

Although a perfect martinet towards many in the various departments of the Foreign Office, he was to me always kind and generous. My father, Sir Reginald Deedes, had, as many will doubtless remember, represented Her Majesty at the Netherlands Court for fifteen years until his death. He was thus an old friend of the Earl, and it was this friendship that caused him to appoint me five years ago his private secretary, and, much to the chagrin of young Lord Gaysford, the Under Secretary, repose such implicit confidence in me that very frequently he entrusted to my care the keys of the ponderous safe wherein were deposited the State secrets of the nation.

"You'd better register this, and we'll lock it away from prying eyes at once," Lord Warnham said a few moments later, handing me the envelope after he had sealed it. Taking it, I went straight to my own room across the corridor at the head of the fine central staircase. It was part of my duty to receive the more important dispatches, number those which were sealed, and prior to depositing them in the safe, register the number in my book, stating the source whence they came, the date received, and the name of the messenger who brought them.

Alone in my room, I closed the door, took the register from my own small safe, numbered the precious envelope with the designation "B27,893," and carefully made an entry in the book. Having finished, a clerk brought me two letters from other Departments, both of which needed immediate replies, therefore I sat down and scribbled them while he waited. Then, having been absent from the Chief's room nearly a quarter of an hour, I went back with the dispatch in my hand. In the room I found Lord Gaysford, who, in reply to my question, stated that the Earl had been compelled to leave in order to attend a meeting of the Cabinet, which he believed would be a protracted one.

To me this was provoking, for the great statesman had taken with him the key of the safe; thus was I left with this important document in my possession. But I said nothing of the matter to the Under Secretary, and returning to my room placed the dispatch in my inner pocket for greater security, determined to keep it there until his Lordship returned. I feared to lock it away in my own safe lest anyone else might possess a key, and felt that in the circumstances my own pocket was the safest place.

For nearly two hours I continued my work, it being Friday, an unusually busy day, until, just as the clock at the Horse Guards chimed one o'clock, a clerk entered with the card of Dudley Ogle, my college chum, with whom I was now sharing, during the summer months, a cottage close to the Thames at Shepperton. On the card was the pencilled query, "Can you come and lunch with me?"

For a few moments I hesitated. I was busy, and I was compelled to deliver the dispatch in my pocket to Lord Warnham before he left for home. I knew, however, that the meeting of the Cabinet must be a long one, and recognising the fact that I must lunch somewhere, I gave the clerk a message that I would join Mr Ogle in the waiting-room in a few moments. Then, locking my safe, I assured myself that the dispatch was still in my pocket, brushed my hat, and joined my friend.

Dudley Ogle was the best of good fellows. After a rather wild college career, it had been his fancy to roam for about two years on the Continent, and on his return, his father, with whom he was not on the best of terms, conveniently died, leaving him possessor of about twenty thousand pounds. By this time he had, however, sown his wild oats, and instead of spending his money as most young men of his age would have done, he invested it, and now lived a careless, indolent existence, travelling where he pleased, and getting as much enjoyment out of life as was possible. He was about my own age—twenty-eight, well set-up, smart-looking, with rather aquiline features, dark hair, and a pair of merry eyes that were an index to a contented mind.

"Didn't expect me, I suppose, old fellow?" he exclaimed breezily, when we met. "I found after you'd left this morning that I was compelled to come up to town, and having nothing to do for an hour or so, it occurred to me that we might lunch together."

"I thought you intended to pull up as far as 'The Nook,'" I said, laughing.

"So I did, but I received a wire calling me to town on some rather urgent business. Where shall we lunch?"

In descending the stairs and turning into Downing Street we discussed the merits of various restaurants, and finally decided upon a small, old-fashioned, unpretentious, but well-known place a few doors from Charing Cross, in the direction of Whitehall, known as "The Ship." Here we ate our meal, spent an hour together, and then parted, he leaving to return to Shepperton, I to finish my work and rejoin him later at our riparian cottage.

On my return to the Foreign Office the Earl had, I found, just come in, and I handed him the secret document which some day, sooner or later, would control the destiny of an empire.

"This has, of course, not been out of your possession, Deedes?" inquired his Lordship, looking keenly at me with his grey eyes, as he stood before the open door of the great safe.

"Not for a single instant," I replied.

"Good. I trust you," he said, carefully placing the sealed envelope in a pigeon-hole to itself, and closing the door with a loud clang, locked it.

"I think," he said, his ascetic features relaxing into a self-satisfied smile, "I think we have once again checkmated our enemies, and swiftly too. The whole thing has been arranged and concluded within a week, thanks to the clever diplomacy of Emden at Berlin."

"And to your own forethought," I added, laughing.

"No, no. To Emden all credit is due, none to me, none," he answered modestly; then, turning, he gave me some instructions, and a few minutes later put on his hat and left for home. At four o'clock I also left, and driving to Waterloo, caught my train to Shepperton, where I found Dudley Ogle awaiting me. Ours was a pretty cottage. Facing the river, it was covered with creepers, sweet-smelling jasmine and roses, with a rustic porch in front, and a large old-world garden around. Life was delightful there after the stuffiness of London chambers, and as we both had with us our men, in addition to Mrs Franks, my trusty housekeeper, we were prevented from being troubled by the minor worries of life.

"Hulloa, old chap!" cried Dudley, hastily rousing himself from a lazy attitude on the couch in our sitting-room as I entered. "Stifling hot, isn't it? There's a wire from the Laings. They want us to dine with them to-night. Going?"

I hesitated, and my reluctance did not escape him.

"Isn't Ella's company sufficient inducement?" he asked chaffingly.

"Going? Of course I am," I answered quickly, glancing at my watch. "We have a full hour before dressing. Let's go for a row. It'll improve our appetites."

Within a few minutes I had exchanged the frock coat of officialdom for flannels, and very soon we were pulling upstream towards a delightful backwater that was our goal. As we rowed, the silence being broken only by the sound of the oars in the row-locks, I calmly reviewed the situation. Why the Laings invited me that night puzzled me. Truth to tell, I loved Ella Laing with all the strength of my being, and had foolishly believed she reciprocated my affection until two nights ago, when I had called at the house near Staines, where she lived with her mother during the summer months. I had discovered her in the garden walking in lover-like attitude with Andrew Beck, a retired silk manufacturer, who had lived in France so long that he had become something of a cosmopolitan, and who had lately entered Parliament at a bye-election as representative of West Rutlandshire. I confess to having conceived an instinctive dislike to this man from the very first moment we had been introduced by a mutual friend in the Lobby of the House of Commons, for he was a parvenu of the most pronounced type, while his grey, beetling brows and flat, broad nose gave his face an expression anything but pleasing.

Nevertheless he walked jauntily, spoke loudly in bluff good-natured tones, gave excellent dinners, and, strangely enough, was voted a good fellow wherever he went. Yet there was an ostentatiousness about his actions that was sickening; his arrogant, self-assertive manner was, to me, extremely distasteful. The discovery that he was endeavouring to supplant me in Ella's affections filled my cup of indignation to the full.

I had left the garden unobserved on that fateful night, returned at once to our riverside cottage, and written her an angry letter, charging her in plain terms with having played me false. In reply, next morning she sent by the gardener a long letter full of mild reproach, in which she asserted that she had no thought of love for anyone beside myself, and that I had entirely misconstrued her relations with Mr Beck. "Strange, indeed, it is that you, of all men, should declare that I love him," she wrote. "Love! If you knew all, you would neither write nor utter that sacred word to me; and even though you are the only man for whom I have a thought, it may, after all, be best if we never again meet. You say you cannot trust me further. Well, I can only reply that my future happiness is in your hands. I am yours."

Deeply had I pondered over this curious, half-hysterical, half-reproachful letter, re-reading it many many times, and becoming more and more puzzled over its vague, mysterious meaning. On several occasions I had been upon the point of calling and questioning her, but had refrained. Now, however, this formal invitation to dine had come no doubt through Ella, and I saw in it her desire to personally explain away my jealousy. So I accepted.

Chapter Two
"The Nook"

When, a couple of hours later, we entered Mrs Laing's garden, the first person we encountered was the man I hated, Andrew Beck, in his ill-fitting dress clothes and broad, crumpled shirt-front, with its great diamond solitaire, lounging in a wicker chair at the river's brink, smoking, and in solitude enjoying the glorious sunset that, reflecting upon the water, transformed it into a stream of rippling gold. "The Nook," as Mrs Laing's house was called, was a charming old place facing the river at a little distance above Staines Bridge—long, low, completely covered with ivy and surrounded by a wide sweep of lawn that sloped down to the water's edge, and a belt of old elms beneath the cool shade of which I had spent many delightfully lazy afternoons by the side of my well-beloved.

"Ah! Deedes," exclaimed Beck, gaily, rising as we approached, "I was waiting for somebody to come. The ladies haven't come down yet."

"Have you seen them?" I asked.

"Not yet," he replied; then turning to my friend Dudley, he began chaffing him about a young and wealthy widow he had rowed up to Windsor in our boat a few days before.

"We saw you, my boy. We saw you?" he laughed. "You were talking so confidentially as you passed, that Ella remarked that you were contemplating stepping into the dead man's shoes."

"No, no," Dudley retorted good-humouredly. "No widows for me. She was merely left under my care for an hour or so, and I had to do the amicable. It's really too bad of you all to jump to such rash conclusions."

At that instant a soft, musical voice behind me uttered my name, and, turning, I met Ella, with a light wrap thrown about her shoulders, coming forward to me with outstretched hand. "Ah! Geoffrey, how are you?" she cried gaily, with joy in her brilliant, sparkling eyes. Then, as our hands clasped, she added in an undertone, "I knew you would come; I knew you would forgive."

"I have not forgiven," I answered, rather coldly, bending over her slim white hand.

"But I have committed no fault," she said, pouting prettily.

"You have given me no satisfactory explanation."

"Wait until after dinner. We will come out here together, where we can talk without being overheard," she whispered hurriedly, then left me abruptly to greet Dudley and Andrew Beck. There was something significant in the swift, inquisitive glance she exchanged with the last-named man, and turning away I strode across the lawn annoyed. A moment later I met Mrs Laing herself. She was elderly and effusive; tall, and of stately bearing. Her hair was perfectly white but by no means scanty, her face was clever and refined without that grossness that too often disfigures a well-preserved woman of fifty, and in her dark eyes, undimmed by time, there was always an expression of calm contentment. Her husband had been a great traveller until his death ten years ago, and she, accompanying him on his journeys in the East, had become a clever linguist, an accomplishment which her only daughter, Ella, shared.

As we stood together chatting, and watching the boats full of happy youths and maidens gliding past in the brilliant afterglow, I thought that never had I seen Ella looking so handsome, as, standing with Dudley, she had taken up Beck's theme, and was congratulating him upon his trip with the skittish widow.

Hers was an oval face, perfect in its symmetry, clear cut and refined, a trifle pale perhaps, but from her eyes of that darkest blue that sometimes sparkled into the brightness of a sapphire, sometimes deepened into softest grey like the sky on a summer night, there shone an inner beauty, indicative of a purity of soul. The mouth was mobile, short and full, with an exquisite finish about the curve of the lips, the nose short and straight, and the hair of darkest gold—the gold that cannot be produced artificially, but has a slight dash of red in it, just sufficient to enrich the brown of the shadows and give a burnish to the ripples in the high lights. Her eyebrows were set rather high up from the eye itself, and were slightly drooped at the corner nearest the ear, imparting to her face a kind of plaintive, questioning look that was exceedingly becoming to her. Her gown was of soft clinging silk of palest heliotrope, that bore the unmistakable stamp of Paris, while on her slim wrist I noticed she wore the diamond bangle I had given her six months before. As she chatted with Dudley, she turned and laughed at me gaily over her shoulder from time to time, and when we entered the house a few minutes later, it was with satisfaction that I found myself placed beside her at table.

Dinner was always a pleasant, if slightly stately, meal at Mrs Laing's. She was a brilliant and accomplished hostess, whose entertainments at her house in Pont Street were always popular, and who surrounded herself with interesting and intellectual people. Bohemia was generally well represented at her receptions, for the lions of the season, whether literary, artistic, or musical, were always to be met there—a fact which induced many of the more exclusive set to honour the merry widow by their presence. Wearied, however, of the eternal small talk about new books, new plays, new pictures, and the newest fads, I was glad when, after smoking, we were free to rejoin the ladies in the quaint, oak-panelled drawing-room.

The moon had risen, and ere long I strolled with Ella through the French windows, and out upon the lawn, eager to talk alone with her.

"Well," she said at length, when we were seated in the shadow beneath one of the high rustling elms, "so you want an explanation. What can I give?"

"Your letter conveys the suspicion that there exists some secret between Beck and yourself," I said, as calmly as I could.

"My letter!" she exclaimed, in a voice that seemed a little harsh and strained. "What did I say? I really forget."

"It's useless to prevaricate, Ella," I said, rather impatiently. "You say that if I knew all I would never utter words of love to you. What do you mean?"

"Exactly what I wrote," she answered huskily, in a low voice.

"You mean to imply that you are unworthy of the love of an honest man?" I observed in astonishment.

"Yes," she gasped hoarsely. "I do not—I—cannot deceive you, Geoffrey, because I love you." The last sentence she uttered passionately, with a fierce fire burning in her eyes. "You are jealous of Andrew Beck, a man old enough to be my father. Well, I confess I was foolish to allow him to walk with me here with his arm around my waist; yet at that moment the indiscretion did not occur to me."

"But he was speaking to you—whispering into your ready ears words of love and tenderness. He spoke in persuasive tones, as if begging you to become his wife," I said angrily, the very thought of the scene I had witnessed filling me with indignation and bitter hatred.

"No, you are entirely mistaken, Geoffrey. No word of love passed between us," she said quietly, looking into my eyes with unwavering glance.

I smiled incredulously.

"You will perhaps deny that here, within six yards of this very spot, you stopped and burst forth into tears?" I exclaimed, with cold cynicism.

"I admit that. The words he uttered were of sufficient significance to bring tears to my eyes," she replied vaguely.

"He must have spoken words of love to you," I argued. "I watched you both."

"I deny that he did, Geoffrey," she cried fiercely, starting up. "To satisfy you, I am even ready to take an oath before my Creator that the subject of our conversation was not love."

"What was Beck persuading you to do?" I demanded.

"No, no," she cried, as if the very thought was repulsive to her. "No, do not ask me. I can never tell you, never!"

"Then there is a secret between you that you decline to reveal," I said reproachfully.

She laughed a harsh metallic laugh, answering in a tone of feigned flippancy,—

"Really, Geoffrey, you are absurdly and unreasonably suspicious. I tell you I love no other man but yourself, yet merely because it pleases you to misconstrue what you have witnessed you brand me as base and faithless. It is unjust."

"But your letter!" I cried.

"I had no intention of conveying the idea that any secret existed between Mr Beck and myself. He was, as you well know, an old friend of my father's, and has known me since a child. Towards me he is always friendly and good-natured, but I swear he has never spoken to me of love."

"But you cannot deny, Ella, that a secret—some fact that you are determined to keep from me—exists, and that if not of love, it was of that secret Beck spoke to you so earnestly in the garden here!"

Her dry lips moved, but no sound escaped them. She shivered. I saw my question had entirely nonplussed her, and I felt instinctively that I had uttered the truth.

At that instant, however, a servant crossed the lawn in the moonlight, and approaching, handed me a telegram, stating that Juckes, my man, had brought it over from Shepperton, fearing that it might be of importance.

Hastily I thrust it into my pocket unopened, and when the servant was out of hearing I repeated the plain question I had put to my well-beloved.

In the bright moonlight I watched how pale and agitated was her face, while involuntarily she shuddered, as if the thought that I might ascertain the truth terrified her.

"Geoffrey," she said at last, in a low, plaintive voice as, sitting beside me, her slim fingers suddenly closed convulsively upon mine, "why cannot you trust me, when you know I love you so dearly?"

"Why cannot you tell me the truth instead of evading it? You say you are unworthy of my love. Why?"

"I—I cannot tell you," she cried wildly, breaking into hysterical sobs. "Ah! You do not know how I have suffered, Geoffrey, or you would not speak thus to me. If you can no longer trust me, then we must, alas! part. But if we do, I shall think ever of you as one who misjudged me and cast me off, merely because of my inability to give you an explanation of one simple incident."

"But I love you, Ella," I cried. "Why should we part—why should—"

"Hulloa, Deedes!" interrupted Beck's high-pitched, genial voice. "I've been looking for you everywhere. We're all going for a moonlight row. Come along."

Further conversation was, I saw, out of the question, and a few minutes later we had all embarked, with the exception of Mrs Laing, and were gliding slowly down the stream, now glittering in the brilliant moonbeams. Dudley had brought Ella's mandoline from the house, and as our prow cut the rippling waters he played a soft, charming gondolier's song. My love sat beside me in the stern, and her eyes mutely asked forgiveness as ever and anon she turned to me. I saw how beautiful she was, how full of delicate grace, and how varying were her moods; yet she seemed nervous, highly-strung, with a strange harshness in her voice that I had never before noticed. She spoke no word to Beck, and I remarked within myself that she avoided him, while once, when he leant over to grasp her hand, she shrank shudderingly from its contact.

An hour later, when, after rowing down to Laleham, we had returned to the "Nook" and, at the instigation of the ladies, were enjoying cigars, I accidentally placed my hand in the breast-pocket of my dress-coat and there felt the telegram which I had until that moment entirely forgotten. Opening it, I was amazed to find it in cipher. The cipher signature was that of the Earl of Warnham, and I saw it had been transmitted over the private wire from Warnham, his seat in Sussex.

Taking a pencil from my pocket I at once proceeded to transcribe the mysterious array of letters, and when I at last discovered the purport of the message, I sat back in my chair, breathless and rigid, while the flimsy paper nearly fell from my nerveless fingers.

"Why, Geoffrey!" cried Ella, starting up in alarm and rushing towards me, "what's the matter? You are as pale as death. Have you had bad news?"

"Bad news!" I answered, trying to laugh and slowly rousing myself. "No bad news at all, except that I must leave for town at once."

"Well, you certainly look as if you've been hard hit over a race," Beck exclaimed, laughing.

"You can't possibly get a train now till 11:30. It's hardly ten yet," said my well-beloved, exchanging a strange, mysterious glance with Dudley.

"Then I must go by that," I answered, again re-reading the pink paper, replacing it in my pocket, and endeavouring to preserve an outward calm.

Presently, when Ella was again alone with me, her first question was,—

"What bad news have you received, Geoffrey?"

"None," I answered, smiling. "It is a private matter, of really no importance at all."

"Oh, I thought it must have been something very, very serious, your hand trembled so, and you turned so pale."

"Did I?" I laughed cheerily. "Well, it's nothing, dearest; nothing at all."

Thus reassured, she continued to chat with that bright vivacity that was one of her most engaging characteristics. I have, however, no idea of what she said; I only answered her mechanically, for I was too full of gloomy apprehensions to heed her gossip, even though I loved her with all my soul.

Half-an-hour later, Dudley, finding that I had to go to town, announced his intention of walking back to Shepperton.

"The night is lovely, and the moon bright as day," he said, as we all shook hands with him in the hall. "I shall enjoy the walk."

"Beware of widows!" shouted Beck, standing at the top of the wide flight of steps.

We all laughed heartily.

"None about to-night," my friend shouted back good-humouredly, and, setting out briskly, disappeared a moment later down the long, winding carriage drive.

"It's really too bad to tease Mr Ogle about widows," Ella protested when we went in.

"He enjoys the joke hugely," I said. "Dudley's an excellent fellow. I've never in my life seen him out of temper."

"In that case he ought to make a good husband," she replied, laughing, as together we all entered Mrs Laing's pretty drawing-room, with its shaded lamps and cosy-corners, where we spent another three-quarters of an hour chatting until, finding we had just time to catch our train, Beck and I made our adieux. When I shook hands with Ella she whispered an earnest appeal for forgiveness, which, truth to tell, I feigned not to hear. Then we parted.

With Beck at my side, I walked sharply down the drive, rendered dark by the thick canopy of trees overhead, and had almost gained the gate leading to the high road when suddenly, catching my foot against some unseen object in the pathway, I fell heavily forward upon the gravel, just managing to save my face by putting out both hands.

"Hulloa!" cried Beck; "what's the matter?"

"The matter!" I gasped, groping at the mysterious object quickly with my hands. "I believe I've fallen over somebody."

"Drunk, I suppose. Come along, or we sha'n't catch our train."

But, still kneeling, I quickly took my vestas from my pocket and struck one. By its fitful light I distinguished the prostrate body of a man lying face downwards, with arms outstretched beyond his head. Turning him over with difficulty, I lit another vesta and held it close down to his face.

Next second I drew back with a loud cry of dismay and horror. It was Dudley Ogle.

His bloodless features were hideously distorted, his limbs rigid, his wildly-staring eyes were already glazed, and his stiffened fingers icy cold.

In an instant I knew the truth. He was dead.

Chapter Three
A Mystery

"Why!" gasped Beck, recognising the cold, drawn features by the light of the match he struck. "It's Dudley! Run back to the house and get assistance quickly. I'll remain here. Life may not be extinct after all, poor fellow!" At this suggestion I sprang up, and dashing away along the drive, burst into the drawing-room from the lawn.

"Geoffrey!" cried Mrs Laing, starting up quickly from a cosy-corner wherein she had settled to read. "What has happened? You look scared."

"A very painful thing has occurred," I gasped breathlessly, striving to preserve a calm demeanour. "We have found poor Dudley lying in the drive yonder. He's dead!"

"Dead!" she screamed hysterically. "Dudley dead!"

"Yes, alas!" I replied. "Beck is with him, awaiting assistance."

"I can't believe it," she cried, clutching at a chair for support. Her face was ashen pale, and her bejewelled hands trembled violently. "Poor Dudley! If he is dead, it is certain that he has been the victim of foul play," she added mechanically, in a low tone. Then suddenly recovering herself, she inquired the circumstances in which we had found him.

"I will explain later," I cried impatiently. "May I ring for the servants?"

"No," she cried, starting forward with a strange, wild look. "Return to him, and leave all to me. For the present the truth must be kept from Ella. There are reasons why my daughter should not know of this tragic affair until to-morrow. As you are aware, she is weak and unstrung to-night, and has already gone to her room. I fear that any sudden shock may prove extremely detrimental to her, and I therefore trust you will respect my wishes."

"Certainly," I answered. "But we are not yet convinced that life is extinct, so while you arrange for his removal here, I'll go at once for a doctor."

"Yes, do. Dr Allenby is nearest. The first house over the bridge," she replied hastily, and as she rang the bell I sprang out again upon the lawn and rushed away along the drive.

Beck was still kneeling beside the prostrate man, supporting his head upon his knee, and approaching, I asked whether he had detected any signs of respiration.

"None whatever," he answered. "I'm afraid, poor fellow, he has gone."

Briefly I explained my errand and rushed off for medical assistance, returning to "The Nook" with the grey-haired practitioner a quarter of an hour later. We found Dudley lying in the drawing-room on the large couch of yellow silk, with Beck and Mrs Laing standing calmly on either side. In Mrs Laing's eyes were traces of tears. The doctor, after a brief examination, shook his head gravely, saying,—

"Life has, unfortunately, been extinct for fully an hour."

"What is the cause of death?" inquired Mrs Laing, eagerly.

"I have not yet examined the body, but there are no marks of violence whatever, as far as I can observe. At the *post-mortem* we may be able to discover something."

She drew a deep breath. I chanced at that moment to glance at her, and was surprised to observe an unmistakable look of terror flit for a brief instant across her haggard countenance. It seemed as though the doctor's hope of determining the cause of death had aroused within her a sudden apprehension. Dr Allenby, however, suggested, in polite terms, that she should leave the room, as he desired to examine the body, and she reluctantly consented, exclaiming, as she moved slowly out,—

"I would have given worlds to have avoided all this. One's name will be bruited about in the papers; and there will be an inquest, I suppose, and all that sort of thing. And dear Ella—what a terrible blow it will be to her!" Then, when the door had closed, while I stood gazing upon my intimate friend who, only an hour before, had been so full of life's enjoyment, buoyant spirits and *bonhomie*, surprised at Mrs Laing's extraordinary manner, and reflecting upon her sudden strange demeanour, the doctor, assisted by Beck, began a minute and careful examination. In a quarter of an hour, they satisfied themselves that no violence had been used, and just as they concluded, the police, who had been sent for, arrived. The local subdivisional inspector, tall, red-faced, and inclined to obesity, a plain-clothes constable, and a sergeant in uniform, who entered the drawing-room, were at once informed of the mysterious circumstances in which the body had been discovered. The inspector scribbled some brief notes, took the names and addresses of all of us, remarking with politeness that we should be compelled to attend the inquest.

Afterwards, the body was removed to the billiard-room and the plain-clothes constable left in charge of it, while, with Beck and Dr Allenby, I entered the dining-room where Mrs Laing, pale, agitated and nervous, was eagerly awaiting us. The arrival of the police in her house had apparently filled her with dread, for almost the first question she asked me was,—

"Have they gone? Have they gone?"

"They have left one officer on duty to prevent the body being touched," I answered.

"Then the police are absolutely in possession of my house! Will they search it?" she inquired hoarsely.

"Search it! Certainly not," I answered. "Of course, if foul play were suspected, they might. Otherwise they have no power without a search-warrant properly signed by a magistrate."

"But no violence is suspected," she exclaimed in a half whisper, glancing over to where the doctor and Beck were standing in earnest conversation. "I shall therefore be spared the indignity of having my house searched, sha'n't I?"

"I trust so, Mrs Laing," I replied. "But it is not such a dreadful ordeal, after all, to have one's place rummaged."

"No, perhaps not," she answered thoughtfully; then, smiling, she added, "Perhaps I am foolish to regret that this terrible affair has occurred at my very door. Poor Dudley has died suddenly, and it is only right that I, his intimate friend, should do what I can to ensure the last rite being carried out in decency. But the very thought of the police unnerves me! and I fear, too, on Ella's account. Only yesterday Dr Allenby told her that she must carefully avoid any shock."

"But she must know the truth to-morrow," I observed.

"Will you break the dreadful news to her?" she urged. "As her betrothed, you, perhaps, can tell her better than anyone else."

"Unfortunately I shall be unable," I said. "This evening I received a very urgent telegram which recalls me to town, and having now lost my last train, I must go by the 6:30 in the morning. I cannot get back before late in the evening, or it may be next day. But as soon as possible I will return straight here, and render you whatever assistance is in my power."

"Thanks. But is your business so very urgent?" she asked.

"Of greatest importance. Poor Dudley's tragic end has delayed me, and even this brief delay may be of most serious consequence."

"Ah! you men in the Foreign Office are always full of deep schemes and clever diplomacy," she smiled, toying with her mass of rings.

I laughed, but did not reply.

"Is it on Foreign Office business that you are compelled to leave us?" she persisted, glancing at me keenly, I thought, as if intent upon ascertaining the purport of the telegram I had received.

"Yes," I replied, in wonder that she should thus evince such a strong desire to glean the nature of my business. But next instant it occurred to me that possibly she might suspect me of being implicated in some mysterious manner with my friend's sudden end, and that, believing I desired to escape, was determined at least to know where I was going, and upon what errand.

At that moment Beck crossed to us, saying, —

"This affair is certainly most distressing, Mrs Laing. Dudley was such an excellent fellow that we must each one of us regret his loss very deeply indeed. I have just been discussing the matter with the doctor; but, of course, he can at present form no conjecture as to the cause of death."

"Natural causes, no doubt," chimed in the medical man, in a dry, business-like tone. "I think we may at once dismiss all idea that violence was used."

"You think so?" inquired Mrs Laing, with eagerness. "You don't believe, then, he has been a victim of foul play?"

"Not at all. Beyond the slight bruise on the forehead, evidently caused by the fall upon the gravel, there is no mark whatever," the doctor answered. "Until I have made a thorough examination I cannot, of course, determine the nature of the fatal cause. By noon to-morrow we shall, I hope, know the truth."

"He must have fallen and expired within ten minutes of leaving the house," Beck exclaimed. "Yet when he shook hands with us he was in the highest possible spirits. How terribly sudden his end was."

"Terrible!" I exclaimed, myself dazed by the peculiarly tragic and mysterious affair. "When he wished us adieu he could not have dreamed that his life had so nearly run its course."

"He complained of no pain during the evening, I suppose?" the doctor inquired.

"Not to my knowledge," Beck answered, and this statement I was compelled to endorse.

"He dined here?" Dr Allenby exclaimed, turning to Mrs Laing.

"Yes."

"There are some remains of the food left, I presume?"

"No doubt," she answered quickly. "But—but what do you suspect! Are the symptoms those of poisoning?" she gasped.

"I suspect nothing," replied the doctor, with hesitation. "The fact that the hands are tightly clenched suggests a final paroxysm of pain which might possibly accrue from poison. The remains of the dinner may be required for analysis, therefore it would be advisable to keep them."

"Very well," she answered, a shadow of annoyance upon her face. "I'll give orders to that effect. But surely, doctor, you do not think poor Dudley can have been poisoned in my house. If anything we had for dinner had been deleterious, all of us must have suffered."

"No, pardon me for disagreeing," he answered politely. "In many cases known to toxicologists, families have eaten of the same meal, and one person only has been seized with sudden illness that has proved fatal. By analysis we may obtain some clue as to the cause of Mr Ogle's unfortunate end."

Mrs Laing's thin lips moved, but no sound escaped them. At last, turning suddenly, she covered her face with her hands, as if to shut out from her gaze the white, haggard countenance she had so recently looked upon.

"Come," exclaimed the doctor, sympathetically, laying his hand upon her arm. "You are trembling. This unfortunate occurrence has no doubt upset you, but you must bear up. Immediately I get home I shall send you a draught that will brace up your nerves. Take care how the sad news is broken to Miss Ella. The slightest undue excitement may affect her very seriously."

"I have not forgotten your words yesterday, doctor," she replied. "You are very kind. Good-night!"

They shook hands, and Dr Allenby, taking up his hat, left—an example Beck and I soon afterwards followed, passing the night at the Angel Hotel.

Throughout the dark, breathless hours sleep came not to my eyes, so full was my mind of the tragic discovery. As I lay awake, hour after hour, listening to the chiming bells, and watching the dawn struggling in between the curtains, I reflected deeply upon the strange events of that evening, and the more I pondered, the more mysterious appeared the circumstances. Foremost in my mind was the strange, inviolable secret that I felt convinced existed between Ella and Beck. Although strenuously denied by her, she had nevertheless admitted her unworthiness of my love. Yet I adored her. No woman had ever stirred my soul as she had; no woman had so completely held me under her spell. I remembered how she had seemed a trifle wan and distressed; yet that look enhanced rather than detracted from her refined beauty. Her steady refusal to enlighten me regarding the subject of her earnest conversation with Beck when I had watched them in the garden, and the significant glances she had exchanged with him across the dinner-table, had aroused within me a suspicion that, notwithstanding her declaration, she loved Beck. Again, the tone of her letter was, I now saw distinctly, such as a woman would write if she desired to break off her engagement. Yet had I not a right to demand full explanation of her extraordinary statement? had I not a right to seek the truth of her relations with this loud-spoken parvenu? Nevertheless, as I pondered, I felt half inclined to believe that my estimate of Beck was a distorted one, for his regret at the death of Dudley, and his sympathy for Mrs Laing were, I felt assured, deep, heartfelt and genuine. When at last I carefully analysed my feelings towards him, I was bound to admit within myself that jealousy was now the only cause of my bitter antipathy.

Again, other incidents increased the mystery. Mrs Laing's dread that Ella should know of Dudley's death was very curious, and her exclamations and inquiries of the doctor regarding his conjecture of poison seemed to point to the fact that she entertained certain suspicions, or was aware of certain facts. But, after fully reviewing the tragic affair in all its phases, I arrived at the conclusion that Dr Allenby did not anticipate for one moment finding poison at the *post-mortem*. On the contrary, from the words he had let drop, he undoubtedly believed death due to heart-disease. I could not, however, rid myself of a vague suspicion that Ella's mother feared analysis of the remains of the dinner, and that the presence of the police unnerved her, as it invariably does those who are guilty.

Until the sun shone out, casting a long bright beam across the dingy carpet, I pondered over these curious facts in their sequence, unable to elucidate the deep mystery underlying them. After a dismal, sleepless night, haunted by a nameless spectral fear, that ray of sunshine brought back hope and banished despair I found myself at last reflecting that, after all, Dudley had expired suddenly from a cause to which any of us might be liable, and it was probable that I had been scenting mystery and tragedy where there were none.

I rose, and actually smiled at the weird and horrible nature of the thoughts that throughout the wearying night had held me spellbound in indescribable dread and terror.

Chapter Four
The Click of the Telegraph

When at noon, in accordance with the urgent and strangely-worded telegram I had received from the Earl of Warnham, I alighted at Horsham Station, in Sussex, I found one of the carriages from the Hall awaiting me. As I entered it, I was followed by a man I knew slightly, Superintendent Frayling, chief of the Criminal Investigation Department at Scotland Yard, who had apparently travelled down by the same train from Victoria.

Greeting me, he took the place beside me, and a moment later the footman sprang upon the box and we sped away towards the open country. To my question as to his business with the Earl, he made an evasive reply, merely stating that he had received a telegram requesting an immediate interview.

"This summons is rather unusual," he added, smiling. "Has anything serious occurred, do you know?"

"Not that I'm aware of. Perhaps there's been a burglary at the Hall?" I suggested.

"Hardly that, I think," he replied, with a knowing look, stroking his pointed brown beard. "If burglars had visited the place, he would have asked for a clever officer or two, not for a personal interview with me." With this view I was compelled to agree, then, lighting cigarettes, we sat back calmly contemplating the beautiful, fertile country through which we were driving. The road, leaving the quaint old town, descended sharply for a short distance, then wound uphill through cornfields lined by high hedges of hawthorn and holly. On, past a quaint old water-mill we skirted Warnham Pond, whereon Shelley in his youthful days sailed paper boats, then half-a-mile further entered the handsome lodge-gates of Warnham Park. Through a fine avenue, with a broad sweep of park on either side well stocked with deer, emus and many zoological specimens, we ascended, until at last, after negotiating the long, winding drive in front of the Hall, the carriage pulled up with a sudden jerk before its handsome portico.

As I alighted, old Stanford, the white-haired butler, came forward hurriedly, saying, —

"His Lordship is in the library awaiting you, sir. He told me to bring you to him the moment you arrived."

"Very well," I said, and the aged retainer, leading the way along a spacious but rather cheerless corridor, stopped before the door of the great library, and throwing it suddenly open, announced me.

"At last, Deedes," I heard the Earl exclaim in a tone that showed him to be in no amiable mood; and as I entered the long, handsome chamber, lined from floor to ceiling with books, I did not at first notice him until he rose slowly from a large writing-table, behind which he had been hidden. His face, usually wizened and pale, was absolutely bloodless. Its appearance startled me.

"I wired you last night, and expected you by the 9:18 this morning, Why did you not come?" was his first question, uttered in a sharp tone of annoyance.

"The sudden death of a friend caused me to lose the train I intended to catch," I explained.

"Death!" he snapped, in the manner habitual to him when impatient. "Is the death of a friend any account when the interests of the country are at stake? On the night my wife was dying I was compelled to leave her bedside to travel to Balmoral to have audience of Her Majesty regarding a document I had sent for the Royal assent. When I returned, Lady Warnham had been dead fourteen hours. In the successful diplomat there must be no sentiment—none."

"The five minutes I lost when I discovered my friend dead caused me to miss my train from Staines to London," I explained.

"But you received my telegram, and should have strictly regarded its urgency," he answered, with an air of extreme dissatisfaction. "The fact of its being in cipher was sufficient to show its importance."

"I was out dining, and my man brought it along to me," I said.

"Why did he do so?" he inquired quickly.

"Because he thought it might be urgent."

"Did he open it?"

"No. Even if he had it was in cipher."

"Is your man absolutely trustworthy?" he asked.

"He has been in the service of my family for fifteen years. He was my father's valet at the Hague."

"Is his name Juckes?" he inquired.

"Yes."

"Ah! I know him. He is absolutely trustworthy; a most excellent man."

The Earl's manner surprised me. His face, usually calm, sphinx-like and expressionless, betrayed the most intense anxiety and suspicion. That my delay had caused him great annoyance was apparent, but the anxious expression upon his ashen, almost haggard face was such, that even in moments of extreme perplexity, when dealing with one or other of the many complex questions of foreign policy, it had never been so intense.

Standing with his back to one of the great bay windows that commanded extensive views of the picturesque park, he was silent for a moment, then turning his keen, grey eyes upon me, he suddenly exclaimed, in a tone of extreme gravity,—

"Since yesterday, Deedes, a catastrophe has occurred."

"You briefly hinted at it in your telegram," I answered. "What is its nature?"

"The most serious that has happened during the whole of my administration," he said in a voice that plainly betrayed his agitation. "The clauses of the secret defensive alliance which Hammerton brought from Berlin yesterday are known in St Petersburg."

"What!" I cried in alarm, remembering the Earl's words, and his elaborate precautions to preserve its secrecy. "Surely they cannot be already known?"

"We have been tricked by spies, Deedes," he answered sternly. "Read this," and he handed me a telegram in the private cipher known only to the Minister himself. Its transcript was written beneath, and at a glance I saw it was from a Russian official in the Foreign Office at St Petersburg, who acted as our secret agent there and received a large sum yearly for his services. The dispatch, which showed that it had been handed in at Hamburg at six o'clock on the previous evening—all secret messages being sent in the first instance to that city—and re-transmitted—read as follows:—

"*Greatest excitement caused here by receipt by telegraph an hour ago of verbatim copy of secret defensive alliance between England and Germany. Have seen telegram, which was handed in at 369, Strand, London, at 3:30. Just called at Embassy and informed Lord Strathavon. Council of Ministers has been summoned."*

"It is amazing," I gasped, when I had read the dispatch. "How could our enemies have learned the truth?"

Without replying he took from his writing-table another message, which read:—

"From Strathavon, St Petersburg. To the Earl of Warnham, London.— Defensive alliance known here. Hostilities feared. French ambassador has had audience at Winter Palace, and telegraphed to Paris for instruction. Shall wire hourly."

One by one he took up the telegraphic dispatches which, during the night, had been re-transmitted from the Foreign Office over the private wire to the instrument that stood upon a small table opposite us. As I read each of them eagerly, I saw plainly that Russia and France were in complete accord, and that we were on the verge of a national disaster, sudden and terrible. With such secrecy and rapidity were negotiations being carried on between Paris and St Petersburg, that in Berlin, a city always well-informed in all matters of diplomacy, nothing unusual was suspected.

A further telegram from our secret agent in the Russian Foreign Office, received an hour before my arrival at Warnham, read:—

"The secret is gradually leaking out. The Novosti *has just issued a special edition hinting at the possibility of war with England, and this has caused the most intense excitement everywhere. The journal, evidently inspired, gives no authority for its statement, nor does it give any reason for the startling rumour."*

I laid down the dispatch in silence, and as I raised my head the Minister's keen, penetrating eyes met mine.

"Well," he exclaimed, in a dry, harsh tone. "What is is your explanation, sir?"

"My explanation?" I cried, in amazement, noticing his determined demeanour. "I know nothing of the affair except the telegrams you have shown me."

"Upon you alone the responsibility of this catastrophe rests," he said angrily. "It is useless to deny all knowledge of it and only aggravates your offence. Because you come of a diplomatic family I have trusted you implicitly, but it is evident that my confidence has been utterly misplaced."

"I deny that I have ever, for a single instant, betrayed the trust you have placed in me," I replied hotly. "I know nothing of the means by which the Tzar's army of spies have obtained knowledge of our secret."

He snapped his bony fingers impatiently, saying,—

"It is not to be expected that you will acknowledge yourself a traitor to your country, sir; therefore we must prove your guilt."

"You are at liberty, of course, to act in what manner you please," I answered. "I tell you frankly, however, that this terrible charge you bring against me is as startling as the information I have just read. I can only say I am entirely innocent."

"Bah!" he cried, turning on his heel with a gesture of disgust. Then, facing me again, his eyes flashing with anger, he added, "If you are innocent, tell me why you were so long absent yesterday when registering the dispatch; tell me why, when such an important document was in your possession, you did not remain in the office instead of being absent over an hour?"

"I went out to lunch," I said.

"With the document in your pocket?"

"Yes. But surely you do not suspect me of being a spy?" I cried.

"I do not suspect you, sir. I have positive proof of it."

"Proof!" I gasped. "Show it to me."

"It is here," he answered, his thin, nervous hands turning over the mass of papers littering his writing-table, and taking from among them an official envelope. In an instant I recognised it as the one containing the treaty.

"This remains exactly as I took it from the safe with my own hands and cut it open."

With trembling fingers I drew the document from its envelope and opened it.

The paper was blank!

I glanced at him in abject dismay, unable to utter a word.

"That is what you handed me on my return from the Cabinet Council," he said, with knit brows. "Now, what explanation have you to offer?"

"What can I offer?" I cried. "The envelope I gave you was the same that you handed to me. I could swear to it."

"No, it was not," he replied quickly. "Glance at the seal."

Taking it to the light I examined the seal carefully, but failed to detect anything unusual. It bore in black wax the Warnham coat of arms impressed by the large, beautifully-cut amethyst which the Earl wore attached to the piece of rusty silk ribbon that served him as watch chain.

"I can see nothing wrong with this," I said, glancing up at him.

"I admit that the imitation is so carefully executed that it is calculated to deceive any eye except my own." Then, putting on his *pince-nez*, he made an impression in wax with his own seal and pointed out a slight flaw which, in the impression upon the envelope, did not exist.

"And your endorsement. Is it not in your own hand?" he inquired.

I turned over the envelope and looked. It bore the designation "B27,893," just as I had written it, and the writing was either my own or such a marvellously accurate imitation that I was compelled to confess my inability to point out any discrepancy.

"Then the writing is yours, eh?" the Earl asked abruptly. "If it is, you must be aware who forged the seal."

"The writing certainly contains all the characteristics of mine, but I am not absolutely sure it is not a forgery. In any case, I am confident that the document you gave me I handed back to you." Then I explained carefully, and in detail, the events which occurred from the time he gave the treaty into my possession, up to the moment I handed it back to him.

"But how can you account for giving back to me a blank sheet of paper in an envelope secured by a forged seal?" he asked, regarding me with undisguised suspicion. "You do not admit even taking it from your pocket, neither have you any suspicion of the friend with whom you lunched. I should like to hear his independent version."

"That is impossible," I answered.

"Why?" he asked, pricking up his ears and scenting a mystery.

"Because he is dead."

At that moment our conversation was interrupted by the sharp ringing of the bell of the telegraph instrument near us, and an instant later the telegraphist in charge entered, and seated himself at the table.

Click, click, click—click—click began the needle, and next moment the clerk, turning to the Earl, exclaimed,—

"An important message from St Petersburg, your Lordship."

"Read it as it comes through," the Earl replied breathlessly, walking towards the instrument and bending eagerly over it.

Then, as the rapid metallic click again broke the silence, the clerk, in monotonous tones, exclaimed, —

"From Lobetski, St Petersburg, via Hamburg. To Earl of Warnham.—A proclamation signed by the Tzar declaring war against England has just been received at the Foreign Office, but it is as yet kept secret. It will probably be posted in the streets this evening. Greatest activity prevails at the War Office and Admiralty. Regiments in the military districts of Charkoff, Odessa, Warsaw and Kieff have received orders to complete their cadres of officers to war strength, recalling to the colours all officers on the retired list and on leave. This is a preliminary step to the complete mobilisation of the Russian forces. All cipher messages now refused."

The Earl, with frantic effort, grasped at the edge of the table, then staggered unevenly, and sank back into a chair, rigid and speechless.

Chapter Five
Lord Warnham's Admission

"Anything further?" inquired the great statesman in a low, mechanical tone, his gaze fixed straight before him as he sat.

"Nothing further, your Lordship," answered the telegraphist.

The Earl of Warnham sighed deeply, his thin hands twitching with a nervous excitement he strove in vain to suppress.

"Ask if Lord Maybury is in town," he said hoarsely, suddenly rousing himself.

Again the instrument clicked, and a few moments later the telegraphist, turning to the Foreign Minister, said, —

"The Premier is in town, your Lordship."

The Earl glanced at his watch a few seconds in silence, then exclaimed, —

"Tell Gaysford to inform Lord Maybury at once of the contents of this last dispatch from St Petersburg, and say that I will meet the Premier at 5:30 at the Foreign Office." The telegraphist touched the key, and in a few moments the Minister's orders were obeyed. Then, taking a sheet of note-paper and a pencil, he wrote in a private cipher a telegram, which he addressed to Her Majesty at Osborne. This, too, the clerk dispatched at once over the wire, followed by urgent messages to members of the Cabinet Council and to Lord Kingsbury, Commander-in-Chief of the British Army, asking them to meet informally at six o'clock that evening at the Foreign Office.

When all these messages had been transmitted with a rapidity that was astonishing, the telegraphist turned in his chair and asked, —

"Anything more, your lordship?"

"Nothing for the present," he answered. "Leave us." Then, when he had gone, the Earl rose slowly, and with bent head, and hands clasped behind his back, he strode up and down the library in silent contemplation. Suddenly he halted before me where I stood, and abruptly asked, —

"What did you say was the name of that friend who lunched with you yesterday?"

"Ogle," I answered. "Dudley Ogle."

"And his profession?"

"He had none. His father left him with enough to live upon comfortably."

"Who was his father?" he inquired, with a sharp look of doubt.

"A landowner."

"Where?"

"I don't know."

The Earl slightly raised his shaggy grey brows, then continued, —

"How long have you known this friend?"

"Several years."

"You told me that he has died since yesterday," his lordship said. "Is not that a rather curious fact—if true?"

"True!" I cried. "You apparently doubt me. A telegram to the police at Staines will confirm my statement."

"Yes, I never disguise my doubts, Deedes," the Earl snapped, fixing his grey eyes upon mine. "I suspect very strongly that you have sold the secret to our enemies; you have, to put it plainly, betrayed your country."

"I deny it!" I replied, with fierce anger. "I care not for any of your alleged proofs. True, the man who was with me during the whole time I was absent is dead. Nevertheless I am prepared to meet and refute all the accusations you may bring against me."

"Well, we shall see. We shall see," he answered dryly, snapping his fingers, and again commencing to pace the great library from end to end with steps a trifle more hurried than before. "We have—nay, I, personally have been the victim of dastardly spies, but I will not rest until I clear up the mystery and bring upon the guilty one the punishment he deserves. Think," he cried. "Think what this means! England's prestige is ruined, her power is challenged; and ere long the great armies of Russia and France will be swarming upon our shores. In the fights at sea and the fights on land with modern armaments the results must be too terrible to contemplate. The disaster that we must face will, I fear, be crushing and complete. I am not, I have never been, one of those over-confident idiots who believe our island impregnable; but am old-fashioned enough to incline towards Napoleon's opinion. We are apt to rely upon our naval strength, a strength that may, or may not, be up to the standard of power we believe. If it is a rotten reed, what remains? England must be trodden beneath the iron heel of the invader, and the Russian eagle will float beside the tricolour in Whitehall."

"But can diplomacy do nothing to avert the catastrophe?" I suggested.

"Not when it is defeated by the devilish machinations of spies," he replied meaningly, flashing a glance at me, the fierceness of which I did not fail to observe.

"But Russia dare not take the initiative," I blurted forth.

"Permit me, sir, to express my own opinion upon our relations with St Petersburg," he roared. "I tell you that for years Russia has held herself in readiness to attack us at the moment when she received sufficient provocation, and for that very object she contracted an alliance with France. The Tzar's recent visit to England was a mere farce to disarm suspicion, a proceeding in which, thank Heaven! I refused to play any part whatever. The blow that I have long anticipated, and have sought to ward off all these long years of my administration as Premier and as Foreign Secretary, has fallen. To-day is the most sorry day that England has ever known. The death-knell of her power is ringing," and he walked down the room towards me, pale-faced and bent, his countenance wearing an expression of unutterable gloominess. He was, I knew, a patriot who would have sacrificed his life for his country's honour, and every word he had uttered came straight from his heart.

"How the secret agents of the Tzar obtained knowledge of the treaty surpasses comprehension," I exclaimed.

"The catastrophe is due to you—to you alone!" he cried. "You knew of what vital importance to our honour it was that the contents of that document should be kept absolutely secret. I told you with my own lips. You have no excuse whatever—none. Your conduct is culpable in the highest degree, and you deserve, sir, instant dismissal and the publication in the *Gazette* of a statement that you have been discharged from Her Majesty's service because you were a thief and a spy!"

"I am neither," I shouted in a frenzy of rage, interrupting him. "If you were a younger man, I'd—by Heaven! I'd knock you down. But I respect your age, Lord Warnham, and I am not forgetful of the fact that to you I owe more than I can ever repay. My family have faithfully served their country through generations, and I will never allow a false accusation to be brought upon it, even though you, Her Majesty's Foreign Secretary, may choose to make it." He halted, glancing at me with an expression of unfeigned surprise.

"You forget yourself, sir," he answered, with that calm, unruffled dignity that he could assume at will. "I repeat my accusation, and it is for you to refute it."

"I can! I will!" I cried.

"Then explain the reason you handed me a sheet of blank paper in exchange for the instrument."

"I cannot, I—"

He laughed a hard, cynical laugh, and, turning upon his heel, paced towards the opposite window.

"All I know is that the envelope I gave you was the same that you handed to me," I protested.

"It's a deliberate lie," he cried, as he turned in anger to face me again. "I opened the dispatch, read it through to ascertain there was no mistake, and, after sealing it with my own hands, gave it to you. Yet, in return, you hand me this!" and he took from the table the ingeniously-forged duplicate envelope and held it up.

Then, casting it down again passionately, he added,—

"The document I handed to you was exchanged for that dummy, and an hour later the whole thing was telegraphed *in extenso* to Russia. The original was in your possession, and even if you are not actually in the pay of our enemies, you were so negligent of your duty towards your Queen and country that you are undeserving the name of Englishman."

"But does not London swarm with Russian agents?" I said. "Have we not had ample evidence of that lately?"

"I admit it," he answered. "But what proof is there to show that you yourself did not hand the original document to one of these enterprising gentlemen who take such a keen interest in our affairs?"

"There is no proof that I am a spy," I cried hotly. "There never will be; for I am entirely innocent of this disgraceful charge. You overlook the fact that after it had been deposited in the safe it may have been tampered with."

"I have overlooked no detail," he answered, with calmness. "Your suggestion is an admirable form of excuse, but, unfortunately for you, it will not hold water. First, because, as you must be aware, there is but one key to that safe, and that never leaves my person; secondly, no one but you and I are possessed of the secret whereby the safe may be opened or closed;

thirdly, the packet you gave me did not remain in the safe. In order that you should believe that the document was deposited there, I put it in in your presence, but when you left my room I took it out again, and carried it home with me to Berkeley Square, intending to show it to Lord Maybury. The Premier did not call as he had promised, but I kept the document in my pocket the whole time, and at six o'clock returned to the Foreign Office and deposited it again in the safe. Almost next moment—I had not left the room, remember—some thought prompted me to reopen the envelope and reassure myself of the wording of one of the clauses. Walking to the safe, I took out the envelope and cut it open, only to discover that I had been tricked. The paper was blank!"

"It might have been stolen while in your possession just as easily as while in mine!" I exclaimed, experiencing some satisfaction at being thus able to turn his own arguments against himself.

"Knowing its vital importance, I took the most elaborate precautions that such circumstances were rendered absolutely impossible."

"From your words, when Hammerton arrived from Berlin, it was plain that you suspected treachery. On what ground were your suspicions founded?"

Upon his sphinx-like face there rested a heavy frown of displeasure as he replied,—

"I refuse to submit to any cross-examination, sir. That I entertained certain suspicions is enough."

"And you actually accuse me without the slightest foundation?" I cried with warmth.

"You are in error," he retorted very calmly, returning to his writing-table and taking up some papers. "I have here the original of the telegram handed in at the branch post-office in the Strand yesterday afternoon."

"Well?"

"It has been examined by the calligraphic expert employed by the police, and declared to be in your handwriting."

"What?" I gasped, almost snatching the yellow telegraph form from his hand in my eagerness to examine the mysterious jumble of letters and figures composing the cypher. My heart sank within me when next instant I recognised they were in a hand so nearly resembling my own that I could scarcely detect any difference whatever.

As I stood gazing at this marvellous forgery, open-mouthed in abject dismay, there broke upon my ear a short, harsh laugh—a laugh of triumph.

Raising my head, the Earl's penetrating gaze met mine. "Now," he exclaimed, "come, acknowledge the truth. It is useless to prevaricate."

"I have told the truth," I answered. "I never wrote this."

For an instant his steely eyes flashed as his blanched face assumed an expression of unutterable hatred and disgust. Then he shouted, —

"You are a thief, a spy and a liar, sir! Leave me instantly. Even in the face of such evidence as this you protest innocence with childish simplicity. You have betrayed your country into the hands of her enemies, and are, even now, seeking to throw blame and suspicion upon myself. You — "

"I have not done so. I merely suggested that the document might have been exchanged while in your possession. Surely — "

"And you actually come to me with a lame, absurd tale that the only man who can clear you is dead! The whole defence is too absurd," he thundered. "You have sold your country's honour and the lives of your fellow-men for Russian roubles. Go! Never let me see you again, except in a felon's dock."

"But surely I may be permitted to clear myself?" I cried.

"Your masters in St Petersburg will no doubt arrange for your future. In London we require your faithless services no longer," the Earl answered, with intense bitterness. "Go!"

Chapter Six
The Veil

Leaving the Earl's presence, I refused old Stanford's invitation to take some refreshment, and, walking along the corridor on my way out, came face to face with Frayling, who was being conducted to the library.

"Going?" he inquired.

"Yes," I answered, and passing on, engrossed in bitter thoughts that overwhelmed me, strode out into the park, wandering aimlessly across the grass to where a well-kept footpath wound away among the trees. Taking it, heedless of my destination, I walked on mechanically, regardless of the brilliant sunshine and the songs of the birds, thinking only of the unjust accusation against me, and of my inability to clear myself. I saw that the stigma upon me meant ruin, both social and financial. Branded as a spy, I should be spurned by Ella, sneered at by Mrs Laing, and avoided by Beck. Friends who had trusted me would no longer place any confidence in a man who had, according to their belief, sold his country into the hands of her enemies, while it was apparent from the Earl's words that he had no further faith in my actions.

Yet the only man who could have cleared me, who could have corroborated my statement as to how I spent my time during my absence at lunch, and shown plainly that I had never entered the Strand nor visited the branch post-office next to Exeter Hall, was dead. His lips were for ever sealed.

I went forward, plunged deeply in thought, until passing a small gate I left the park, and found myself in Warnham Churchyard. For a moment I stood on the peaceful spot where I had often stood before, admiring the quaint old church, with its square, squat, ivy-covered tower, its gilded clock face, and its ancient doors that, standing open, admitted air and sunshine. Before me were the plain, white tombs of the departed earls, the most recent being that in memory of the Countess, one of the leaders of London society, who had died during her husband's absence on his official duties; while across the well-kept lawn stood a quaint old sun-dial that had in silence marked the time for a century or so. From within the church the organ sounded softly, and I could see the Vicar's daughter, a pretty girl still in her teens, seated at the instrument practising.

Warnham was a quiet Sussex village unknown to the world outside, unspoiled by modern progress, untouched by the hand of the vandal. As presently I passed the lych-gate and entered its peaceful street, it wore a distinctly old-world air. At the end of the churchyard wall stood the typical village blacksmith, brown-faced and brawny, swinging his hammer with musical clang upon his anvil set beneath a great chestnut tree in full bloom; further along stood the schools, from the playground of which came the joyous sound of children's voices; and across the road was the only inn—the Sussex Arms—where, on more than one occasion, I had spent an hour in the bare and beery taproom, chatting with the garrulous village gossips, the burly landlord and his pleasant spouse. The air was heavy with the scent of June roses and the old-fashioned flowers growing in cottage gardens, whilst the lilacs sent forth a perfume that in my perturbed state of mind brought me back to a realisation of my bitterness. Lilac was Ella's favourite scent, and it stirred within me thoughts of her. How, I wondered, had she borne the news of Dudley's tragic and mysterious end? How, I wondered, would she greet me when next we met?

Yet somehow I distrusted her, and as I walked on through the village towards the Ockley road, nodding mechanically to a man I knew, I was seriously contemplating the advisability of never again seeing her. But I loved her, and though I strove to reason with myself that some secret tie existed between her and Beck, I found myself unable to break off my engagement, for I was held in her toils by the fascination of her eyes.

For fully an hour I walked on, ascending the hill swept by the fresh breeze from the Channel, only turning back on finding myself at the little hamlet at Kingsfold. In that walk I tried to form resolutions—to devise some means to regain the confidence of the Earl, and to conjecture the cause of Dudley's death—but all to no purpose. The blows which had fallen in such swift succession had paralysed me. I could not think, neither could I act.

Re-passing the Sussex Arms, I turned in, dusty and thirsty. In the bare taproom, deserted at that hour, old Denman, a tall, tight-trousered, splay-footed, grey-haired man, who drove the village fly, and acted as ostler and handy man about the hostelry, was busy cleaning some pewters, and as I entered, looked up and touched his hat.

"Well, Denman," I said, "you don't seem to grow very much older, eh?"

The man, whose hair and beard were closely-cropped, and whose furrowed face had a habit of twitching when he spoke, grinned as he answered,—

"No, sir. People tells me I bear my age wonderful well. But won't you come into the parlour, sir?"

Declining, I told him to get me something to drink, and when he brought it questioned him as to the latest news in the village. Denman was an inveterate gossip, and in his constant drives in the rickety and antiquated vehicle known as "the fly," to villages and towns in the vicinity, had a knack of picking up all the news and scandal, which he retailed at night for the delectation of customers at the Sussex Arms.

"I dunno as anything very startling has happened lately in Warnham. The jumble sale came off at the schools last Tuesday fortnight, and there's a cricket match up at the Lodge next Saturday. Some gentlemen are coming down from London to play."

"Anything else?"

Denman removed his hat and scratched his head.

"Oh, yes," he said suddenly. "You knows Mr Macandrew what's steward for Mr Thornbury? Well, last Monday week an old gentleman called at his house up street and asked to see him. His wife asked him into the parlour, and Mr Macandrew went in. 'Are you Mr Macandrew?' says the old gent. 'I am,' says Mr Macandrew. 'Well, I shouldn't 'ave known you,' says the old man. And it turned out afterwards that this old man was actually Mr Macandrew's father, who's lived ever so many years in America, and hasn't seen Mr Macandrew since he wor a boy. I did laugh when I heard it."

"Extraordinary. Have you had any visitors down from London?" I inquired, for sometimes people took the houses of the better-class villagers, furnished for the season.

"We had a lively young gent staying here in the inn for four days last week. He was a friend of somebody up at the Hall, I think, for he was there a good deal. He came from London. I wonder whether you'd know him."

"What was his name?"

"Funny name," Denman said, grinning. "Ogle, Mr Ogle."

"Ogle!" I gasped. "What was his Christian name?"

"Dudley, I fancy it was."

"Dudley Ogle," I repeated, remembering that he had been absent from Shepperton for four days, and had told me he had been in Ipswich visiting some friends. "And he has been here?"

"Yes, sir. We made him as comfortable as we could, and I think he enjoyed hisself."

"But what did he do—why was he down here?" I inquired eagerly.

"Do you know him, sir? Jolly gentleman, isn't he? Up to all manners o' tricks, and always chaffing the girls."

"Yes, I knew him, Denman," I answered gravely. "Tell me, as far as you know, his object in coming to Warnham. I'm very interested in his doings."

"As far as I know, sir, he came to see somebody up at the Hall. I drove him about a good deal, over to Ockley, to Cowfold, and out to Handcross; and I took him into Horsham every day."

"Do you know who was his friend at the Hall?"

"No, I don't, sir. He never spoke about it; but I did have my suspicions," he answered, smiling.

"Oh! what were they?" I asked.

"I fancy he came to see Lucy Bryden, the housekeeper's daughter. She's a good-looking girl, you know," and the old man winked knowingly.

"What made you think that, eh?"

"Well, from something I was told," he replied mysteriously. "He was seen walking with a young lady across the park one night, and I 'eard as 'ow it was Mrs Bryden's daughter. But next day I 'ad a surprise. A young lady called here for him, and she was dressed exactly as the young woman who had been in the park with him was. But it wasn't Mrs Bryden's daughter."

"Then who was it?"

"I heard him call her Ella. She came from London."

"Ella?" I gasped. "What the deuce do you mean, Denman? What sort of a girl was she? A lady?"

"Yes, sir, quite a lady. She was dressed in brown, and one thing I noticed was that she had on a splendid diamond bracelet. It was a beauty."

"A diamond bracelet!" I echoed. There was no doubt that Ella had actually been to Warnham without my knowledge, for the bracelet that the old ostler, in reply to my eager questions, described accurately, was the one I had given her.

"What time in the day did she call? Where did they go?" I demanded, in surprise.

"She came about mid-day, and they both went for a walk towards Broadbridge Heath. They were gone, I should reckon, about three hours, and when they returned, it was evident from her eyes that she'd been crying."

"Crying! Had Ogle been talking to her angrily, do you think?"

"No. I don't believe so. They remained here and had some tea together in the parlour, and then I drove 'em to Horsham, and they caught the 6:25 to London."

I was silent. There was some remarkable, unfathomable mystery in this.

"Now, Denman," I said at last, "I know you've got a sharp pair of ears when you're perched up on that box of yours. Did you overhear their conversation while driving them to Horsham?"

Again the old man removed his battered hat and calmly scratched his head.

"Well, sir, to tell you the truth, I did 'ear a few words," he answered. "I 'eard the young lady say as 'ow she wor powerless. He seemed to be a-begging of her to do something which horrified her. I 'eard her ask him in a whisper whether he thought they would be discovered, and he laughed at her fear, and said, 'If you don't do it, you know the consequences will be fatal.'"

"Do you think they went up to the Hall when they went out walking?"

"I don't know, sir. They could, of course, have got into the park that way. But you don't look very well, sir. I hope what I've told you isn't—isn't very unpleasant," the old ostler added, with a look of apprehension.

"No. Get me some brandy, Denman," I gasped.

While he was absent I rose and walked unsteadily to the window that overlooked a comfortable-looking corner residence surrounded by a belt of firs, a wide road, and a beautiful stretch of valley and blue downs beyond. The landscape was peaceful and picturesque, and I sought solace in gazing upon it. But this latest revelation had unnerved me. Dudley and Ella had met in that quiet, rural place for some purpose which I could not conceive. Their meeting had evidently been pre-arranged, and their object, from the words the old man had overheard, was apparently of a secret and sinister character.

The strange, inquiring look I had detected in Ella's face whenever she had glanced surreptitiously at Dudley on the previous night was, I now felt assured, an index of guilty conscience; and Mrs Laing's dread that Ella should know the truth of my friend's tragic end appeared to prove, in a certain degree, the existence of some secret knowledge held by all three.

Yet I could not bring myself to believe that my well-beloved had wilfully deceived me. From what Denman had said, it appeared as if Ogle had held her under some mysterious thrall, and was trying to compel her to act against her better judgment. Her pure, womanly conscience had, perhaps, revolted against his suggestion, and she had shed the tears the old ostler had noticed; yet he had persisted and held over her a threat that had cowed her, and, perhaps, for aught I knew, compelled her to submit.

My thought that the man who was my friend should have thus treated the woman I adored filled me with fiercest anger and hatred. With bitterness I told myself that the man in whom I placed implicit confidence, and with whom I had allowed Ella to spend many idle hours punting or sculling while I was absent at my duties in London, was actually my enemy.

With sudden resolve I determined to travel back to Staines and, by possession of the knowledge of her mysterious visit to that village, worm from her its object. At that moment Denman entered, and I drank the brandy at one gulp, afterwards ordering the fly and driving back to Horsham station, whence I returned to London.

At my flat in Rossetti Mansions, Chelsea, I found a telegram from the Staines police summoning me to the inquest to be held next morning at eleven o'clock, and also one from Ella asking me to return. The latter I felt inclined to disregard; the former I could not. Her words and actions were, indeed, beyond comprehension, but in the light of this knowledge I had by mere chance acquired, it seemed plain that her declaration of her unworthiness of my love was something more than the natural outcome of highly-strung nerves and a romantic disposition. Women of certain temperaments are prone to self-accusation, and I had brought myself to believe her words to be mere hysterical utterances; but now, alas! I saw there was some deep motive underlying them. I had been tricked. I had, it seemed, been unduly jealous of Beck, and unsuspecting of my real enemy, the man whose lips were closed in death.

I now regretted his end, not as a friend regrets, but merely because no effort would be availing to compel his lying tongue to speak the truth. Yet, if he were my rival for Ella's hand, might he not have lied when questioned regarding the events of that fateful afternoon when the secret defensive alliance had been so mysteriously exchanged for a dummy? Jealousy knows neither limit nor remorse.

Next morning, after spending the greater part of the night sitting alone smoking and endeavouring to penetrate the ever-increasing veil of mystery that had apparently enveloped her, I travelled down to Staines, arriving there just in time to take a cab to the Town Hall, where the inquest was to be held. The town was agog, for a crowd of those unable to enter because the room was already filled to overflowing, stood in the open space outside, eagerly discussing the tragic affair in all its various aspects, and hazarding the wildest and most impossible theories. Entering the hall, I elbowed my way forward, and as I did so I heard my namé shouted loudly by a police constable. I was required as a witness, and succeeded in struggling through to the baize-covered table whereat the grave-faced Coroner sat.

He stretched forth his hand to give me the copy of Holy Writ whereon to take the oath, when suddenly my eyes fell upon a watch and a collection of miscellaneous articles lying upon the table, the contents of the dead man's pockets.

One small object alone riveted my attention. Heedless of the Coroner's words I snatched it up and examined it closely.

Next second I stood breathless and aghast, dumbfounded by an amazing discovery that staggered belief.

Chapter Seven
Ella's Suspicions

The formula of the oath fell upon my ears in a dull monotone, as mechanically I raised the Bible to my lips, afterwards replying to the Coroner's formal questions regarding my name, address and occupation. The discovery I had made filled me with fierce, bitter hatred against my dead companion, and, dazed by the startling suddenness of the revelation, I stood like a man in a dream.

Dr Diplock, the Coroner, noticed it, and his sharp injunction to answer his question brought me back to a knowledge of my surroundings. I was standing in full view of an assembly of some three hundred persons, so filled by curiosity, and eager to hear my story, that the silence was complete.

"I beg your pardon, but I did not hear the question," I said, bracing myself with effort.

"The deceased was your friend, I believe?"

"Yes," I answered. "He shared a furnished cottage with me at Shepperton. I have known him for some time."

"Were you with him at the day of his death?"

"I left him at Shepperton in the morning, when I went to town, and he called upon me at the Foreign Office about one o'clock. We lunched together, and then, returning to Downing Street, parted. We met again at Shepperton later, and came here, to Staines, in response to an invitation to dinner at 'The Nook.' I—"

A woman's low, despairing cry broke the silence, and as I turned to the assembly I saw, straight before me, Ella, rigid, almost statuesque. Her terror-stricken gaze met mine; her eyes seemed riveted upon me.

"Kindly proceed with your evidence," exclaimed the Coroner, impatiently.

"We dined at 'The Nook,'" I went on, turning again to face him. "Then we went for a row, and on our return Mr Ogle left us to walk back to Shepperton."

"Alone?"

"Yes."

"Why did you not accompany him?"

"Because I had, during the evening, received a telegram summoning me away."

"Who was the message from?"

"The Earl of Warnham," I replied. Then obeying his request to continue, I explained how, on leaving "The Nook" about an hour later to catch my last train, I had stumbled upon the body of my friend.

Then, when I had concluded, the Coroner commenced his cross-examination. Many of his questions were purely formal in character, but presently, when he began to take me through the events which occurred at the Foreign Office, I experienced a very uncomfortable feeling, fearing lest I should divulge the suspicions that had during the last half-hour been aroused within me. It was, I recognised, absolutely necessary that I should keep my discovery a strict secret, for upon my ability to do so everything depended.

"Was there any reason why he should call for you at the Foreign Office and ask you to lunch with him? Was he in the habit of doing this?" inquired the Coroner.

"No; there seemed no reason, beyond the fact that he was compelled to come to town, and merely wanted to pass an idle hour away," I said.

"Why did he go to London?"

"I have no idea what business took him there."

"He never told you that he had any enemy, I suppose?" the official asked, with an air of mystery.

"Never. He was, on the contrary, most popular."

"And no incident other than what you have related occurred at the Foreign Office? You are quite certain of this?"

For a moment I hesitated, half inclined to relate the whole story of the mysterious theft of the secret convention; but risking perjury rather than an exposure of facts that I saw must remain hidden, I answered as calmly as I could,—

"No other incident occurred."

"Have you any reason to suspect that he was a victim of foul play?" the Coroner continued, looking at me rather suspiciously, I thought.

At that moment I glanced at Ella, and was astounded to see how intensely excited she appeared, with her white face upturned, her mouth half open, her eyes staring, eagerly drinking in every word that fell from my lips. Her whole attitude was of one who dreaded that some terrible truth might be brought to light.

"I have no reason to suspect he was murdered," I answered in a low tone, and as I surreptitiously watched the face of the woman I loved I saw an instant transformation. Her breast heaved with a heavy sigh of relief as across her countenance there passed a look of satisfaction she was unable to disguise. She was in deadly fear of something, the nature of which I could not conjecture.

"You have no suspicion whatever that the deceased had an enemy?" asked the foreman of the jury, who had the appearance of a local butcher.

"None whatever," I answered.

"I frequently saw Mr Ogle on the river of an afternoon with Miss Laing," the man observed. "Was there, as far as you are aware, any affection between them?"

Glancing at Ella, I saw she had turned even paler than before, and was trembling. The question nonplussed me. In my heart I strongly suspected that some attachment existed between them; but resenting this impertinent question from a man who struck me as a local busybody, I made a negative reply.

"Then jealousy, it would appear, was not the cause of the crime," the foreman observed to his fellow-jurymen.

The Coroner, however, quickly corrected him, pointing out that they had not yet ascertained whether death had, or had not, been due to natural causes.

Turning to me, he said, —

"I believe I am right in assuming that you are engaged to be married to Miss Laing, am I not?"

"I was engaged to her," I replied hoarsely.

"Then you are not engaged at the present moment? Why was the match broken off?"

I hesitated for several moments, trying to devise some means to avoid answering this abrupt question. The bitter thought of Ella's double dealing occurred to me, and with foolish disregard for consequences I resolved not to spare her.

"Because of a confession she made to me," I said.

"A confession! What of?"

"Of unworthiness."

"She acknowledged herself unfaithful to you, I presume?" observed one of the jurymen who had not before spoken; but to this I made no reply.

"Now, have you any suspicion that any secret affection existed between her and the deceased?" the Coroner asked, in a dry, distinct voice, that could be heard all over the room.

"I—I cannot say," I faltered.

The movement among the audience showed the sensation my reply had caused, and it was increased by Ella suddenly rising from her place and shrieking hysterically: "That answer is a lie—a foul lie!"

"Silence!" shouted the Coroner, who, above all things, detested a scene in his Court. "If that lady interrupts again, she must be requested to leave."

"Have you any further question to ask Mr Deedes?" he inquired, turning to the jury; but as no one replied, he intimated that the examination was at an end, and I felt that I had, at last, successfully passed through the ordeal I had dreaded.

Retiring to a seat, my place as a witness was at once taken by Beck; but scarcely had I sunk into a chair near where Ella was sitting when I felt within my hand the object I had taken from among the things found in the dead man's possession. It had not been missed, and I wondered whether its loss would ever be detected. To keep it was, I felt, extremely dangerous; nevertheless I sat holding it in my palm, listening to the evidence of the well-known member for West Rutlandshire. His story, related in that loud, bombastic tone that had at first so prejudiced me against him, was much to the same effect as mine regarding the discovery of the body, its removal into the house, and the subsequent examination by the doctor, until there commenced the minute cross-examination.

"How long have you known the deceased?" the Coroner inquired, looking up suddenly from his notes.

"A few months. About six, I should think," he answered.

"Have you any suspicion that he had an enemy?"

"No. He was about the last man in the world who would arouse the hatred of anybody. In fact, he was exceedingly popular."

"You say you have been a frequent visitor at Mrs Laing's. Now, from your own observations, have you seen anything that would lead you to the belief that he loved Miss Laing?"

"Nothing whatever," he replied. "Ella was engaged to Mr Deedes, and although she was on the river a great deal with Ogle, I am confident she never for a moment regarded him as her lover."

"Why are you so confident?"

"Because of certain facts she has confided in me."

"What are they?"

He was silent. Evidently he had no intention of being led on in this manner, but, even finding himself cornered, his imperturbable coolness never deserted him, for he calmly replied, with a faint smile, —

"I refuse to answer."

"Kindly reply to my question, sir, and do not waste the time of the Court," exclaimed the Coroner, with impatience. "What were these facts?"

Again he was silent, twisting his gloves around his fingers uneasily.

"Come, answer if you please."

"Well," he replied, after considerable hesitation, "briefly, she gave me to understand that she loved Deedes, and had refused to listen to the deceased's declaration of affection."

"How came she to confide this secret of hers to you?" the Coroner asked eagerly.

Through my memory at that moment there flashed the scene I had witnessed in secret in the garden on that memorable night when I had detected this man with his arm around Ella's waist, and I looked on in triumph at his embarrassment.

"I am a friend of the family," he answered, with a calm, irritating smile a moment later. "She has told me many of her secrets."

I knew from the expression upon his face that he lied. Was it not far more likely that on that night when I had discovered them he was uttering words of affection to her, and she, in return, had confessed that she loved me?

"Are you aware whether Mr Deedes had any knowledge that the deceased was his rival for Miss Laing's hand?" inquired the Coroner, adding, self-apologetically, "I much regret being compelled to ask these questions, for I am aware how painful it must be to the family."

"I believe he was utterly ignorant of it," Beck replied. "He regarded Mr Ogle as his closest friend."

"A false one, to say the least," Dr Diplock observed in tones just audible. Beck shrugged his shoulders, but did not reply.

The inquisitive foreman of the jury then commenced a series of clumsy, impertinent questions, many of which the witness cleverly evaded. He resented this man's cross-examination just as I had done, and during the quarter of an hour's fencing with the tradesman no noteworthy fact was elicited. The Coroner, seeing this, suddenly put an end to the foreman's pertinacious efforts to draw from the Member of Parliament further facts regarding home life at "The Nook," and called Dr Allenby.

The doctor, who had apparently had long experience of inquests, took the oath in a business-like manner, and related the facts within his knowledge clearly and succinctly, describing how I had summoned him, his visit to "The Nook," and the appearance of the dead man.

"Have you made a *post-mortem?*" the Coroner asked, without looking up from the notes he was making.

"I made an examination yesterday, in conjunction with Dr Engall. We found no trace of disease, with the exception of a slight lung trouble of recent date."

"Was it sufficient to cause death?"

"Certainly not; neither was the bruise upon the forehead, which had, no doubt, been caused by the fall upon the gravel. The heart was perfectly normal, and we failed utterly to detect anything that would result fatally. The contents of the stomach have been analysed by Dr Adams, of the Home Office, at the instigation of the police, I believe."

"Then, as far as you are concerned, you are unable to determine the cause of death?"

"Quite. It is a mystery."

The next witness was a thin, white-haired, dapper little man, who, in reply to questions, explained that he was analyst to the Home Office, and had, at the request of the police, submitted the contents of the deceased's stomach to analysis, the position of the hands pointing to a slight suspicion of poison.

"And what have you discovered?" inquired the Coroner, the Court being so silent that the proverbial pin, if it had been dropped at that moment, might have been heard.

"Nothing," he answered clearly. "There was no sign of anything of a deleterious nature whatsoever. The deceased was certainly not poisoned."

The assembly of excited townspeople again shifted uneasily, as it was wont to do after every important reply which might elucidate the mystery. It seemed as though a rumour had been circulated that Dudley had been poisoned, and this declaration of the renowned analyst set at rest for ever that wild, unfounded report. People turned to one another, whispering excitedly, and a shadow of disappointment rested upon their inquisitive countenances. They had expected it to be pronounced a case of murder, whereas it would now be proved that death had occurred from some natural but sudden and unknown cause.

"Then you have no opinion to offer as to the cause of death!" the Coroner exclaimed.

"None whatever," was the reply, and that concluded the analyst's important testimony.

The foreman of the jury expressed a wish to put a question to Ella, and a few moments later she stood where I had stood, and removing her glove, took the oath with trembling voice.

"Have you any reason to suppose, Miss Laing, that Mr Ogle's declaration of love to you had aroused the enmity of Mr Deedes?" asked the man, seriously.

"No," she answered in a tone so low that I could scarcely distinguish the word.

"Mr Deedes was your lover, wasn't he?"

"I am still engaged to him," she replied, tears welling in her eyes. "He tells a falsehood when he says that our love is at an end."

"Then why did you not tell him of Mr Ogle's declaration?"

"Because they were friends, and I did not wish to arouse animosity between them."

Slight applause followed this reply, but it was instantly suppressed.

The Coroner, to bring matters to a conclusion, asked, "Now, knowing Mr Ogle as intimately as you did, do you suspect that he might have been murdered?"

She gasped, swayed slowly forward and gripped the corner of the baize-covered table to steady herself.

"Yes," she answered in a clear but tremulous voice. "I—I believe he was murdered."

A thrill of excitement and wonder ran through the onlookers. Her handsome face was ashen pale, and her breast, beneath her blouse of cool-looking muslin, rose and fell quickly, showing how intense was her agitation.

"And what causes you to believe this?" asked the Coroner, raising his brows in interrogation.

"I have suspicions," she answered in a low voice, striving to remain calm, and glancing quickly around the silent assembly.

"You suspect some person of having been guilty of murder?" he asked, interested.

"Not exactly that," she said quickly. "That Mr Ogle was murdered I feel confident, but who committed the crime I am unaware. It is a mystery. Knowing Mr Ogle so well as I did, he entrusted to me knowledge of certain facts that he strenuously kept secret from others. Yet I cannot conceive who would profit by his death."

At this point the inspector of police rose and expressed a desire to know, through the Coroner, whether she had quarrelled with Mr Ogle.

"The day prior to his death we had a few words," she faltered.

"Upon what subject?" asked the Coroner.

She at first refused to reply, but after being pressed, said, "We quarrelled about my engagement to Mr Deedes."

So she acknowledged with her own lips that the dead man had been my bitter enemy, as I, too late, had discovered.

"He wished you to marry him?" suggested the Coroner. She did not answer, but burst into a fit of hysterical tears, and a few moments later was led out of the Court.

"I think, gentlemen," the Coroner observed, turning to the jury, "no end can be obtained in pursuing this very painful inquiry further. You have heard the evidence, and while on the one hand the exact cause of death has not been established, on the other we have Miss Laing declaring that the unfortunate gentleman was murdered. The evidence certainly does not point to such a conclusion, and there are two courses that may be pursued; either to adjourn the inquiry, or to return an open verdict and leave the elucidation of the mystery in the hands of the police."

The jury, after consulting among themselves, retired, but only for five minutes, coming back into court and returning an open verdict of "Found dead."

Then, as the Coroner thanked the twelve tradesmen for their attendance, I rose and crossed to Beck, afterwards walking with him to "The Nook."

Chapter Eight
"I Dare Not!"

"What do you think of Ella's statement?" Beck asked, as we were crossing Staines Bridge on our way to Mrs Laing's.

"I can't understand it," I replied.

"Neither can I," he said. "Girls of her excitable temperament are apt to make statements of that character utterly without foundation. No doubt Dudley was her intimate friend, and finding him dead, her romantic mind at once conjured up visions of murder."

"Yes. There is a good deal in your argument," I admitted, with a touch of sorrow at the remembrance that Ogle had aspired to her hand.

"I never spoke to you on the subject, for fear of making mischief, but I have many times been amazed at your blindness when Dudley and Ella used to flirt openly before your very eyes," he observed, glancing at me.

"Ah! you are right," I cried angrily. "I foolishly trusted him, believing implicitly in his honour and in Ella's purity."

"Of the latter you surely have no cause for suspicion," he exclaimed quickly.

"I am not so certain," I replied with bitterness. "The more deeply I attempt to probe this mystery, the more sorrow I heap upon myself. I was happy in the belief that she loved no other man except me, yet apparently she is as tactful as an adventuress, and delights in toying with a man's affections."

"Every woman is fickle," my friend remarked sympathetically. "If she is thrown into the society of one man frequently, and passes idle hours alone with him, she either ends in loving him or hating him. There is little purely platonic friendship between men and women nowadays."

"Yes, alas!" I echoed, as we entered the carriage drive and passed the well-remembered spot where I had discovered the body. "There is very little indeed."

A quarter of an hour later I stood alone before the window of the bright morning-room which commanded a beautiful view of the brilliant, sunlit Thames, and the row of tall, swaying poplars and drooping, wind-whitened willows on the opposite shore. I was awaiting Ella, who had, her maid told me, gone to her room.

Presently, pale-faced and trembling, she entered, and, closing the door, moved slowly towards me, stretching forth her hand in silence, her tearful eyes downcast. I grasped the slim, white fingers, and found them cold as marble.

"Geoffrey," she exclaimed, low and huskily. "Geoffrey, forgive me!"

"Forgive! For what reason?" I inquired sternly, looking at her in admiration, yet determined to be firm. This was, I resolved, to be our last interview.

"Because I—I was foolish and weak, and—" She paused, sighing deeply.

"Well?" I said cynically. "What other excuse?"

"Yes, yes," she cried brokenly. "I know they are mean, paltry excuses. I know I am trying to make you believe it was not my own fault, yet—" and pausing again, she raised her clear blue eyes to mine with passionate glance, "and yet, Geoffrey, I love you in a manner I have loved no other man before."

"You have a strange way of exhibiting this so-called affection," I observed coldly. "You actually encouraged the advances of the man in whom I reposed foolish and ill-placed confidence."

"For a purpose. I never loved him—never," she protested, trembling.

"You had a reason? A strange one, I should think," I exclaimed angrily. "Indeed, at this very moment you are mourning the loss of this man."

"Dudley Ogle was not your enemy, Geoffrey. He was your friend," she answered, with a tremor in her voice. "Some day I will prove this to you. I cannot now. It is impossible."

"Why?"

"I dare not!"

"Dare not! What do you fear?" I demanded in surprise, instantly releasing her hand.

"The consequences would be fatal to our love," she gasped. Then, after a pause, she clutched my arm, and, burying her beautiful face upon my shoulder, sobbed bitterly.

"Our love!" I echoed contemptuously. Notwithstanding the fierceness of my anger, I smoothed her dark gold hair, and presently, when she grew a trifle calmer, endeavoured to discover the meaning of her strange, enigmatical words.

"You cannot know—you will never know—how dearly I have loved you, Geoffrey," she cried, in answer to my eager questions. "Neither will you ever know how much I have suffered, how hard I have striven for your sake."

"For my sake! Yet you admit having allowed Dudley Ogle to utter words that I alone had a right to utter!"

"Yes, I admit all," she said, with a tragic touch of sorrow in her strained voice. "I deny nothing."

"And you come to me asking forgiveness, believing that I can again trust you without hearing any explanation of your recent strange conduct with Beck, as well as with Dudley! I think you must regard me, Ella, as a weak, impressionable fool," I added, with bitter sarcasm.

"No, I do not," she cried quickly. "I appeal to your generosity towards a woman. I have been compelled to act against my own inclinations, compelled, in order to outwit my enemies, to act a part despicable and revolting. I can now only ask forgiveness," and, throwing herself suddenly upon her knees before me, she cried, "See! Geoffrey, I crave one grain of pity from you, my old friend, the only man I have loved!"

"No, Ella," I answered, quickly withdrawing my hand that she was pressing to her hot, fevered lips. "I may pity you, but forgive you never."

"Never!" she gasped, clasping her breast with her hands as if to stay the wild beating of her heart, and struggling unevenly to her feet. "Why never?"

"Because you have deceived me."

"Yes, yes!" she wailed. "I admit it, I admit it all, but I swear my actions were imperative. Ah! alas that you cannot know everything, or you would kiss me as fondly as you used to do. You, Geoffrey, would love me with a love even more tender and passionate than before, if only you were aware of what I have suffered for your sake."

I turned from her in disgust. Her tragic attitude filled me with loathing and contempt, for I knew she was lying.

"Can you never again trust me?" she asked, in a low, hoarse voice. "Will you never forgive?"

"I can have no further confidence in a woman who has practised such artful deception as you have," I answered, turning again towards her, and noticing the look of unutterable sadness in her tearful eyes.

"Deception!" she cried, starting. "What do you mean? What have I done?"

"You acknowledge having deceived me wilfully with all the deep cunning of an adventuress, yet you refuse me one word of explanation, either in regard to Beck or Dudley?"

"There is nothing to explain, as far as Mr Beck is concerned," she answered demurely. "He is an old friend, and your suspicions that there was any love between us are absolutely absurd."

"Why, then, did you confess in your letter that you were unworthy of my love!" I demanded with warmth, walking towards her.

She hung her head. There was a deep silence, broken only by the low ticking of the clock. In a few moments her hand stole in search of mine, and, engrossed in my own sad thoughts, I let it linger there.

"Geoffrey," she said at length, timidly.

I gazed out upon the sunlit river, watching a boatful of happy holiday folk pass by, and remained stolidly unconscious.

"Geoffrey," she repeated, "I tried ever so long to refrain from that confession, yet was unable. But I did not allude to Mr Beck. It was my conduct with Dudley that caused me to become a conscience-stricken wretch. I feared from day to day that you might discover our many long excursions and the idle afternoons we spent up the backwaters; he lazy and indolent, I using all my woman's wiles to fascinate him and bring him to my feet."

"And you succeeded," I interrupted huskily.

"Yes, I succeeded," she went on, speaking slowly, almost mechanically. "I had set my mind upon victory, and I achieved it after weeks and weeks of striving, dreading always that you might discover the truth, and fearing lest my conduct should appear in your eyes too serious for forgiveness. The blow that I dreaded has now fallen," she cried, with a choking sob. "Dudley is dead, and I, compelled to speak the truth, have publicly acknowledged myself unworthy of your love."

"Is it not best that I should know the truth?" I asked seriously. "You render your behaviour the more unpardonable by the absurd falsehoods you wish me to believe."

"I do not wish you to believe any falsehoods," she cried resentfully, her bright eyes flashing as she glanced at me. "What I have now told you is the truth. I swear it before Heaven!"

"You deliberately flirted with Dudley, with an object in view. Oh, no!" I laughed with contempt, "that is too lame a tale."

"It is the truth," she said, looking me straight in the face, her nervous hands toying with her rings. "Even though you may believe ill of me, I have lost neither honour nor self-respect. I acted under compulsion, to achieve one object."

"And I hope you have gained the mysterious end you had in view," I said, with bitter sarcasm.

"Yes, I have," she replied, with an intenseness in her voice that surprised me. "I have gained my object even at risk of being discarded by you, Geoffrey, and being branded as a base adventuress."

"Even at the cost of the life of the man you deceived?" I hazarded.

She started at my words. Her pale lips trembled, and in her eyes was a strange look, as if haunted by some spectral fear. The effect of this remark was extraordinary, and I at once added, —

"Remember, you suspect that Dudley's death was not due to natural causes."

"Suspect?" she cried. "I know he was foully murdered."

"By whom?" I inquired, with breathless eagerness.

"I have yet to discover that," she answered, in a low voice. "But I will make the elucidation of the mystery the one object of my life. It is I alone who will avenge his murder."

"Your very words betray your love for him," I exclaimed, disgusted.

"I tell you it is not because I loved him," she protested, with indignation.

"Then why do you seek revenge?" I demanded ruthlessly.

"For reasons known to myself—reasons I refuse for the present to disclose," she replied, regarding me with unwavering glance.

"And you expect me to again repose confidence in you, notwithstanding your steady refusal to explain anything?" I observed, with a laugh.

"All I have told you now, Geoffrey, is the truth," she replied, looking earnestly into my eyes. "Once I deceived you, but I will never do so in future. I promise some day before long to explain all the facts to you; when

I do so they will astound you. For the success of my plans I am compelled at present to preserve my secret, even from you."

"What are your plans?"

"Be patient, and you shall see."

"You intend to avenge Dudley's death?"

"I do; and something further," she said. "Only by the most careful investigation and the strictest secrecy can my plans be successfully carried out. Trust in me, Geoffrey. Tell me that you will reconsider your decision not to forgive me," she whispered, leaning upon my shoulder with one arm entwined affectionately about my neck, as was her habit. "And I will yet prove to you that I am an honest woman who has acted only in your interests."

"In my interests? How?" I asked, amazed.

"You shall know all later, when I have ascertained the truth."

"Tell me one thing, Ella," I exclaimed, after a pause. "Have you any idea whether Dudley had any occupation?"

"Occupation? I always understood he had enough money to be independent."

Then taking from my vest pocket the object I had picked up from among the contents of the dead man's pockets displayed on the table in the Coroners's Court, I held it up to her, saying seriously, —

"Now, tell me truthfully, Ella, have you ever seen this in Dudley's possession?"

She glanced at it for an instant, holding her breath, as across her blanched countenance there passed an expression of bewildered amazement.

The object I held beneath her gaze was insignificant in itself, merely a small brass seal, but it bore the Warnham arms in exact imitation of the cut amethyst worn by the Earl. It was the seal which had been used to manufacture the duplicate of the envelope containing England's secret alliance with Germany.

The suddenness with which I had produced it startled and nonplussed her. As I transfixed her blue eyes with my keen, suspicious gaze, her white lips moved, but no sound fell from them. Embarrassment held her dumb.

Chapter Nine
The Bond of Secrecy

I held the small brass stamp towards her, inviting her to examine it, but she shrank back with an expression of terror and repulsion, refusing to touch it.

"Have you ever seen Dudley with this in his hand?" I asked, repeating my question seriously, determined upon learning the truth.

"Where did you find it?" she inquired, a look of bewilderment upon her haggard face.

"You have not answered my question, Ella," I said sternly.

"Your question? Ah!" she cried, as if in sudden remembrance of my words. "I—I have never seen Dudley with it. I—I swear I haven't."

"Is that the absolute truth?" I asked in doubt.

"The truth!" she echoed. "Did I not, a moment ago, promise you I would never again deceive you by word or action? Can you never have confidence in me?" she asked, in a tone of mingled regret and reproach.

"But this was found in Dudley's possession," I said, holding it nearer my gaze, and detecting in the bright sunlight streaming through the window small portions of black wax still adhering to the cleverly-cut coat of arms. Black wax, I remembered, had been used to secure the dummy envelope.

"And even if that were so, is it such a very remarkable fact that a man should carry a seal?" she asked suddenly, raising her brows and assuming a well-feigned air of surprise. At that instant it occurred to me that she was an adept in preserving a mystery; she could practice deception with a verisimilitude little short of marvellous.

"But this," I observed, "is no ordinary seal."

"It looks ordinary enough," she answered, smiling. "It's only brass."

"But its discovery forms a clue to a most serious and startling crime," I said.

"A crime!" she gasped. "What do you mean? Dudley's murder?"

I did not fail to notice that she used the word "murder" as if she had absolute proof that death had not been due to natural causes. Yet the effect of my announcement had been to fill her with sudden apprehension. She strove to appear amazed, but I thought I could detect in her attitude and bearing a fear that I had knowledge of her secret.

"It is most probably connected with that tragic event," I answered meaningly, looking her straight in the face. "The police will no doubt pursue their investigations and clear up the matter."

"The police!" she whispered hoarsely, just as Mrs Laing had done when the officers had entered her house. "Do you think they will discover the cause of poor Dudley's death?"

"I cannot say," I answered calmly. "They will, however, discover the reason he had this seal in his possession."

"I tell you it was not his—I mean I never saw him with it," she protested.

"But he may have had it in his pocket and not shown it to you. Indeed, there were reasons that he should not do so because it was used for a nefarious purpose."

"For what?" she asked, suddenly evincing an interest in the stamp, taking it from my hand and examining it closely.

It was on my tongue to relate to her the whole circumstances, but suddenly remembering that for the present the secret of England's peril must be preserved if the identity of the spy were to be discovered, I refrained, and answered,—

"The man who used that seal committed one of the worst crimes of which a man can be guilty."

"What was it; tell me?" she asked quickly. "Surely Dudley never committed any offence!"

"I am not certain," I answered gloomily. "An enemy who would pose as a friend, as he has done, might be capable of any deceit."

"Have I not already told you that he was not your enemy, Geoffrey?" she observed calmly.

"Ah, Ella," I cried in disgust, "all these falsehoods only render your conduct the more despicable. You will deny next that you went down to Warnham to meet him surreptitiously."

"To Warnham?" she cried, white to the lips.

"Yes. Do you deny it?"

"No. I—it is quite true that I met him there," she faltered.

"You spent the day with my rival, unknown to me," I went on bitterly. "Yet you declare that you never loved him?"

Her breath came and went in short, quick gasps, her haggard eyes were fixed; she stood silent, unable to make reply.

"It is useless to further prolong this painful interview," I exclaimed at last, turning from her.

"I swear I never loved him," she cried suddenly. "Some day, when you know the truth, you will bitterly regret how you have misjudged me, how, while striving to serve you, I have fallen under suspicion."

"But your visit to Warnham!" I said. "Is that an act such as can be overlooked without explanation?"

"I only ask you to place trust in me, and I will prove ere long that I acted under compulsion."

"You want me to believe that he held you irrevocably in his power, I suppose?" I said with biting sarcasm.

She nodded, and held her head in downcast, dejected attitude.

"It is easy enough to allege all this, now that he is dead," I observed doubtingly.

"I have told you the truth. I feared him, and was compelled to obey," she exclaimed hoarsely.

"What was the object of your visit? Surely you can explain that?"

"No. I cannot."

"You absolutely refuse?"

"Absolutely," she answered, in a low, strained voice, looking straight at me with an expression of determination.

"Then we must part," I said, slowly but firmly disengaging myself from her embrace.

"No, no," she wailed, sobbing bitterly and clinging more closely to me. "Do not be so cruel, Geoffrey. You would never utter these words could you know all."

"But you will not tell me," I cried.

"At present I dare not. Wait; be patient, and you shall know everything."

"How long must I remain in doubt and ignorance?" I asked.

"I know not. To-morrow the bond of secrecy may be removed from my lips, or it may be many months ere I can fearlessly speak and explain," she answered in a strange voice, almost as if speaking to herself.

"From your words it would appear that some person still holds power over you, even though Dudley is dead," I said, looking into her eyes seriously.

She sighed deeply, and her hand, resting upon my shoulder, trembled violently. "Yes, you guess the truth," she answered. "I would tell you all— explain all these facts that no doubt puzzle you and cause me to appear base, heartless and deceitful—yet I fear the consequences. If I did so we should be parted for ever."

"But if you told the truth and cleared your conduct, I should then have confidence again, and love you. How should we be parted?"

Pale and silent she stood, with her eyes resting upon the distant line of drooping willows. Not until I had repeated my question did she move and answer in a voice almost inaudible, as she clung to me,—

"We should be parted by death," she whispered hoarsely.

"By death!" I cried, dismayed. "What do you mean, Ella? Do you fear that the same tragic fate that has overtaken Dudley will overtake you?"

She shuddered, and burying her white face upon my shoulder, again burst into a torrent of tears. Hers was indeed a woeful figure, bent, dejected and grief-stricken. Raising her head at last, she stifled her sobs with an effort, and implored with earnestness,—

"Tell me, Geoffrey, that you will not prejudge me. Tell me with your own lips that you will be content to wait in patience until I can present the facts to you in their true light. I am not an adventuress, as you think. I have never, I swear before Heaven, looked upon any other man with thought of affection. I have told you of my inability to speak; I can tell you no more."

I made a movement, steady, stern and deliberate, to put her from me; but, with her arms around my neck, she cried in an agonised tone,—

"No, Geoffrey. At least show me a single grain of pity. Be patient. If you desire it I will not come near you until I can reply to your questions and clear my conduct of the stigma upon it; I will do anything you ask so long as you give me time to pursue my investigations and free myself from this terrible thraldom. Say you will, and bring back peace to my mind and happiness to my heart. I love you, Geoffrey, I love you!" and her hot, passionate lips met mine in a manner that showed plainly her terrible agitation, and her fear lest I should cast her off.

Slowly, during those moments of painful silence that followed, my anger and bitterness somewhat abated, and, even against my better judgment, feelings of pity swayed my mind. It seemed to me, as I reflected upon the past, that Dudley Ogle had been unfortunate in his early surroundings and education; his character had received a wrong bias from the very beginning, and the possession of wealth had increased it. And yet, in spite of all that, there had been something pleasant and good in him. No man is altogether hideous when truly known, and I had not yet accurately ascertained the character of his mysterious relations with my well-beloved. I had, during this interview, caught glimpses of the real, true woman beneath the veil of falsehood and evasion of the truth; I had seen a wistful look occasionally in Ella's eyes, as though she were haunted constantly by some terrible dread.

Yea, I pitied her. Perhaps, if I waited, the time would come when her nature would recover from the blight that had fallen upon it; when the alien element that had grafted itself upon her true life would be expelled by those avenging powers that vex and plague the erring soul, not in mockery, but to save it from the death that cannot die.

The strangeness of her manner, and the tragic apprehension of her words would, I knew, never fade from my memory; yet half inclined to believe I had misjudged her, I at length, although feeling that the world could never again be quite the same for me, drew her slight form towards me, and imprinting a long, passionate kiss upon her ready lips, said,—

"I will try and think of you as a woman who has been wronged, Ella. I will wait until you can explain, but remember that until you relate to me truthfully the whole of the facts there can be no love between us."

"No love!" she wailed in a voice of poignant grief. "Is your love for me so utterly dead, then, that you should say this?"

"No," I answered, caressing her, stroking her wealth of gold-brown hair fondly as of old. "I love you still, Ella; yet, speaking candidly, I cannot trust you further until you explain the truth."

"But you will be patient, will you not?" she urged. "Remember that I have before me a task so difficult that it may require all my woman's tact and cunning to accomplish it. But I will—I must succeed; failure will mean that I lose you, my best beloved. Therefore wait, and ere long I will convince you that I have not lied."

"Yes, I will wait," I said, kissing her once again. "Until you have cleared yourself, however, remember that I cannot love you as I have done."

"Very well," she answered, her tear-stained face brightening. "If such is your decision, I am content. Before long I will explain all the facts, and then, I feel confident, you, noblest and dearest, will love me even better than before."

"I trust I shall," I answered with heartfelt earnestness, taking her small hand and pressing it softly; "for I love you, Ella."

"I care for nothing else," she answered, raising her face to mine and smiling through her tears. "I am happy in the knowledge that you still think of me. You have enemies; yes, many. But there was one that loved you always—ay, and loves you now, and ever shall love you."

For a moment I gazed into the deep blue depths of her clear, trusting eyes, still grasping her tiny hand in mine, but almost at that instant the door opened and Mrs Laing, fussy, good-natured, and full of sympathy, entered, and seating herself, commenced to chat about the events of that memorable morning.

Chapter Ten
England's Peril

By the discovery of the duplicate of Lord Warnham's private seal in the possession of my dead companion, it became impressed upon my mind that Dudley Ogle, the man in whom I had placed implicit trust, had not only abused my confidence by making love to Ella, but was a spy in the Russian secret service. Try how I would I could see no extenuating circumstances, and as next morning, when sitting alone in my London flat, moody and disconsolate, I calmly reflected upon the startling events of the past few days, I saw plainly, from Ella's attitude when I had exhibited the brass stamp, that, notwithstanding her declaration to the contrary, she had seen it before.

It seemed placed beyond all doubt that Dudley had acted in conjunction with certain agents, who had by some means ascertained the very day and hour that the secret convention would arrive from Berlin. Then Dudley, armed with the forged duplicate, called upon me, and while we were together extracted the document from my pocket and substituted the envelope. Yet there was the registration mark upon it, so cleverly imitated as to defy detection. How that had been placed upon the dummy puzzled me, for the designation I had written could not be known until the envelope, with its precious contents, had been filched from my pocket.

The reason of Dudley's visit to Warnham was now, to a certain extent, explained. More than probable it seemed that through bribery he had obtained from one of the servants an impression in wax of the Earl's private seal, and from it the brass stamp had been cut. The theft of the document had been accomplished with a neatness that seemed almost miraculous; and if Dudley really had stolen it, he must have been a most adroit pickpocket. Nevertheless, even though his every action had now corroborated up to the hilt the suspicion that he was a spy, I could not, somehow, believe him capable of such crafty, nay devilish, deception. Friends that we were, I could have trusted him with any secret, or with any of my possessions; but these revelations startled and amazed me.

Still there was a more remarkable and puzzling phase of the mystery. If Ella's fears were well grounded, why had he been murdered, and by whom?

The mysterious secret possessed by the woman I adored, the woman who held me under the spell of her marvellous beauty, was of a tragic and terrible nature, I felt assured. No doubt it had some connection with Dudley's death, and that sinister circumstance, once elucidated, would, I knew, furnish a very valuable clue to the identity of the spy, if perchance the innocence of my companion should be established, as I hoped it might be.

There was still one fact, too, that required explanation, one that seemed to prove conclusively that Dudley was in the pay of our enemies. I had found, on looking over his possessions in our cottage at Shepperton, some pieces of crumpled foolscap. He had evidently intended to throw them away, but being unable to get rid of them at the moment, had placed them in a drawer and locked them up. On smoothing them out, I found another piece of paper inside. To my astonishment I saw it was a letter written by me, while the pieces of foolscap accompanying it were covered with words and sentences in ink and pencil, showing how carefully he had studied and copied all the characteristics of my handwriting. These papers were, in themselves, sufficient evidence that he had practised the forger's art.

I had, after leaving Staines, returned straight to Shepperton, and in company with a detective carefully investigated all my friend's belongings. We spent the afternoon and evening in reading through heaps of letters, but discovered nothing that would lead to any suspicion of foul play. The detective made notes of one or two of the addresses of the writers, and took charge of several letters relating to money matters. When, however, we had removed all the correspondence from the small wooden box in which it had been kept, the detective ascertained that there was a false bottom, and unable to find out the secret whereby it might be opened, we forced it with a chisel.

At first we were disappointed, only one insignificant-looking paper being therein concealed, but when the officer eagerly opened it I at once recognised its extreme importance, although I preserved silence. The paper was nothing less than a Russian passport of a special character signed by the Chief of Secret Police in St Petersburg, and countersigned by the Minister of the Interior himself. It was not a formally printed document, but written in Russian upon official paper stamped with the double-headed eagle. It was made out in the name of Dudley Ogle, and after explaining that he was an official engaged on secret service, gave him complete immunity from arrest within the Russian Empire.

"What's this, I wonder?" the detective said, puzzled by the unfamiliar characters in the writing.

Taking it from him I glanced through it, and without betraying the slightest surprise, answered, "Merely a passport for Russia."

"That doesn't lead us to anything," he replied, taking it from my form, glancing at it again for an instant, and tossing it back carelessly into the box.

But when he had completed his investigations, removed whatever letters and papers he thought might be of use and departed, I secured the passport and the crumpled foolscap, and giving Juckes orders to remove my belongings back to London and give up possession of the cottage, I returned to Rossetti Mansions.

With these undeniable evidences of Ogle's activity as a spy, I was sitting alone next morning pondering over the best course to pursue, at last resolving to go to the Foreign Office and boldly place the startling facts before Lord Warnham.

About noon I knocked at the door of the Minister's private room, and received, in his deep, hoarse voice, permission to enter. He was alone, seated at his big writing-table, engrossed in a long, closely-written document he was studying.

"Well, sir," he exclaimed, with an expression of displeasure when he saw me, "to what, pray, do I owe this intrusion?"

"I have come," I said, "to clear myself of the charge you have made against me."

"To clear yourself! Bah!" he cried in disgust, returning to his papers. "My time is too valuable for further discussion," and he made a movement to ring the bell for a messenger to conduct me out.

But I placed my hand upon his bony fingers firmly, and stayed it, saying,—

"It is to your interest, Lord Warnham, as well as to my own, that you should know the truth."

"A traitor who will sell his country's honour is capable of any falsehood whereby to justify himself," he snapped savagely.

"I am no traitor," I protested in anger.

His thin, white face relaxed into a bitterly sarcastic smile, and his lip curled in withering contempt.

"The efforts of ten years' delicate diplomacy with Berlin have been rendered futile by your treachery or culpable negligence. Now you come to me with some lame, paltry tale or other, in an endeavour to convince me that you are neither thief nor spy! Each word of yours only aggravates your offence. I have dismissed you, and I tell you I decline to reopen the question."

"But you have accused me of a crime, and I demand to be judged," I cried.

"I have already judged you," he said, after a pause, laying down his pen with a sudden calmness, and fixing his grey eyes keenly upon me.

"Yes, falsely."

"You have come to me to prove that I have misjudged you," he said at last, leaning back in his chair. "Very well. Let me hear your story."

"I have no story further than what I have already told you," I answered. "You have made a charge against me; I have come to you to refute it."

"By what means?"

"By documentary evidence."

"Documentary evidence!" he exclaimed. "Of what kind?"

"You will remember that I told you of the death of the only man who could speak regarding my absence from the office and my return."

"Yes. He died mysteriously. The inquest was held yesterday;" and, taking up a letter from his table, the Earl added, "They report from Scotland Yard that an open verdict was returned, although one witness, a woman, alleged murder. Well, what was the allegation? Against yourself?" he asked, raising his grey, shaggy brows.

"No," I said with emphasis. "I am not a murderer."

"Then why did this woman—what's her name?—Ella Laing," he said, referring to the letter, "why did she allege foul play?"

"I cannot tell; but all the facts I have ascertained point to the same conclusion, although the medical evidence negatived any such suggestion."

"Then what is your contention?"

"That the man who was my friend was a spy," I said.

"You would shift the responsibility upon one who, being dead, can tell us nothing," he said in a tone of reproachful contempt. "I suspected this. It was but what might have been expected."

"But I have evidence indisputable that he was a spy," I exclaimed excitedly. "Read this," and I handed to him Dudley's passport.

Spreading it out before him, he carefully adjusted his gold *pince-nez*, and after a little difficulty translated it. Then, without expressing any surprise, he turned it over and held the paper to the light of the window, examining the water-mark.

"Well," he exclaimed calmly at last, "what else?"

I placed before him the crumpled sheets of foolscap whereon attempts had been made—and successfully too—to imitate my handwriting, explaining where I had discovered them. These he also examined very minutely, giving vent to a low grunt, as was habitual to him when reassured.

"Anything more?" he asked impatiently. "I can't waste time. The outlook is too serious."

"But you must—you shall spare time to fully investigate this mystery," I cried. "You will remember that the dummy envelope you took from your safe bore an imitation of your private seal?"

"Yes. What of that?"

"Here is the seal with which that impression was made," I replied in triumph, handing to him the little brass stamp. "I have had the portions of wax microscopically examined, and they are of the same wax as was used to seal the dummy."

He took it between his thin fingers that now trembled with excitement. The production of this object was, I saw, entirely unexpected. Suddenly rising from his chair he unlocked his great safe and took therefrom the dummy envelope. Then, returning to his table, he lit a taper and carefully made an impression in wax of the seal I had given him, afterwards taking it to the light, and by the aid of a large magnifying glass compared it closely with the seal upon the dummy.

"And where did you find this seal?" he inquired, glancing across to me.

"Among the contents of the dead man's pockets," I answered.

"Impossible!" he retorted. "The police have possession of everything found on the man."

"Yes, they had, but this came into my possession yesterday at the inquest."

"How?"

I hesitated, then, determined to conceal no fact from the great statesman, I answered boldly,—

"I stole it from the table whereon it was displayed."

"Stole it!" he echoed.

Slowly he turned the brass stamp over in his hand as if deep in thought; then, with brows knit in anger, he looked me straight in the face, exclaiming bluntly,—

"Your story is an absolute tissue of lies from beginning to end."

His words staggered me. I had expected him to be eager to further probe the mystery, and try and elucidate the manner in which Dudley had manufactured the dummy and exchanged it for the secret convention. Instead of this he was distrustful and suspicious; indeed, he boldly accused me of attempting to wilfully mislead him and conceal the truth.

"I have told you no lies. Every word I have uttered is the truth," I answered, with fierce indignation.

"You certainly never obtained possession of this seal in the manner in which you would have me believe, for the detectives sent to Staines had strict injunctions to search for any object that would lead them to suppose the dead man was not what he represented himself to be, and I made a special request that any seals discovered might be submitted to me for examination. If this had been in the dead man's pockets it would have been brought to me."

"But I tell you it was among the articles found upon him. I picked it up from the Coroner's table, and finding it was not missed, brought it to you, rather than inform the police of our suspicions, which I understood you desired should, for the present, be kept secret."

"I do not believe you," he retorted angrily.

"Ask whoever searched the body, and they will no doubt remember finding the seal," I answered.

"It is quite unnecessary," he exclaimed.

"Unnecessary? Why?"

"Because I don't believe one word of this elegantly romantic story of yours."

"But I have brought you evidence in black and white that Ogle was a spy!" I cried.

"Evidence of a sort," he answered carelessly, returning to his table and sinking into his armchair. "You have brought these things to me in order to induce me to believe that they were in the dead man's possession instead of where they really were—in your own."

"It is false," I protested, flushing at his base and dogged insinuations.

"So is this elaborate so-called evidence you have brought me," he answered.

"In what way?" I demanded.

"You wish to know," he cried. "Well, I will tell you. First, the passport is a forged one, and was never written in St Petersburg."

"Why?" I cried in dismay. "How can you tell?"

"Because its water-mark shows it to be English paper, whereas all Russian official paper, as this is supposed to be, is manufactured by Yaronovski, of Moscow, and bears his name."

This fact had never occurred to me, and taking up the paper I examined the water-mark, finding, to my surprise, the name of a well-known English mill.

"Then the attempts at imitating your handwriting are quite as unsatisfactory," he went on. "Indeed, I have no proof that all those letters and words have not been made by yourself."

"They have not," I protested. "You seem determined not to believe in my innocence."

"And the seal," he continued, heedless of my interruption. "You expected that it would be regarded as irresistible proof. Well, in the first place I do not believe it was discovered on the body, as you allege; and, secondly, even if it had been, it is no absolute proof that the dead man was the culprit."

"Why?" I inquired eagerly.

"Because it was not with that seal that the dummy envelope was secured," he answered slowly, at the same time handing me the two impressions, and inviting me to compare them.

This I did with breathless eagerness, by the aid of the magnifying glass, and in astonishment was compelled to admit that he spoke the truth. There were several discrepancies in the quarterings of the arms that I had not before noticed, and I saw instantly that they did not correspond with those impressed upon the envelope. The amazing worthlessness of my discoveries held me embarrassed, and I stood helpless, and in silence, as the Minister hurled at me some bitter invectives, declaring that I had come to him with an ingenious story, and evidence that might have convinced a man less shrewd.

"Take your clumsily-forged documents and your attempt to reproduce my seal, and leave me at once!" he cried, in a terrible ebullition of wrath, gathering up the objects I had brought and tossing them back to me. "Your dastardly conduct is too despicable for words; but remember that to you, and you alone, your country owes the overwhelming catastrophe that must now inevitably fall upon it."

With these ominous words ringing in my ears I stumbled out, knowing not whither I went, and scarcely responding to the greetings of the men I knew, who regarded me in askance. The great central staircase, up which climbed the brilliantly-uniformed representatives of all civilised countries on the face of the earth whenever the Minister held his receptions, I descended with heavy heart, and crossing the grey, silent courtyard, soon found myself amid the bustle of Parliament Street.

I saw with chagrin how utterly I had failed in my endeavour to elucidate the mystery, for not only had I been unable to throw any further light upon the theft of the treaty, or the tragic end of the man I suspected, but I had actually heaped increased suspicion upon myself. On reflection, I found myself in accord with the Minister's declaration that the passport was a forgery, and that the brass stamp was not the seal used by the spy. These facts were absolutely incontestable. The only thing remaining was the paper whereon attempts had been made to imitate my writing. I tried to explain this fact away, and clear the memory of the dead man of all suspicion, but, alas! could not bring myself to believe in his innocence. There rankled in my breast the bitter thought that he had uttered words of love to Ella, and had tried to induce her to break off her engagement to me. She herself had acknowledged on oath before the Coroner that they had quarrelled because she loved me. No. Although this passport was a clumsy imitation, and the seal had been cut without due regard to the Warnham quarterings, the plain, incontestable evidence of his forgery remained.

He was, after all, a cunning, despicable scoundrel, who had brought dishonour upon my name and ruined me both socially and financially. I found myself smiling grimly at the thought of how quickly retribution had fallen upon him. If he had died from natural causes it was but a judgment for his misdeeds; if struck down by an unknown hand it was but vengeance for his treachery towards his Queen, his country, and his bosom friend.

Heedless of where I went I walked on, called at my club, I remember, and thrust my letters into my pocket unopened; then, pursuing my way, arrived home late in the afternoon. As I entered, Juckes handed me a note from Ella, telling me that they had left Staines owing to the tragic affair, and asking me to call that evening at Pont Street, adding that she wished to see me upon a very important matter. For a long time I sat alone, smoking and thinking, trying to devise some means by which I could bring the Earl to believe in my loyalty; but at last, in desperation, I rose, dressed, and took a cab to Mrs Laing's.

The house was not large, but well ordered, exquisitely furnished, and there was about everything an air of elegant refinement that betokened wealth, taste and culture. It was nearly seven when I arrived, and I was gratified to learn that, with the exception of Beck, who came later, I was the only guest. Dinner was a much more stately meal at Pont Street than it had been at Staines, where very often we sat down in flannels, and I was not sorry when it was over, and I found myself free to talk alone with Ella. It was plain, from the dark rings about her eyes, that she had passed a sleepless night, and that her terrible and mysterious secret bore her down beneath its oppressive weight. Yet she had greeted me with the same joyous smile, the same hearty hand-shake as of old, and I had, while sitting at dinner chatting with her, felt myself wondering how I could ever have brought myself to utter such bitter reproaches and recriminations as I had done on the previous day. Her kiss, now that we were alone, thrilled me; her speech, soft and musical, held me enraptured by its charm.

She told me, in answer to my questions, how she had fared after I left "The Nook"; how dismal the place had appeared, and how many bitter memories it would always possess for her. Then, in response to her suggestion, we walked out upon the balcony, where, under the striped awning, a table and chairs were set. Here, in the cool night air, the quiet only broken by an occasional footfall or the tinkle of a passing cab-bell, we sipped our coffee and gossiped on as lovers will.

Suddenly, while she was telling me of the plans her mother had prepared for their sojourn for a couple of months at the seaside, the loud, strident cry of a running newsman broke upon our ears. At first, in the distance, the voice did not attract our attention, but when it neared us, the words, hoarse, yet indistinct, held me speechless. I sat stunned.

Ella herself sprang from her chair, and leaned over the balcony, straining her ears to catch every sound of the rough, coarse voice. The man had paused for breath before the house, a bundle of papers across his shoulder, and the ominous words he shouted were, —

"Extra spe-shall! Probable war against England! Spe-shall! War against England! Startling statement! Spe-shall!"

Chapter Eleven
Beck's Prophecy

"Hark!" gasped Ella, turning to me, pale in alarm. "What is that man crying? Listen!"

Again the hoarse voice broke the silence, dear, distinct, ominous,—

"War against England! Spe-shall!" his cry being followed by the sound of hurrying feet as people rushed from their houses, purchased copies of the paper at exorbitant prices, and eagerly devoured the amazing news.

"Surely it must be some absurd story that the papers have got hold of," Ella exclaimed a few moments later, when, after again watching the excitement below, she returned and stood beside my chair. "The idea of war against us is absolutely absurd. You Foreign Office people would have known if such were actually the case. Evening papers are so often full of exaggerated reports, contradicted next morning, that one ceases to believe in them."

"I have every reason, unfortunately, to believe in the truth of this sudden probability of war," I answered gloomily, scarce knowing what I said.

"You believe it's true!" she cried. "How do you know? Will Russia actually dare to challenge us?"

"Yes," I replied. "But how were you aware that Russia was our enemy?"

She started and held her breath. Her attitude was that of one who had unconsciously betrayed herself.

"I—I—merely guessed it," she answered lamely, with a forced smile a moment later. "I've been reading the papers lately."

"The papers have given no hint of any impending complication," I answered abruptly, removing the cigarette from my lips and looking up at her keenly.

"But I read something the other day which stated that Russia and France had combined with the object of attacking England in the near future."

I did not answer. I could only gaze at her, amazed at the calm, circumstantial manner in which she lied. That she had some knowledge of the political situation—of what character or extent I knew not—was certain, for other words she had let drop in unguarded moments had once or twice aroused within me increasing suspicion. When I reflected upon her alarm on hearing the strident cry of the newsman, I was compelled to admit that her fears were not genuine. The questions she put to me regarding the relative strengths of England and Russia, and the probable course of events, were naïve enough, but they were uttered, I knew, with a view to disarm any suspicion I might entertain.

At last, wearied of her eternal masquerade, I roused myself, tossed away my dead cigarette, and, declaring that in the circumstances my presence at the Foreign Office was imperative, suddenly said,—

"You asked me to come here this evening because you had something particular to say to me, Ella. You have not yet referred to it."

"I wanted to ask you a question," she exclaimed in a low tone, slowly moving towards me and bending until she placed her arm tenderly around my neck.

"Well, what is it?"

For a moment she remained silent in hesitation, but at last spoke in that harsh, strained voice that had so frequently puzzled me of late.

"I know you have investigated Dudley's belongings," she said. "And I wanted to know whether you discovered among them some scraps of paper bearing imitations of your own handwriting."

I regarded her in surprise; her question amazed me. In her eyes I noticed a look of intense earnestness and appeal for sympathy.

"Well, what if I have?" I inquired.

"If you have, they will, I know, be regarded by you as evidence that Dudley was a forger."

"That is what I believe him to have been," I said with bitterness.

"You judge him wrongly," she replied quite calmly, her face nevertheless as white as the simple-made dinner gown she wore. "I have already seen those papers, and know their authorship."

"Did not Dudley trace my writing?"

"He never did," she replied. "As his death was encompassed by his enemies, so is dishonour cast upon his memory."

"Then you allege that he was the victim of conspiracy!" I exclaimed, surprised.

"No doubt. When I am at last free to speak I shall prove it, and by so doing remove from myself the suspicion now resting upon me." She spoke earnestly, with an intense ring in her voice that told me she now uttered the truth.

"For what reason was it desired to imitate my handwriting?" I asked, pressing her hand tenderly. "Come, tell me, Ella."

"I really don't know," she replied. "All I am aware is that your writing was most carefully traced and imitated, and for that purpose two of your letters to me were stolen."

"By whom?"

"I have never been able to discover."

At that moment our conversation was interrupted by a voice crying, "Here, Deedes! Have you seen this alarming news?" and turning I saw Beck standing beside the tall, amber-shaded lamp in the drawing-room, a pale pink news-sheet in his hand. Rising quickly I re-entered the room, and walking over to him, followed by Ella, took the newspaper, and devoured the dozen lines of leaded type placed beneath the bold, alarming head-lines.

My well-beloved was peering over my shoulder as, in breathless eagerness, I read that, according to Reuter's correspondent at St Petersburg, the *Novoë Vremya* had that afternoon issued a special edition containing the amazing statement that Russia would, in the course of a few hours, formally declare war against England, and that this fact was corroborated by the issue of telegraphic orders to the commanders of military districts as a preliminary to a general mobilisation of the forces. This announcement was similar to that of our secret agent in St Petersburg, with the additional facts that the greatest activity had commenced in the War Office and Admiralty, and that the Tzar had, in consequence, abandoned his visit to Odessa, which he was about to undertake that day.

"The outlook is certainly most alarming," I observed, handing on the paper to Ella.

"It's extraordinary!" cried Beck, intensely excited, as became a patriotic legislator. "We have not had the slightest inkling of any diplomatic deadlock, or any disagreement with Russia. The whole thing is absolutely amazing."

"But what will happen?" asked Ella, eagerly, with white, scared face. "Will England be invaded and battles fought here in the manner prophetic writers have foretold?"

"I fear so," I said despondently. "If war is really declared, a conflict must very soon occur, and the struggle will then be long and deadly."

"But surely the Government will not allow an enemy to land upon English soil," she exclaimed, still holding the paper in her trembling hands. "What are ambassadors for but to avert such catastrophes as this?"

"Ambassadors," exclaimed Beck, "appear to me to be useless pawns. Surely our Embassy at St Petersburg must have been asleep not to have given the Government warning of the plans of Russia long ago. Preparations for war against a power like England are not made without very careful deliberation."

"But can we be invaded?" I queried.

"No doubt," Beck replied promptly. "The opinions of our greatest strategists are unanimous that, under certain conditions, France and Russia combined could invade our island. It is all very well for people to talk about England's maritime power; but is it what we believe it to be? I think not."

Having made a deep study of this very question, I was, although a loyal and patriotic Englishman, compelled to agree with him in a certain measure. Once, not so very long ago, it was generally believed, even by our greatest military and naval experts, that should England become engaged with a first-rate foreign Power, she could, single-handed, in a week close every one of her enemy's ports and have a fleet ready to reduce at its leisure everything he held beyond the seas. Indeed, some authorities went so far as to declare that with almost any two Powers against her, she could do as much; and it was that recognition of this power abroad that gave England, in spite of her military weakness, so commanding a position in Europe. But since the Franco-Russian Alliance the increase in the fleets of the Powers had been so rapid that we had utterly failed to keep pace with them. We built huge, unwieldy battleships, while our enemies constructed the fastest cruisers and torpedo-boat destroyers afloat, thereby sweeping away our hitherto undisputed mastery of the sea.

"The great danger that appears to me," Beck said presently, after we had been discussing the serious outlook at considerable length, "is that we may be blockaded by these two hostile powers, so as to reduce us near starvation, and compel us to surrender."

"But not before we have engaged the enemy at sea and given them a taste of the lion's paw," I observed.

"Of course. First, we must expect a great naval battle or battles, followed by a dash upon our territory and the landing of the hostile armies. If England received one serious reverse at sea, she could never recover from it. The loss of her maritime power would paralyse her."

"I know," I said. "That argument is trite enough. But I, nevertheless, believe that England is still, and will be for many centuries to come, Queen of the Sea."

"Oh! yes," he said, rather contemptuously. "The cheap, clap-trap patriotism of the pot-house and the music-hall is all very well, but we, in the House of Commons, entertain a very different opinion. The belief in England's greatness held by the lower classes is admirable, and, of course, ought to be carefully fostered, because it leads men to enlist in the Services. But you know, as well as I do, that in the Government Departments our naval strength is regarded as over-estimated in comparison with the power of some other European nations, and our military strength utterly inadequate. If it is really true that Russia is about to declare war against us, I fear the awakening of those confident of our insular security will be a terrible one."

"Terrible no doubt it will be, on account of the fearful loss of life and property such a war must entail, but I anticipate that when the struggle comes every Englishman will bear arms for the defence of his home and loved ones, and that the foreign invader will meet with a reception the warmth of which he never expected."

"Geoffrey is a patriot," exclaimed Ella, laughing. "So am I. I don't believe Russia and France will ever dare to land soldiers on our coasts."

"Well spoken," I exclaimed. "I do not share the fears of these so-called experts."

"I do," Beck went on excitedly. "If hostilities occur our defences will soon be found weak and utterly unreliable. That's my opinion."

"Then you declare that England is great no longer," I observed, with a smile.

"No, I don't go so far as that; but I contend, as I did in my speech in the House a fortnight ago, that those charged with maintaining our defences in a proper state of efficiency have for years been culpably negligent. The power of England to-day is still the same as it has been—on paper. But, in ascertaining it, we always close our eyes wilfully to the true fact that other nations have awakened during the past ten years, and have now actually overtaken us."

"I don't think that," I answered. "Until our country is actually invested I shall still believe in its strength."

But Beck, greatly to the amusement of Ella, was firm in his opinions, and, when I argued with him, commenced to quote statistics with a glibness which told how carefully he had studied the speech he recently delivered before the House, a speech which, by the way, had been dismissed in one line by all the newspapers. Ella, standing beside me in her pale cream dress, girdled narrow with a band of mauve silk, looked charming, and supported me in all my views, exhibiting a knowledge of politics and of the Continental outlook that I had not in the least suspected. Indeed, she now and then attacked the arguments of the member for West Rutlandshire with a vehemence that surprised me, for more than once she completely upset his declarations by citing some fact he had overlooked.

Even while we discussed these things we knew how wildly-excited must be the seething world of London. The news, although, alas! not fresh to me, had fallen that night upon the metropolis like a thunderbolt. Mrs Laing, who presently entered the room, was shown the paper by Ella, and was utterly unnerved by the startling intelligence. I had noticed that she had never since been the same stately, composed woman as before the discovery of Dudley. The tragic affair at "The Nook" seemed to have upset her, and in her face there were now traces of extreme nervousness and excitability.

"Surely the paper has printed an unwarrantable untruth, Mr Beck," she exclaimed, after reading the statement by the aid of her glasses. "I really can't believe it."

"I scarcely think we ought to credit it before we receive some confirmation," the burly legislator replied. "It may, of course, be a mere idle rumour set afloat for Stock Exchange purposes."

At that moment they exchanged swift, mysterious glances that somehow appeared to me significant, yet next instant I found myself convinced that the unusual expression in their eyes had merely been due to a chimera of my own imagination. With a foolish disregard for probability, I seemed somehow to scent mystery in everything, and it now occurred to me that to successfully probe the truth of Ella's relations with the two men, I must never allow myself to be misled by misconstruing words or actions. I felt almost confident that I had noticed Beck and Mrs Laing exchange looks akin to approbation; nevertheless, on reflection, I convinced myself that I had been quite mistaken, and half an hour later laughed at my suspicions.

Presently Beck announced his intention of going down to the House to ascertain the latest official news, and I, bidding Ella and her mother farewell, accompanied him. It was about eleven o'clock when we drove up, but the cab could not get much further than Broad Sanctuary, so dense was the crowd that had gathered at St Stephen's on the startling news being spread. From the high summit of Big Ben the electric light was streaming westward, showing the excited thousands assembled there that Parliament was already deliberating upon the best course to pursue on the outbreak of hostilities, and as we elbowed our way through the turbulent concourse war was on everyone's tongue. Men and women of all classes of society, wildly-excited, with pale, scared faces, discussed the probable course of events; many sang patriotic songs, the choruses of which were taken up and shouted lustily, while here and there, as we proceeded, loud invectives against the Tzar and his French allies greeted our ears.

At last we reached St Stephen's Hall, and, passing its zealously-guarded portals, hurried forward to the Lobby. Here the scene was of a most exciting character. Members were standing in small groups, eagerly discussing the serious and unexpected turn affairs had taken, and, in answer to our inquiries, we learnt that a quarter of an hour before an official reply had been given in the House to a question addressed from the Opposition benches, admitting that, according to the latest advices from St Petersburg, there was, no doubt, foundation for the rumour published by the *Novoë Vremya*, and that it was very probable that in the course of an hour or two war would formally be declared.

A tiresome topic was being discussed in the House, but it was being carried on without spirit or enthusiasm, all the members being on tiptoe with expectation regarding the next telegram from the enemy's camp. The amazing intelligence that had spread like wildfire throughout the metropolis had brought every member in town down to the House, until the Lobby became so thronged that locomotion was difficult. I chatted with many legislators I knew, and found all held similar views—that an attempted invasion of England had been planned by France and Russia. The Cabinet had been hastily summoned, and was at that moment deliberating with the Commander-in-Chief regarding the immediate steps to be taken for the complete mobilisation of the forces.

One fact had impressed itself upon me as, accompanied by Beck, I had struggled through the ever-increasing crowd outside, namely, the intense patriotism of the Volunteers. There were dozens who, on hearing the news, had at once put on their uniforms in readiness to bear their part in the defence of their homes, and everywhere as they swayed to and fro in the crowd they were lustily cheered. The sight of a uniform in those wild moments was sufficient to send the multitude half mad with enthusiasm, and in one or two instances volunteers had been raised shoulder-high in order that all should unite in giving them ovations.

Within the sombre, smoke-blackened walls of Parliament it was a breathless period of eager waiting. There was no cheering, there was no cheap patriotism, no outburst of enthusiasm. Some of the little knots of white-hatted politicians condemned the Government unmercifully for failing to obtain news of a pending catastrophe which might have been avoided by diplomacy, while others declared that the action of the Opposition in the past was alone responsible for the present disaster. Wherever I went I found an opinion, almost unanimous, that England could not withstand the blow now threatened. In that time of wild theories and wilder apprehensions Beck's arguments and prophetic utterances were listened to eagerly, until quite a crowd stood around him. Of late he had written one or two articles on the subject of England's unpreparedness for war, notably one in the *Nineteenth Century*, which had attracted considerable attention, and his opinions were now listened to and afterwards discussed, even among men whose names were household words.

As I stood watching and listening, I was compelled to admit that during the short time my friend had been in Parliament he had certainly won good opinions, and even among the most level-headed politicians his views, notwithstanding his blustering manner, were regarded as worthy of serious consideration. I confess to having previously looked upon him rather as a crank upon this subject, but I did so no longer, now that I recognised what weight his arguments carried.

Chapter Twelve
An Important Dispatch

Half an hour later I stood at the door of the small post-office in the Lobby, after discussing the situation with that most cheery and courteous of officials, Mr Pike, the postmaster, who had left me for a moment to give some instructions to his subordinates. My mind was filled by gloomy thoughts, as I reflected that all this national terror and excitement had been produced by the dastardly and almost miraculous ingenuity of some unknown person.

But was he unknown? Was it not more than probable that the person to whom all this was due was Dudley Ogle, the man who lay lifeless without a single sorrowing friend to follow his body to the grave? Sometimes I felt entirely convinced of this: at others I doubted it. If Ella spoke the truth, as it now appeared, then it was plain that Dudley had been the victim of a terribly cruel and crafty conspiracy that culminated in his death. Might not this be so, I argued within myself. Yet the words and actions of Ella were all so remarkable, so veiled by an impenetrable mystery, that any endeavour to elucidate her reasons only puzzled me the more, driving me almost to the verge of madness.

Truth to tell, I loved her with a fond, passionate love, and had, only after months of trepidation and uncertainty, succeeded in obtaining her declaration that she reciprocated my affection, and her promise to be my wife. Yet within a month of my new-born life in happiness supreme, all these untoward events had, alas! occurred, stifling my joy, replacing confidence by doubt, and driving me to despair.

While I stood there alone, Lord Warnham hastily approached the post-office window with a telegram, and, seeing me, exclaimed,—

"Ah! I want you, Deedes. An hour ago I sent telegrams everywhere for you. Come with me to my room."

He handed in his telegram, and together we went along the corridors to his own private room, where, in an armchair, with some papers in his hand, sat the Marquis of Maybury, Prime Minister of England. We had met before many times when the burly, elderly peer had been a guest at Warnham Hall, and on many occasions I had acted as his secretary when he had been alone.

"Well, Deedes," he exclaimed gravely, looking up suddenly from the papers, "Lord Warnham has explained to me the mysterious theft of the secret convention, and I am anxious to see you regarding it."

The Foreign Minister seated himself at his table in silence, with folded arms, as the world-renowned statesman proceeded to question me closely regarding the events of that memorable day when the document had been so ingeniously stolen.

"Have you not the slightest clue to the culprit, even now?" Lord Maybury asked at last, stroking his full grey beard. "Remember that England's honour and her future depends absolutely upon the issue of this serious complication. If you can furnish us with any information, it is just possible that diplomacy may do something, even at the eleventh hour. You see we have lost the original of the convention, and this, if produced in Petersburg, is sufficient evidence against us to upset all our protestations."

"I have told Lord Warnham all I know," I answered calmly. "To him I have explained my suspicions."

"That this friend of yours called Ogle, who died mysteriously on that very same day, was the actual spy," he observed. "Some of the facts certainly point to such a conclusion; but, now tell me, did Ogle enter your room at the Foreign Office on that day?"

"Certainly not," I replied. "No one is allowed in my room except the clerks."

"Could he have seen the envelope sticking out of your pocket?"

"No," I answered. "I am confident he could not, because, on placing it in my pocket, a deep one, I took precaution to notice whether it were visible."

"Then, if such is the case, I maintain that Ogle could not possibly have known what designation you had written upon the envelope," the Premier observed; adding, "Did you meet anyone you knew during your walk to the Ship, or while you were in Ogle's company?"

"No one whatever," I said.

"I know the Ship. At which table did you sit?"

"At the first table on the left, in the inner room beyond the bar. I sat in the corner, with my back to a high partition. Therefore, the envelope could not possibly have been extracted from my pocket without my knowledge."

"Then I should like to hear your theory of the affair," said the Prime Minister, his dark, penetrating eyes fixed upon me.

"It is so remarkable," I answered, "that I am utterly unable to form any idea how the theft was accomplished."

"You believe, however, that Ogle was a spy?"

"At present, yes," I said. "And further, I have grave suspicions that he was murdered."

"Ah, that was alleged at the inquest," his Lordship observed. "At present the police are sparing no effort to determine the cause of his death, and to find out who manufactured the duplicate of Lord Warnham's seal."

"The seal I picked up from among the contents of Ogle's pockets was not the identical one used to secure the dummy envelope," I said quickly.

"I am fully aware of all the facts," he answered rather coldly. "My desire is to find out something fresh. Even the police seem utterly baffled. Who is this young woman, Ella Laing, who at the inquest alleged murder?"

"The daughter of Mrs Laing, of Pont Street."

"Do you know her intimately?"

"She is engaged to be married to me," I replied.

"It is apparent that she was very friendly with this Ogle. Surely you can induce her to tell you something about him."

"She knows but little more than what I already know. He lived with me at Shepperton, and had few secrets from me."

"Did you ever suspect him to be a spy?"

"Not for one moment. He had plenty of money of his own, and was in no sense an adventurer."

"Well," exclaimed the Premier, turning to his colleague at last. "It is extraordinary—most extraordinary."

Lord Warnham nodded acquiescence, and said, "Yes, there is a deep and extraordinary mystery somewhere: a mystery we must, for the sake of our own honour, penetrate and elucidate."

"I entirely agree," answered the other. "We have been victimised by clever spies."

"And all owing to Deedes's culpable negligence," added Lord Warnham, testily, glancing at me.

"No, I am inclined to differ," exclaimed the Premier. He had never acted very generously towards me, and I was surprised that he should at this moment take up the cudgels on my behalf. "To me it appears, as far as the facts go, that Deedes has been victimised in the same manner as ourselves."

"But if he had exercised due caution this terrible catastrophe could never have occurred," the Foreign Minister cried impatiently, tapping the table with his pen in emphasis of his words.

"A little more than mere caution, or even shrewdness, is required to defeat the efforts of the Tzar's spies," the Premier said quietly. "In my opinion, Deedes, although in a measure under suspicion, cannot be actually condemned. Remember, among Ogle's correspondence he discovered evidence of an undoubted attempt to forge his handwriting."

"We have no corroboration that he really did find that actually among the dead man's possessions," exclaimed Lord Warnham quickly. "I have myself seen the detective who accompanied him to Shepperton, and he tells me that no sheets of paper of that character were discovered. He—"

"I found them while he was engaged in an adjoining room," I interrupted. "I did not mention it to him, preferring to bring the evidence straight to you."

"It is just possible that Deedes's version is correct," observed the Premier. "Personally, I must say, Warnham, that I cannot see any ground for the dismissal of a hitherto trustworthy servant of Her Majesty upon this extraordinary evidence. I have always found Deedes upright, loyal and patriotic, and coming as he does of a well-known family of diplomats, I really do not suspect him of having played his country false."

"I am obliged for your Lordship's words," I exclaimed fervently. "I assure you that your merciful view is entirely correct. I am innocent, and at this moment am utterly at a loss to account for any of the amazing events of the past few days."

Lord Warnham was silent in thought for a few moments, then, turning his sphinx-like face to me, he said, in a tone rather more conciliatory than before, "Very well. As it is Lord Maybury's wish, I will reinstate you in the Service; but remember, I have no confidence in you."

"Then you still suspect me of being a spy?" I cried reproachfully. "I am to remain under suspicion!"

"Exactly," he answered dryly. "Until the truth is ascertained I, at least, shall believe you had something to do with the theft of that secret convention. Even the telegram sent from the Strand Post-Office to St Petersburg is in your handwriting—"

"Forged!" I interposed. "Have you not already seen the careful attempts made to copy the formation of my letters and figures?"

"The greatest calligraphic expert of the day has pronounced the telegram to be undoubtedly in your own hand, while the counter-clerk who took in the message and received payment for it, has seen you surreptitiously, and recognised you by the shape of the silk hat you habitually wear."

Here was an astounding case of mistaken identity. I had never entered the post-office near Exeter Hall for six months at least.

"I should like to meet that clerk face to face," I burst forth. "He tells a distinct falsehood when he says he recognises me. I did not go into the Strand at all on that day." Then a thought suddenly occurred to me when I reflected upon the shape of my hat, and I added, "I admit that my hat is of a rather unusual shape," taking it up and exhibiting it to them. "But when I bought this in Piccadilly two months ago Ogle was with me, and he purchased one exactly similar."

"Again the evidence is against the dead man," the Premier said, turning to Lord Warnham. "Where is his hat?" he inquired of me sharply.

"At Shepperton. I can produce it if required. Its shape is exactly like mine."

"You had better speak to Frayling upon that point," observed Lord Warnham. "It may prove important. At any rate, Deedes, perhaps, after all, I have been just a trifle unjust in condemning you, therefore consider yourself reinstated in the same position as before, although I must admit that my previous confidence in your integrity is, to say the least, seriously—very seriously—impaired."

"I hope it will not remain so long," I said. "If there is anything I can do to restore your belief in my honesty, I will do it at whatever cost."

"There is but one thing," he exclaimed. "Discover the identity of the spy."

"I will regard that the one endeavour of my life," I declared earnestly. "If the mystery is to be fathomed I will accomplish it."

"While we've been talking," the Premier interposed, "a thought has occurred to me, and for mentioning it I hope you, Deedes, will pardon me. It has struck me that if, as seems even more than likely, this man Ogle was actually a spy who had carefully cultivated your acquaintance with an ulterior motive, is it not within the range of possibility that the lady, who was also your most intimate friend, as well as his, either knew the true facts, or had a hand in the affair?"

"I can trust Ella," I said, glancing at him resentfully. "She is no spy."

The elderly statesman stroked his beard thoughtfully and smiled, saying, "Ah, I expected as much. I myself was young once. When a man loves a woman he is very loth to think her capable of deceit. Yet in this instance we must not overlook the fact that more than one female spy has been brought under our notice."

"I am aware of that," I replied, angry that he should have made such a suggestion against my well-beloved, yet remembering her strange utterances when she heard the news of impending war shouted in the street. "But I have the most implicit faith in the woman who is to be my wife."

"Has she explained, then, the character of the secret existing between herself and Ogle?" asked Lord Warnham, raising his grey, shaggy brows. "From the evidence at the inquest it was plain, you will remember, that there was some mysterious understanding between them. Has she given you her reasons for declaring that Ogle has been murdered?"

For a moment I was silent; afterwards I was compelled to make a negative reply.

"That doesn't appear like perfect confidence, does it?" the Foreign Minister observed, with a short, hard laugh. "Depend upon it, Deedes, she fears to tell you the truth."

"No, she fears some other person," I admitted. "Who it is I know not."

"Find out, and we shall then discover the spy," the Premier said, adding, with a touch of sympathy, after a moment's pause, "Remember, I allege nothing against you, Deedes. Do your duty, and regardless of all consequences discover the means by which we have been tricked. Induce the woman you love to speak; nay, if she loves you, force her to do so, for a woman who truly loves a man will do anything to benefit him, otherwise she is unworthy to become his wife. Some day ere long you yourself will become a diplomat, as other members of your family have been. Now is the time to practise tact, the first requisite of successful diplomacy. Be tactful, be resourceful, be cunning, and look far into the future, and you will succeed both in clearing yourself and in explaining this, the most remarkable mystery that has occurred during the long years of my administration."

I thanked him briefly for his advice, declaring that it should be my firm endeavour to follow it, and also thanked Lord Warnham for my re-instatement, but my words were interrupted by a loud double knock at the door, and in response to an injunction to enter, there appeared, hot and breathless, Frank Lawley, one of the Foreign Office messengers. He wore, half-concealed by his overcoat, his small enamelled greyhound suspended around his neck by a thin chain, his badge of office, and in his hand carried one of the familiar travelling dispatch-boxes.

"Good evening, your Lordships," he exclaimed, greeting us.

"Where are you from, Lawley?" inquired Lord Warnham, eagerly.

"From Paris, your Lordship. My dispatch, under flying seal, is, I believe, most important. The Marquis of Worthorpe feared to trust it on the wire."

In an instant both Premier and Minister sprang to their feet. While Lord Maybury broke the seals Lord Warnham whipped out his keys, opened the outer case, and then the inner red leather box, from which he drew forth a single envelope.

This he tore open, and holding beneath the softly-shaded electric lamp the sheet of note-paper that bore the heading of our Embassy in Paris, both of Her Majesty's Ministers eagerly devoured its contents.

When they had done so they held their breath, raised their heads, and without speaking, looked at each other in abject dismay. The contents of the dispatch held them spellbound.

The window of the room was open, and the dull, distant roaring of the great, turbulent multitude broke upon our ears. The excitement outside had risen to fever heat.

Chapter Thirteen
A Statement to the Press

"This is indeed extraordinary!" exclaimed Lord Maybury, the Premier, at last.

"An amazing development—most amazing!" the Foreign Minister cried, unusually excited.

"What is the best course?" asked the head of the Government.

"There is but one," his colleague answered. "I shall wire to St Petersburg at once and await confirmation."

"The situation is becoming absolutely bewildering," observed the Premier. "It may be best, I think, to convene another meeting of the Cabinet."

Lord Warnham, with that involuntary caution that he had developed during long years of office as Minister of Foreign Affairs, at once dismissed Frank Lawley, but allowed me to remain. As his confidential secretary I had been present on many occasions when delicate matters of diplomacy had been adjusted and plans arranged which, if divulged, would have caused an upheaval throughout Europe.

"No, I don't think another Council is necessary, at least not to-night," answered Lord Warnham, when the cosmopolitan messenger had closed the door behind him.

"But the whole thing is at present a mystery," said the Prime Minister, standing astride with his broad back to the empty grate.

"Exactly. We must have news from the Embassy in St Petersburg before long. Until then, I think we should be patient."

"But hark!" exclaimed the Premier, quite calmly, and as we all three listened we could hear the dull roar of the crowd becoming louder. The popular excitement outside was intense, and the eager multitude increased each moment. "They are clamouring for news. It is, I think, time that another statement should be made in the House."

"As you wish," Lord Warnham answered, with ill grace. It was part of his creed to tell the public absolutely nothing. The Premier was for publicity—he for secrecy always.

"But whatever statement is made regarding the receipt of intelligence it cannot compromise our position at St Petersburg," the Marquis argued.

"Very well. Let the statement be made. But, personally, I cannot see what we can say at present."

"Say something. It will reassure the public that we are endeavouring to readjust diplomatic negotiations. Already we are being hounded down on all sides by wild-haired agitators as having been asleep. Let us show our opponents that we are now fully alive to England's peril."

"Ah, Maybury," laughed the Foreign Minister, "it is always my opinion that the less the public know the easier it is for us to carry on the business of the country. The irresponsible journals are really the cause of nine-tenths of our diplomatic ruptures."

"But the Press assist us in many ways, and if you are averse to a statement in the House why not make one to *The Times*, or to a news agency? Perhaps the latter course would be best, for it will re-establish public confidence."

"But that will not be official," Lord Warnham demurred.

"Nevertheless, we can make the official statement later, when we have received confirmation of this extraordinary dispatch."

"Is the dispatch from Paris very remarkable?" I asked, unable to any longer bear their tantalising conversation, so anxious was I to ascertain the latest development of this conspiracy against our country.

"Read it for yourself," Lord Warnham answered, glancing at the Premier to ascertain whether this course received his approbation, and finding that it did, he handed me the dispatch, which I found a moment later read as follows:—

"From Marquis of Worthorpe, Paris, to Earl of Warnham, Her Majesty's Principal Secretary of State for Foreign Affairs.—My Lord,—In further continuation of my dispatch of this morning, I have the honour to report to your Lordship that the war preparations actively commenced here on receipt of a telegram from St Petersburg (copy of which was enclosed in my last dispatch) have, owing to a later telegram from Russia, been entirely stopped. The orders for mobilisation have everywhere been countermanded. According to a statement just made to me by our secret agent in the Ministry of Foreign Affairs, the French Government have to-day received word that the Tzar's declaration of war will not, for some unexplained reason, be published. I send this by special messenger in the hope that it will reach your Lordship this evening.—Worthorpe."

"This is remarkable!" I cried. "It appears as if Russia has already repented." But the Premier and his colleague, at that moment in consultation regarding the steps to be taken should this astounding and reassuring news prove correct, did not notice my remark. Presently, however, the Prime Minister, turning to me, asked, —

"Are any of the reporters your personal friends, Deedes?"

"Yes, I know several."

"To whom shall we make our statement?" he inquired. "We want it spread throughout the country."

"In that case I should suggest Mr Johns, of the agency that supplies the club tapes and newspapers."

"Then send for him."

At once I went to the door and dispatched the messenger waiting outside to find that well-known figure of the Reporters' Gallery, who makes it his boast that for years without a break he had sat through every sitting of the House of Commons, and whose friends have a legend that he can enjoy a sleep in his "box" over the Speaker's chair and awake at the very moment any question of public interest arises. Ten minutes had elapsed when the chosen representative of the Press entered, hot and breathless, bowing to their Lordships. He was spare, dark-haired, with sharp, aquiline features, a breadth of forehead that denoted considerable learning, a pointed, dark-brown beard, and a pair of sharp, penetrating eyes. He spoke with a broad Scotch accent, his sallow face betraying signs of considerable excitement.

"I desire, Mr Johns, to make a statement to the Press, and have sent for you with that object," exclaimed the Minister for Foreign Affairs, glancing up at him.

"With pleasure, my Lord," exclaimed the reporter, taking from his pocket a pencil and a few loose sheets of "copy paper." "I'm quite ready."

Then, as Lord Warnham dictated his message to the public, the representative of the news agency took it down in a series of rapid hieroglyphics. The words the Minister uttered were as follows: —

"In order to allay undue public alarm, I wish it to be known that, according to advices I have received, the statement in the *Novoë Vremya* to-day, at first believed to be correct, is without foundation."

"Then war is not declared?" interrupted the reporter, excitedly.

"No. The alarming report reproduced by the English Press from the St Petersburg journal is apparently totally incorrect."

"And I presume I may say that there is no rupture of diplomatic negotiations with St Petersburg?"

Lord Warnham, smiling that sphinx-like smile which might be construed into anything the interlocutor chose, turned to the Prime Minister for his opinion upon the point.

"Of course," exclaimed the Marquis. "We have received no intimation of any diplomatic difficulty. Further, you may reassure the public that the Government will do everything in its power to avert any catastrophe; but as no catastrophe has occurred, all this excitement is quite uncalled for."

"May I use your own words, your Lordship?" inquired the reporter, quickly. "I want to reproduce this in the form of an interview."

"You can act as you please about that," the Premier said, smiling as he added, "I suppose we shall see it in every newspaper in England to-morrow, headed, 'The War Against England: Interview with the Prime Minister'—eh?"

"Not to-morrow, your Lordship—to-night," laughed the reporter, fidgeting in his eagerness to get away with the finest bit of "copy" that ever his pencil wrote.

The Premier turned to speak with Lord Warnham, but my friend Johns was not to be delayed, even by the discussion of the nation's peril. If the Archangel had suddenly appeared he would have calmly "taken a note" of how such an occurrence affected the onlookers.

"Is there anything more I can say, your Lordship?" he asked, impatiently interrupting their conversation.

"No, I think not at present," Lord Warnham answered. "If you have any further statement to make, I shall hold myself in readiness," he said, the journalistic spirit of greed being aroused to have the whole of this exclusive information to himself.

"We will send for you if we have anything further to communicate," Lord Warnham answered, and wishing him good evening, intimated that at least for the present the interview was at an end.

After he had left, it was desired, upon the suggestion of the Premier, to slightly amend one of the sentences used by Lord Warnham, and with that object I rushed after the excited interviewer. After a little search I found him in the small room behind the Press Gallery, dictating in breathless haste to the clerk, who sat resting his head on one hand while with the other he worked the telegraph-key. As I approached, I heard him exclaim in broad Scotch,—"Now, then, Ford, look sharp, my lad, look sharp! Send this along, 'Our representative has just interviewed the Marquis of Maybury and the

Earl of Warnham on the situation. The exclusive information imparted is of the greatest possible importance, as it shows'—"

Here I interrupted him, and having requested him to reconstruct the sentence, as desired by Lord Warnham, left him, and returned to where the two Ministers were still in earnest consultation.

Having busied myself with some correspondence lying upon the Foreign Minister's table, while the pair discussed a critical point as to the instructions to be sent to Lord Worthorpe in Paris, there presently came another loud knock at the door. One of the clerks, who had rushed over from the Foreign Office, entered, bearing a telegraphic dispatch.

"Where from?" inquired Lord Warnham, noticing the paper in his hand as he came in.

"From St Petersburg, your Lordship," he answered, handing him the telegram.

The Premier and Foreign Secretary read it through together in silence, expressions of satisfaction passing at once across both their countenances.

"Then we need have no further apprehension," exclaimed the Premier at last, looking up at his colleague.

"Apparently not," observed Lord Warnham. "This is certainly sufficient confirmation of Worthorpe's dispatch," and he tossed it across to the table whereat I sat, at the same time dismissing the clerk who had brought it.

Taking up the telegram, I saw at a glance it was from our secret agent in the Russian Foreign Office, and that it had been re-transmitted from Hamburg. Although he had stated that all cipher messages were refused, this was in our private code, and its transcription, written beneath, was as follows:—

"Remarkable development of situation has occurred. Ministers held a Council this afternoon, and after conferring with the Tzar, the latter decided to withdraw his proclamation of war, which was to be issued to-night. The reason for this sudden decision to preserve peace is a mystery, but the Tzar left half-an-hour ago on his journey south, two of the Ministers have left for their country seats, and telegraphic orders have been issued countermanding the military preparations, therefore it is certain that all idea of war is entirely abandoned. Immediately at the conclusion of the Council, a telegram was sent to the Russian Minister in Paris, informing him of the decision not to commence hostilities against England. The Novoë Vremya, in order to allay public feeling, is to be prosecuted for publishing false news."

When I had read this astounding dispatch, congratulating myself that, after all, our country need not fear a foreign foe, I sat listening to the discussion between the two great statesmen. The Premier advocated an immediate statement in the House in order to reassure the public, but Lord Warnham, with that love of secrecy apparent in all his actions, personal or political, was strenuously opposed to such a course.

"Let us wait until to-morrow," he said. "To-night the papers will publish special editions containing the interview we have just given the Press representative, and this certainly ought to calm the crowd outside." He spoke with a sneer of contempt of the multitude of excited citizens in fear of their lives and property.

"But they are patriots, many of them, Warnham," the Premier protested. "Who have placed us in power but that public?"

"Oh, of course," the other snapped impatiently. "You go in for popularity with the masses. I don't. I've never been popular, not even in my own Department. But I can't help it. I do my duty, and perhaps it is my very unpopularity that has secured me a reputation as head of Foreign Affairs."

"It may be, Warnham. It may be," said the Premier, slowly. "But you are more popular than you imagine."

"In the Press, yes. These modern journals will lick the boots of anybody in power. It is not as it used to be in the old days, when you and I received a sound rating nearly every morning in *The Times*."

"I do not allude to the Press, but contend that you are popular with the public. You would increase that popularity by allowing a statement to be made to-night."

"Let them wait until the morning," he growled. "I haven't the slightest wish to be regarded as the people's saviour. An immediate statement will appear too much like a bid for cheap notoriety."

"Is it not your duty to the people to allay their apprehensions of a coming war?"

"It is my duty to Her Majesty alone," he exclaimed, suddenly remembering that he had forgotten to dispatch the reassuring news to Osborne, and turning, he thereupon dictated to me a telegram, which I quickly reduced to cipher.

"Then you decline to allow any explanation to be given?" said the Premier, in a tone of reproach, stroking his full beard thoughtfully. "You would go home comfortably to bed and allow these thousands of half-scared citizens to remain in fear and doubt throughout the night."

"Why not?" he laughed. "I tell you I am unpopular, therefore a little secrecy more or less does not matter. If a Foreign Minister allowed the Press and public to know all his doings, how could diplomacy be conducted? The first element of success in dealing with foreign affairs is to preserve silence, and not allow one's self to be drawn."

"But in this instance silence is quite unnecessary," exclaimed the Prime Minister, growing impatient at the dogged persistence of his eccentric colleague, whose delight was to be designated as harsh, unrelenting and ascetic. In private life Lord Warnham lived almost alone in his great, gloomy mansion, scarcely seen by any other person save his valet, the telegraph clerk and myself. Some said that a strange romance in his youth had soured him, causing him to become misanthropic and eccentric; but it was always my opinion that the blow which fell upon him years ago; the early death of his young and beautiful wife, whom he loved intensely, was responsible for his slavish devotion to duty, his eccentricity, and the cool cynicism with which he regarded everybody, from his Sovereign to his secretary. As a Foreign Minister, every Government in Europe admired, yet feared him. He was, without doubt, the most shrewd and clever statesman the present century had known.

"I shall preserve silence until to-morrow," he said, decisively, at last.

"If Her Majesty were consulted, she would, I feel sure, advocate an immediate declaration of the exact position of affairs," Lord Maybury said. "She has the welfare of her people at heart. Remember, both you and I are her servants."

"Of course, of course," he said, commencing to pace the room slowly. "Well," he added, after a pause, "suppose we made a statement in the Commons to-night, and to-morrow we find the outlook still threatening and gloomy—what then?"

"Listen!" cried the Prime Minister, at last losing patience, and throwing open the window wide. "Listen! The people of London are clamouring for news. Give it to them, and let them depart."

"They'll be able to read it in the papers presently. Let them pay their pennies for it," he sneered.

"But that is not official," the Premier argued, and before his colleague had time to reply, the messenger stationed outside the door entered, bearing a telegram, which he took to Lord Warnham.

"The representative of Reuter's Agency has brought this telegram, just received from St Petersburg, and desires to know whether you have any confirmation of the abandonment of the proposed hostilities against us," the man said.

"Oh, tell him I have nothing to communicate," cried his Lordship, hastily. "And, look here, don't bother me again with any inquiries from the Press."

"Very well, your Lordship," the messenger answered, and at once withdrew.

"Why not make an official declaration?" the Marquis urged. "It would avoid a great deal of unnecessary worry and anxiety."

For a long time the Foreign Minister held out, until at length he became convinced by Lord Maybury's forcible arguments in favour of publicity, and gave his sanction to a statement being made in the House of Commons. Presently we all three proceeded there, and at once the news spread like wildfire, within Parliament and without, that the latest news from St Petersburg was to be officially announced. From the glass swing door of the Press gallery I watched the House rapidly fill to overflowing, even to its galleries, and when all had assembled the excitement for about ten minutes was intense. It was a memorable scene, more impressive, perhaps, than any of the many that have taken place within those sombre-panelled walls.

Presently, prefaced by the Speaker's loud "Order-r-r! Order!" a slim, grey-haired figure rose from the Government bench and explained that the news contained in the *Novoë Vremya* was entirely false, and assured the House that war had not been, and would not be, declared against England.

The final sentences of this welcome announcement were lost in a terrific outburst of applause. So excited were some of the younger members that they tossed their hats high in the air like schoolboys, and the vociferous cheering of the Foreign Secretary was continued, loud and long, notwithstanding the Speaker's dignified and formal efforts to suppress it. The scene was the most enthusiastic and stirring that I had ever witnessed, but even this was eclipsed by the terrific enthusiasm I found prevailing among the multitude when, a quarter of an hour later, I fought my way though the throng to gaze outside.

The great concourse of citizens, wildly-excited, were almost mad with delight. Publicly, from the steps of St Stephen's Hall, the official statement had been shouted, and the multitude sent up such an outburst of applause that it echoed far and wide from the dark walls of Parliament and Abbey, church and hospital. The more enthusiastic ones yelled themselves hoarse with joyful shouts, while others started to sing "God save the Queen" until, taken up by all, the National Anthem echoed through the streets again and again. Then cheer upon cheer was given for "Warnham" and for "Good old Maybury," the women joining in honouring England's greatest statesman.

It was popularly believed that by the efforts of these two men war had been averted, and it was not therefore surprising when they both left together and entered a carriage to drive to Downing Street, that the crowd unharnessed the horses, and fifty stalwart patriots dragged the carriage in triumph to its destination, while such an ovation was accorded them on every side, that even the excitement of the declaration of the poll at their election was paltry in comparison.

I sat with them on the carriage, and as we were dragged onward through the dense, surging crowd, the Marquis turned to the Foreign Minister and exclaimed, with a smile, —

"Surely you can never regard yourself as unpopular after this?"

"Ah!" exclaimed the other, sadly, with a heavy sigh. "It is you they are cheering, not myself. The people call you 'good old Maybury,' but they have never called me 'good old Warnham,' and will never do so. I am still unpopular, and shall be always."

Chapter Fourteen
Sonia

Notwithstanding official assurances that no alarm need be felt at the political outlook, the popular excitement, fostered by a sensational Press, abated but slowly. On the morning following the memorable scene in the House of Commons, a great panic occurred on the Stock Exchange, and it was fully a week ere confidence was restored. Meanwhile, at Lord Warnham's dictation, I exchanged constant communications with our ambassador in St Petersburg, and although every endeavour was used to elucidate the mysterious reason why the Russian Government so suddenly altered its tactics, it remained as inexplicable as the means whereby they had obtained the original of our secret convention with Germany.

Both the London police and our secret agents in Russia abandoned none of their activity, but all their efforts were to no purpose. The incident was a perfect enigma.

Thus a month went by. Lord Warnham had slightly relaxed towards me as if, after all, he believed that I had spoken the truth, although he frequently, when vexed, would refer in uncomplimentary terms to what he called my "carelessness that nearly cost England her honour." Indeed, although I had been reinstalled in the position of great trust I had previously held, mine was no enviable lot. The Foreign Minister was a man of moods, strangely eccentric, sometimes preserving a rigid silence for hours, and often working for long periods alone during the night, attending to unimportant dispatches that might have been answered by a lower-grade clerk. But it was his object always to know the exact work done in each department, and to be able to do it himself. Thus he was enabled to keep a more careful watch over everything that went on, and was not, like the majority of Cabinet Ministers, a mere figure-head. Times without number I have gone to Berkeley Square early in the morning when some important matter of diplomacy has been in progress, and found the grey, thin-faced peer still seated in his study, the blinds still down, the electric light still on, showing how he had worked on unconsciously throughout the whole night, and was quite unaware of dawn. His servants had strict orders never to disturb him, even for meals, hence, when he was busy, he frequently spent many hours in his chair, regardless of day or night.

These periods of intense mental strain would, however, be followed by exasperating irritability of such a character that I often feared to utter a word lest he should break out into a fierce ebullition of anger. At those times he would scatter broadcast the most severe censures on all and sundry, sparing neither ambassador nor consul, so fierce was his wrath. Knowing this, I would sometimes, after writing an abusive dispatch at his dictation, put it aside and, instead of forwarding it, accidentally overlook it. Then, next day, he would almost invariably relent, and after deep thought, exclaim,—

"Read me the copy of that dispatch I sent yesterday to Vienna, Deedes."

"Oh," I would answer, as if suddenly recollecting, "I quite forgot to forward it, we were so busy yesterday."

"Ah, too late now! too late!" he would grumble, feigning annoyance, yet secretly pleased. "Destroy it, Deedes; destroy it."

Afterwards he would dictate a more temperate and less offensive letter, which the messenger leaving London that night would carry in his valise.

One morning, towards the end of July, I received a strangely-worded letter, written in a foreign hand, asking me to call at an address in Pembroke Road, Kensington, and signed "Sonia." The missive, which had been left at my flat by a commissionaire, stated that the matter upon which the writer desired to see me was extremely urgent, and contained a request that I would telegraph a reply. This I did, accepting the appointment, for, on reflection, I had a very dim recollection of having, at some time or other, written officially to someone named "Sonia," and the letter aroused curiosity within me.

That night, at the time she named, I found myself before a large, substantial-looking detached house, situated in the quiet, rather unfrequented thoroughfare off Earl's Court Road, a house which, to my excited imagination, bore external evidence of mystery within. Why such thought should seize me I know not. Perhaps it was because the writer of the letter was unknown, and the object of my visit at present unexplained; nevertheless I entered the small garden that divided the house from the roadway, and, ascending the steps, rang the bell. My summons was immediately answered by a neat maid, to whom I gave my card, and next moment I was ushered into a well-furnished drawing-room, dimly lit by one tall, shaded lamp, the light of which was insufficient to illuminate the whole room.

For a few moments I remained alone in wonder, when suddenly the door opened, and there entered an extremely pretty girl, scarcely out of her teens, dark-haired, with clear-cut features, bright eyes, and a delicately-rounded chin. It struck me, however, even before she spoke, that in her face was a strange expression of unutterable sadness, a look that told of long suffering and intense agony of mind. Her mannerisms were those of a foreigner, her *chic* was that of the true Parisienne, her dress of black silk crêpon was plainly but well made, and the fact that she spoke in broken French was, next second, conclusive.

"Ah! You have come, m'sieur. You are indeed very good," she exclaimed, with a charming accent, her skirt rustling as she advanced to greet me.

"I am at your service, mademoiselle," I answered, bowing, at the same time accepting the seat she offered.

"Well," she commenced, with a smile, slowly sinking into an armchair near me, "when I wrote to you I feared you would not come. You have been so good to me already that I fear to ask any further favour."

"I must ask your pardon, mademoiselle," I said, "but I really am unaware that I have ever rendered you any service."

"What, do you not remember?" she cried. "You, who were so good to my father and myself; you, to whom we both owed our lives."

"I certainly have some hazy recollection of your name," I answered, puzzled, "but try how I will, I cannot recollect in what connection it has come before me."

"Do you not remember the case of the refugee, Anton Korolénko, the man who, after being hounded all over Europe, in Vienna, in Madrid, in Paris, by the *agents provocateurs* of the Secret Police, found an asylum in London?" she inquired, surprised. "They said we need not fear the *Okhrannoë Otdelenïe* here, in your free England, but no sooner had we arrived than, owing to the treachery of one of our brotherhood, a warrant for our extradition was issued by General Sekerzhinski, chief of the Department in St Petersburg. News of this was telegraphed to us, and I applied to your Minister for protection. You yourself saw me and gave me your promise of assistance, a promise which you kept; the warrant was returned to Russia unexecuted, and you thus saved us from the fate we dreaded."

"Ah, yes," I answered quickly. "Of course, I remember now. It is fully two years ago; but you have so altered that I scarcely knew you."

"I was a girl then," she smiled. "Now I feel quite a woman. Since I saw you last I have sustained a bereavement. My poor father is, alas! dead."

"Dead!" I echoed sympathetically.

"Yes," she sighed, with bitterness. "He died of a broken heart. On the day we escaped from St Petersburg, my mother, who was perfectly innocent, had unfortunately fallen into the drag-net of the police. She was imprisoned for six months, then sent to Siberia, but died of cold and fever on the road there. Her tragic end proved such a terrible blow to my father that, even here in safety, he grew morose, his health, already broken by long years of imprisonment, failed, and six months ago he died, and I was left alone."

"Your life is indeed a sad one, mademoiselle," I said, for I well-remembered the touching story she related when, a mere girl, pale-faced and agitated, she came to implore the protection of the British Government on behalf of her aged father. She had, with tears in her dark, brilliant eyes, told me a narrative of systematic persecution almost incredible; how her father, a wealthy merchant, having fallen into disfavour with General Sekerzhinski, the chief of Secret Police in St Petersburg, that official had formed a cunningly-devised plan to entrap him into a political conspiracy. She admitted that at one time, during the Terror that culminated in the murder of Alexander II, her father had participated in the revolutionary movement, and had spent eight years of solitary confinement in the Peter-Paul Fortress. Although he had long ago renounced all revolutionary ideas, it was, of course, easy enough for an all-powerful official like Sekerzhinski to discover evidence against him. The *agents provocateurs* were quickly at work, with the result that orders were in a few days issued for the arrest of Korolénko for the murder of a woman in a low quarter of the city, and for the apprehension of his wife and their pretty daughter, Sonia, as accomplices. The reason of this allegation was plain. If the General had only alleged a political offence his victims could not be extradited from a foreign country, while for an ordinary crime they could. Korolénko's wife was arrested while shopping in the Nevski Prospekt, but Sonia and her father, fortunately, obtained word from a friend of theirs in the secret service, and fled, succeeding in escaping from St Petersburg into Finland, and after weeks of starvation and terrible hardships found themselves in Stockholm, whence they went to Hamburg. Here they narrowly escaped arrest by the German police, but succeeded in getting to Vienna, and thence to Venice, Marseilles, Madrid, and afterwards to Paris, where they had heard a large colony of Russian refugees resided. After two days, however, owing to a fact they ascertained, they fled to London. Here they believed themselves safe until one day they received another telegram from their friend in the secret police, warning them that a request for their extradition was on its way to London. It was then, in desperation, that Sonia came to crave an interview with Lord Warnham, and I had seen her on his behalf.

Her story of wrong, hatred, and heartless persecution I have only here briefly outlined, but during the half-hour she had sat in the waiting-room at the Foreign Office relating it to me in detail she spoke with such earnestness that I was convinced of the truth, and resolved to assist her. Urging her to be assured that I would do all that lay in my power, she had at last dried her tears, and grasping my hand as she went out, had said,—

"I shall never forget your kindness to us, m'sieur. We are alone, friendless, forsaken, hounded down by a man who has sworn to ruin my father and his family. That you can protect us, I am confident. You can save us from the mines—nay, you can save our lives, if you will. I appeal to you, our only friend. Assist us, and you will ever receive the thanks from one who is to-day on the verge of despair and suicide."

I promised, and she went away hopeful and confident. But to secure their immunity from arrest was by no means an easy matter. Fortunately, however, I was on excellent terms with the Secretary of the Russian Embassy, and having obtained the sanction of Lord Warnham, who was always chivalrous wherever women were concerned, treating them with a charming old-world courtesy, I set about attaining my object, securing it at last, but being compelled in turn to promise my friend assistance in an important matter of diplomacy. The warrant was next day returned to Russia unexecuted, and Sonia and her father were free.

From her I had received a brief note in response to my intimation of the withdrawal of the warrant, apparently hastily written, but thanking me, and declaring that they both owed their future happiness to my exertions. For a few days I reflected upon the strange drama of real life that had been enacted, then the circumstances passed out of my mind.

Now, as she sat before me, older and yet more beautiful, gazing into my eyes with that intense, wistful look that had attracted me when first we had met, all her tragic story came back to me vividly, and I was not surprised at her deep sorrow at the loss of her father she had loved so dearly.

"So you desire my assistance," I exclaimed presently, after she had been explaining how lonely she was in exile from her friends.

"Yes," she said slowly, with emphasis. "But first tell me one thing. You are acquainted with a woman named Ella Laing. Do you know her past?"

Chapter Fifteen
Beyond Recall

"Really your question is a curious one," I exclaimed, smiling, although inwardly I resented her intrusion upon my affairs.

"Do not think I intended to be unduly inquisitive," my youthful hostess said quickly, fidgeting with her golden bangle whereon a tiny bell tinkled musically as she moved, and glancing up at me with her dark, bright eyes.

"Ella's past can concern no one except herself," I observed, rather puzzled. There was a strange, half-suspicious expression in her face that I had not at first noticed.

"If you intend to marry her it concerns you also, does it not?" she asked, in a quiet, grave voice.

"Yes, of course," I answered. "But how do you know I intend to marry her?"

"I have heard so, and have seen you together," she answered, rather evasively.

"Well, let us come to the point at once," I said, still smiling, and feigning to be amused. "Tell me what objection there is to her. Why do you inquire about her past?"

"Because it is a mystery," she replied, regarding me calmly, the strange glint in her penetrating eyes increasing my mistrust.

"In what way?" I inquired. I had known Mrs Laing and Ella for over a year, and certainly nothing I had learnt regarding their antecedents had excited my suspicion. The Yorkshire Laings are a county family, and Edward Laing, Ella's father, had been the head of the great shipping firm that has its headquarters in Hull, and is well-known in the North Sea and Atlantic trades. At his death the concern was turned into a company, and Mrs Laing and her daughter had travelled for nearly three years, returning to London shortly before I met them. The statement that Ella's past was mysterious was certainly puzzling, therefore I added, "When you make an allegation, I really think it is only fair that you should substantiate it."

She shrugged her shoulders with a foreign mannerism that was charming, exclaiming in her broken English, — "Ah, you understand me not, m'sieur. I speak not your language with politeness. Well, it is, oh, so very difficult?"

"Do you tell me that Ella Laing is not what she represents herself to be?" I inquired eagerly.

"Ah, no," she answered. "I ask m'sieur if he knows of her past. M'sieur was once good to me, very good. I forget never those who to me are generous."

"But your words contain a hidden meaning," I said, dropping into French, hoping thereby to induce her to place my mind at rest.

"Yes, I am well aware of that," she answered, with volubility. "You love her; you have offered her marriage—the woman who is your most bitter foe!"

"What do you mean? That Ella is my enemy?" I cried, dismayed.

Her full, red lips parted in a silvery peal of laughter, displaying an even set of pearly teeth, as, throwing back her handsome head, she exclaimed, —

"Ah! I expected it would cause you pain to learn the truth. Yet, after all, is it not best to know now, instead of hereafter?"

"In what way is she my enemy?" I asked, bending forward to her and transfixing her with my eyes.

She remained silent, merely giving her shoulders a slight shrug, sighing the while.

"A moment ago you told me that because I once performed you a service you intended to render me one in return. Come, tell me the truth," I urged.

Again she sighed, but at last said, "The truth has already been forced upon you, I should think."

"In what manner?"

"By the death of your friend, Dudley Ogle," she replied, in a half whisper, the strange look of almost murderous hatred again showing in her eyes.

"Well," I said, "I can see nothing in that tragic incident to lead me to any conclusion that Ella is my enemy."

"Love is blind, of course," she answered, rather contemptuously. "Your blindness extends apparently even to the theft of the important dispatch entrusted to your care."

Her words amazed me, for, with the exception of Lord Warnham, the Marquis of Maybury, and Frayling at Scotland Yard, no living person knew of the theft of the secret convention.

"How, pray, are you aware that any document has been stolen?" I asked quickly, my mind at once filled with suspicion. The fact that this girl was a Russian was in itself sufficient to place me at once upon my guard.

"I have heard so," she answered, with a mysterious smile.

"Well, and what do you allege?" I inquired, keeping my eyes fixed upon her.

"Allege!" she cried. "Why, nothing. I have merely asked you a simple question, whether you are aware of the past of Ella Laing, and you have not answered. You are silent."

"I know sufficient of her past to love her," I answered, determined that the words of this strange-mannered girl should not arouse greater suspicion than that which already dwelt in my mind.

"Love her! Bah! You will hate her when you learn the truth," she cried, with a gesture of disgust.

"Then tell me," I cried impatiently. "Why should I hate her?"

"No," she said slowly, shaking her head, and slightly raising her shoulders. "I make no reflections. If you love her—well, I suppose you desire that your fool's paradise should last as long as possible."

"My fool's paradise, as you term it, will, I trust, last always," I said resentfully, for her manner had suddenly changed, and she treated me reproachfully, with a familiarity that was as surprising as it was annoying.

"Alas! not always, I fear," she smiled, as if pitying my simplicity. "Your present paradise will soon be a veritable hell."

"You speak candidly, at least," I said, angered at her words. "But I did not call here to listen to libellous allegations of which there are no proofs."

"No proofs?" she echoed. "Ah, do not be so confident, m'sieur. You have no knowledge of the character of the woman you love, or you would not say this. I do not wish you to follow my advice; I do not urge you to listen to my words. I only warn you because you have been my best friend," and she gazed straight into my eyes with an earnestness that was intense.

"You warn me. Of what?"

"Of Ella, the woman who has apparently fascinated you as she has done others," and she sighed, as if memories were painful.

"A pretty woman may often unconsciously fascinate many men before meeting the man she marries," I said, as calmly as I could.

"Unconsciously, yes," she answered. "But there are some who use the beauty that their Maker has bestowed upon them to allure their victims."

"You anticipate I am doomed, then?" I laughed.

She regarded me gravely for an instant, then said, in a voice quiet and low, —

"I do not think—I know. The mysterious death that overtook your friend Dudley Ogle should have overtaken you instead. But for an amazing coincidence, by which your life was saved and his taken, you would, ere this, have been in your grave."

"And my assassin would have been the woman I love, I suppose, you are going to tell me?" I observed, amused at her melodramatic manner and the absurdity of the idea.

"No, I leave you to discover the truth," she answered, arching her dark brows, a shadow of annoyance crossing her refined features at that moment.

"You are apparently well acquainted with Miss Laing," I said, after a long pause.

"I know her," she admitted abruptly.

"Then, as I refuse to listen further to any charges against her of which you can give me no corroboration, it may be best for me to bring her here to hear your allegations, even at risk of creating a scene. You said you intended to render me a service, and by facing her you can."

"No, no," she cried, suddenly jumping from her chair and laying her hand upon my arm in earnestness. "She does not know I am in London; she must never know, otherwise our plans will be spoilt. Do not mention my name to her; now promise me," she implored. "Promise me, and I will render you the assistance you will require ere long. The secret knowledge I possess enables me to give you warning. Remember that what I have said is between one friend and another."

Through my perturbed mind there surged vivid recollections of recent events, of Ella's beauty, and of the inscrutable mystery surrounding her. It was amazing, to say the least, that this handsome girl, whose life had been so romantic and full of tragedy, should thus make veiled allegations and denounce as vile and worthless the woman I so deeply loved. That she had some ulterior motive was, of course, apparent, but although I debated within myself its probable cause, I utterly failed to arrive at any satisfactory conclusion. One fact was, however, impressed upon me during our subsequent conversation—namely, that Sonia was in possession of the secret that Ella withheld from me. That the pretty Russian had known Mrs Laing and Ella intimately I could not doubt from what she told me regarding them, yet I did not fail to detect in her voice a harshness whenever she spoke of them, the more so when she mentioned the name of my well-beloved. Once, in trying to determine the cause of this, I felt inclined to attribute it to jealousy, but when I reflected that I had seen Sonia only once before, and that I knew absolutely nothing of her except what she herself had told me, I scouted the idea.

It was plain, too, that she had been intimately acquainted with Dudley, for she spoke of him familiarly, smiled at his little eccentricities, and expressed the most heartfelt regret at his mysterious and tragic end. Times without number, when she had sunk back into her chair, I tried to induce her to impart to me something more regarding the woman I loved, but she declined. She warned me by constant utterances to be circumspect, but regarding the past preserved a silence rigid and severe.

Presently, as my eyes wandered around the well-furnished room, I noticed, standing upon the piano, a photograph frame of oxydised silver containing a portrait. I looked at it astounded, for it was the likeness of my dead friend. She noticed my attention attracted by it, and rising in silence, brought it across to me, and taking it from its frame, said,—

"This, perhaps, will convince you that Mr Ogle was my friend."

I took the portrait from her hand, and read on the back in his well-known handwriting the words,—"From Dudley to dearest Sonia."

No copy of this portrait had I before seen. From the suit of light tweed he wore I knew that he could not have been photographed longer than a month prior to his death, and it seemed likely that he had had this taken specially for her. Although fond of telling me of his flirtations, he had never spoken of his acquaintance with this pretty refugee, yet from her remarks I knew that they had been friends for several years.

Long and earnestly I looked at the picture, then handed it back to her without comment. Truth to tell, even this counterfeit presentment filled me with a fierce hatred against him, for had not Lord Maybury been absolutely correct in remarking that everything pointed to the conclusion that he was a spy? Indeed, his association with this pretty Russian, who had perhaps fascinated him, was another fact which seemed now to confirm my increasing suspicions. It was a romantic story that Sonia told me, but what evidence did I possess that she was actually a political refugee? The warrant issued from St Petersburg for the arrest of her father and herself was for the murder of a foreign woman who, according to the depositions that my friend at the Russian Embassy showed me, had been enticed to a house in a low quarter of the city and strangled with a silken cord. No hint had been given that the pair "wanted" were "apostles of dynamite," and I now remembered that when I had suggested it to my friend he laughed, declaring that I was utterly mistaken. I recollected that the words he used were,—

"They are not revolutionists, but a precocious pair of criminals who, from time to time, have made enormous coups. No doubt the charming girl has told you some ingenious fiction or other about her father's patriotism, but I should advise you to take it all with the proverbial grain of salt. They are the only two of an utterly unscrupulous gang now remaining at liberty, and if your Government will give them up, we will rid society of them by burying them deep in one of our Siberian mines. But as you have come with this offer to readjust the little diplomatic friction in return for their liberty, I will urge my chief to accept it; nevertheless, do not forget that this action of yours will set at liberty a pair of the most fearless and ingenious harpies in Europe."

As I sat opposite her, watching her seductive smiles, these words recurred to me, and I wondered whether the allegations of the Secretary of the Embassy was true. I recollected also, when, with tears in those brilliant eyes, she had besought me to intercede on her father's behalf, how she told me distinctly that Sekerzhinski, the Chief of Police, had made charges against them cruel and false. Certainly when she had come to me humbly imploring the protection of the British Government against the persecution of her accusers she had none of the swagger of the adventuress. Even now, dressed in plain mourning, with no jewellery except the single golden bangle which I remembered she had worn when we before met, I could not bring myself to think that she was actually the desperate criminal that my friend Paul Verblioudovitch would have me believe.

Knowing, as I did, how the Tzar's emissaries followed and captured by all manner of subtle devices those suspected of revolutionary conspiracy, I was again convinced, as I had been two years ago, that Sonia was a conspirator against the life of his Majesty. She certainly was not a common criminal. As she chatted to me, young, refined, sad-eyed, there were in her face unmistakable traces of anxiety and suffering. Finding that she absolutely refused to say anything further regarding the woman I adored, I began to question her as to her own happiness and future.

"Ah," she sighed, "I am lonely, dull, and unhappy now that my father is no longer alive. Together we shared months of terrible hardship, of semi-starvation, hiding in the frozen wilds of the North, and ever pushing forward through that great lonely land towards our goal of freedom. Often and often we were compelled to exist on roots and leaves, and more than once we were compelled to face death," and she shuddered. "The recollection of that terrible journey is to me like some hideous nightmare, for to escape detection we often travelled by night, in terror of the wolves, and guided only by the brilliant stars high in the bright, frosty sky. The knowledge of our fate if caught—the mines in far Siberia—held us in dread and hastened our footsteps. Thus, clad only in tattered rags, we went forward shivering, knowing that to halt meant certain death. Not until after three long months of suffering did we reach Stockholm, where we once more awakened to the joys of life, but then, alas! they had in them the dregs of bitterness. Two days after regaining our liberty, the news reached us that my poor mother had died at the roadside while chained to a gang of desperate convicts on their long and weary journey to Lake Baikal, the most dreaded district in all Asiatic Russia. The Almighty spared her the horrors of the fever-infected *étapes* and the gloom and torture of the mines, but from that moment my poor father, heart-broken, grew careless of the future, and it was only for my sake that he endeavoured to elude the bloodhounds of the Tzar."

"Do you live here, in this house, alone?" I asked.

"No," she replied. "I have Pétrouchka and his wife Akoulina, who were our servants in St Petersburg for many years, in addition to the English maid who admitted you."

"Then you are not quite alone," I said. "Besides, you ought not to be unhappy, for you have enough money to live comfortably, and you should try and forget your sad bereavement."

"Alas! I cannot forget," she said, still speaking in French. "It is impossible. I am exiled here in your country, while all my relatives and friends are so far away. I cannot go into your society, for I have no chaperon; besides, English puzzles me so. I shall never learn it, never. Oh, it is so difficult."

"Yes," I admitted, laughing. "But not so puzzling as your own Russian, with all its bewildering letters."

She smiled, but there was a touch of wistful sadness in her handsome face when, after a slight pause, she looked at me earnestly, saying,—

"It was because I am so lonely and unhappy that I asked you to come here to-night."

"To be your companion—eh?" I observed, laughing. "Well, what you have told me regarding Ella Laing is scarcely calculated to set a man's mind at rest."

"Ah, no. I have only told you in order that you should be forewarned. Let that pass; yet remember the words I have uttered, proof of which you shall have some day. The fact is, I want you to do me a favour. I am tired of this exile from my friends; I have no one as companion except old Akoulina, and I want to return to Russia for a month or so to visit my relatives, and to transact some legal business connected with my poor father's estate."

"But is it safe for you to return?" I hazarded.

"Not unless you will procure me a passport. This you can do if you will," she answered earnestly.

"You would be arrested on the frontier," I said. "Is it wise to run such risk?"

"Of course the passport must not be in my own name," she went on. "You alone can obtain one from your friend at the Embassy."

I shook my head dubiously, feeling assured that I could never induce Verblioudovitch to issue a false passport to a woman he had denounced as a dangerous criminal.

"Ah, you will try, will you not?" she implored, rising and gripping my arm. "It is necessary that I should be in St Petersburg within fourteen days from now, in order to give instructions regarding my late father's property. His brother, my uncle, is endeavouring to cheat me of it, and I must return, or I shall lose everything. I shall be ruined utterly."

She spoke so rapidly, and upon her pale face was a look so wistful, that I felt assured she was in earnest. Hers was not the face of a malefactor, but rather that of a modest girl whose spirit had been broken by her bereavement.

"I obtained your immunity from arrest here in England, it is true," I said. "But I fear that in my efforts to obtain for you a false passport I shall fail. If the police discover you within Russian territory, then nothing can save you from Siberia."

"But they will not find me," she cried hastily. "Obtain for me a passport that will carry me across the frontier, and within an hour I shall be as dead to the police as the stones in the wall."

This expression she had involuntarily let drop struck me as distinctly curious. It certainly was not such a phrase as would be used by any but a constant fugitive from justice. Indeed, it was really the parlance of the habitual criminal. Again I remained silent in doubt.

"Will you try?" she asked, intensely in earnest.

"If it is your wish I will try," I answered. "But only in return for one service."

"Well?" she inquired sharply.

"That when I bring you the passport you will tell me truthfully and honestly the grounds whereon you allege that Ella Laing is my enemy."

She knit her brows for a few brief seconds, as if the possibility of my demand had never occurred to her. Then, suddenly smiling, she answered, extending her hand,—

"It's a bargain. But, remember, I must be in St Petersburg within fourteen days."

"I shall not forget," I answered, with a sudden resolve to do my utmost to obtain the permit allowing this strange but handsome girl to re-enter her native land, and thus learn the truth regarding my well-beloved. "I shall call on Verblioudovitch to-morrow."

"You are good to me, m'sieur, very good," she cried, joyfully. "In return, I will tell you one thing, even now. If you doubt what I say regarding the woman you love, look calmly into her face, pressing her hand affectionately the while, and ask her if she knows anyone with diamond eyes."

"Is Diamond Eyes a pet name?" I inquired. I was puzzled, for I had a faint consciousness of having heard that designation before, but to whom applied I know not.

"Discover for yourself," she answered, smiling. "I have given you the clue. Follow it, and seek the truth."

Many times during our subsequent conversation I besought her to tell me something further, but she would not, and at last, after remaining with her over an hour, I left, promising I would at once set about obtaining the passport she desired. Hers was a strange personality, yet I, by some vague intuition, felt myself on the verge of a discovery. I was convinced that she knew of the theft of the secret convention, and could, if she wished, impart to me some startling truth.

Chapter Sixteen
Advice Gratis

Soon after noon next day I called at the Russian Embassy at Chesham House, and was ushered into the private room of my friend, Paul Verblioudovitch, the secretary to the urbane old gentleman who acted as the Tzar's representative at the Court of St James. It was a large but rather gloomy room, well stocked with books, containing a writing-table and several easy-chairs, into one of which I sank after the hall-porter, a gigantic, liveried Russian, had conducted me thither, and announced the immediate arrival of my official friend.

While waiting, I reflected that my errand was scarcely one that would commend itself to the favour of Lord Warnham. Official relations between the Russian Embassy and the British Foreign Office, never very cordial, were, owing to our knowledge of the suppressed declaration of war, now seriously strained. Nevertheless, Paul and I were very intimate friends. I had first met him in St Petersburg, where for six months I had occupied an unimportant post in the British Embassy. Being compelled to pay frequent visits to the Minister of Foreign Affairs, I was always seen by Verblioudovitch, an official who spoke excellent English. Then I left and returned to London under Lord Warnham, and for nearly two years entirely lost sight of him, until I was one day delighted to find he had been promoted as Secretary of Embassy in London. Since that time our friendship had been renewed, and we had spent many a pleasant evening together.

"Ah, my dear fellow!" he cried, almost without any trace of accent, as he suddenly opened the door and interrupted my reflections. "You're an early visitor," he laughed, shaking hands cordially. "Well, what is it? A message from your indefatigable chief?"

"No, not exactly," I smiled, sinking again into my comfortable chair as he walked to the opposite side of his writing-table, afterwards seating himself at it. He was a well-preserved man of about forty-five, tall, erect, of military bearing, with closely-cropped, dark hair, a well-trimmed moustache, and a face that was an index to his happy, contented disposition. The Tzar's officials are supposed to be a set of the most stern, hard-hearted ruffians on earth, but there was certainly nothing of the heartless persecutor about him. Indeed, he was quite the reverse—a devil-may-care, easy-going fellow, who enjoyed a joke hugely, and when outside the sombre walls of the Embassy was full of genuine good humour and buoyant spirits. He may have been able to disguise his careless demeanour beneath the stern, strictly business-like manner of officialdom, but I, for one, had never seen him assume the loftiness of his position as secretary of the chief among the Embassies in London.

"Our people at home have recently been playing an amusing little game at your expense, haven't they?" he laughed, passing over to me his silver cigarette case and selecting one himself when I gave it back to him.

"I believe they have," I answered.

"I would have given anything to have seen the look on your old chief's face when first he heard that we were going to declare war," he laughed. "How did he take it? You had a rough half-hour, I expect."

"Of course," I smiled. "Things looked so serious."

"Yes, so they did," he admitted, his face growing grave. "I quite expected that we should have to pack up our baggage and go back to St Petersburg. The fact is it's a puzzle to us why the Imperial declaration wasn't actually published. A hitch somewhere, I suppose."

"Fortunately for us—eh?" I observed, lighting up calmly. He imported his own cigarettes, and they were always excellent.

"Yes," he answered, adding after a moment's reflection, "but why have you come to me now that we are officially at daggers drawn?"

"Only officially are we bad friends," I said. "Personally we shall be on good terms always, I hope, Paul. It was because I know I can count upon your assistance that I've come to ask you a favour."

"Ask away, old chap," he said, deftly twisting his cigarette in his fingers, afterwards placing it between his lips.

"I have a friend who wants to go to Russia, and desires a passport."

"Well, he can get one at the Consul-General's office," my friend answered, without removing his cigarette. "I'll give you a note, if you like."

"No," I said. "First, it is not a man who is going, but a woman; and, secondly, I want a passport viséd by the Embassy in a name other than the real name of its bearer."

"Oh," he exclaimed suspiciously, glancing straight at me. "Something shady, oh? Who's the woman?"

"Well, she's hardly a woman yet," I answered. "A pretty girl who has lost her father and desires to return to her friends in St Petersburg."

"What's her name?"

"You know her," I said slowly. "I came to you on her behalf some time ago when a warrant was out for the arrest of her and her father. I—"

"Of course, I quite remember," he answered quickly, interrupting me. "Anton Korolénko escaped with his daughter, that ingenious little nymph, Sonia, who came and pitched you a long, almost idyllic yarn, and you came here to intercede. I did as you requested and secured their freedom by endorsing the report of the agent of police told off to watch them by a statement that both father and daughter were dead. I then kept my promise by returning the warrant, but I tell you I narrowly escaped getting into a devil of a scrape about it."

"But you can manage to give me a false passport for her, can't you?" I urged.

"Where's her father? If he goes back their whole game will be given away."

"Her father is dead," I answered.

"Dead! Well, the grave is, I think, about the best place for such an enterprising old scoundrel, and as for his daughter, hang it, old chap, ten years in Nerchinsk wouldn't hurt her. What story has she been telling you this time, eh?" he asked.

"She is lonely without her father, and in order to secure her property, which is about to be seized by her uncle, she is bound to be in St Petersburg within fourteen days."

"Fourteen days," repeated my friend, reflectively. "Let's see, to-day's the twelfth," and he made some rapid calculations upon his blotting-pad. "Well, what else?" he inquired, looking up at me keenly.

"Nothing, except that she dare not return under her own name."

"I should scarcely think she'd better," he laughed, "unless she wants to spend the remainder of her days in that rather uncomfortable hotel called Schlusselburg, where the beds are not aired, and there are no toilet-glasses. But, tell me," he added gravely, a moment later, "why do you interest yourself in her welfare? She's entertaining and rather pretty, I've been told, but surely you, who are engaged to that charming girl to whom you introduced me at the Gaiety one evening a few weeks ago, really ought not to associate yourself with Anton Korolénko's daughter? She's a criminal."

"I have an object," I said briefly.

"Every man says that when a girl has taken his fancy. I know the world, old fellow."

"But it so happens that I've not been captivated by her charms," I retorted.

"Well, my dear Geoffrey," he said, in a tone of unusual gravity, "take my advice and keep away from her. Ever since you induced me to secure her her liberty, I have honestly regretted it, knowing as I do the terrible crimes alleged against the gang of which she and her villainous old father were prominent members."

"What kind of crimes were they?"

"Everything, from picking pockets to murder," he answered. "They stuck at nothing, so long as they secured the huge stakes for which they played. Has she been again weaving for your benefit any more of her tragic romances? She'd make a fortune as a novelist."

I paused in deep thought.

"Truth to tell," I said at last, "she has made an allegation against the woman I love."

"Against Ella Laing?" he exclaimed, a faint shadow of anger crossing his brow. "What has she said? Tell me; perhaps I can suggest a way of dealing with her," he added quickly. "She's most unscrupulous; her tongue is tipped with venom."

"She has given me to understand that Ella is an adventuress, and my most bitter enemy," I blurted out suddenly.

He flung down his pen in anger, a fierce imprecation in Russian upon his lips. The reason of his sudden annoyance was a mystery, but his quick eyes noticed my amazement, and in on instant he assumed a calm demeanour, saying, in a voice of reproach, —

"So this woman, who has libelled Ella, you are striving to assist, eh? Well, what ground has she for her allegation?"

"She will tell me only on one condition."

"And what is that?"

"If I induce you to give her a false passport, and promise not to inform the frontier police of her intended departure, she will relate to me the truth," I said.

"And are you actually prepared to accept as truth the allegations which this woman uses as a lever to compel you to exercise your good offices on her behalf?" he observed, in a tone of reproach.

I was silent, for I now recognised for the first time the strength of his argument.

"You see her position is this," he continued. "She has nothing to lose and everything to gain. You get her the permit she desires; and she, in return, will tell you some absurd romance or other, concocted, perhaps, because she has taken a fancy to you and is jealous of Ella. We are friends, Deedes, or I should not speak so plainly. But I tell you that if I were in your place I would refuse to hear any lies from this pretty, soft-spoken criminal."

"I quite appreciate your argument," I answered, reflectively, "and I thank you for your good advice." Were the words she had uttered lies, I wondered? Assuredly, her allegation that Ella was my enemy was a foul falsehood; nevertheless that she was well aware of the tragic end of Dudley Ogle I could not doubt, and her assertion that it had been intended that I should be the victim had startled me and aroused my curiosity. I was determined, at all hazards, to ascertain the truth.

"Do not be entrapped by a pretty face or a fine pair of eyes, that's my advice," my companion said, slowly striking a match.

"I can assure you, old fellow, I shall not be misled by any pretty face, even if it has diamond eyes," I said, quite unthinkingly, Sonia's strange words recurring to me at that moment.

"Diamond eyes!" gasped Paul Verblioudovitch, starting visibly and holding the burning match still between his fingers without lighting his cigarette. He had in that instant grown paler, and I thought I detected that his hand trembled, almost imperceptibly be it said. "What do you mean?" he demanded, with a strange fierceness in his gaze. "What do you know of Diamond Eyes?"

Chapter Seventeen
A Spy's Story

"I know nothing of diamond eyes," I replied, surprised at Paul's excited inquiry. Instead of showing a good-natured friendliness towards me as usual, he had suddenly become agitated and suspicious. He glanced at me in doubt, saying,—

"Sonia has been revealing something. It is useless now to try and disguise the fact."

"No," I replied quickly. "She has not explained anything. What do you expect her to reveal?"

"Oh, nothing, my dear fellow, nothing," he answered, smiling, with that indifference cultivated by the diplomat. "The expression you used was as original as it was unusual, that's all."

"I don't claim originality for it," I laughed. "To Sonia is the credit due."

"To Sonia?" he exclaimed uneasily, glancing sharply at me. "Then it is true, as I suspected, that she has been telling you some of her ingenious falsehoods."

"Scarcely that," I replied, thrusting my hands deeply into my pockets. "She has merely urged me to go to Ella and ask her whether she is acquainted with anyone with diamond eyes."

"As I thought," he cried, rising and pacing the room furiously. "It is exactly as I expected. She is trying to entrap you as she has the others, and has embarked upon the first step by speaking thus of Ella, and sowing seeds of suspicion in your mind. This is the character of the woman you seek to help, and you invoke my assistance in your efforts! No, Geoffrey," he said, halting suddenly, and looking me straight in the face, "I shall not stir on her behalf."

"But remember, that in return for the passport, she has promised to tell me all regarding Ella," I cried anxiously.

"All?" he echoed, in surprise. "Is she such a mysterious person, then? Surely you have confidence in her, or you would not have asked her to be your wife?"

"There is a mystery connected with her," I said quietly. "A mystery, deep and inscrutable, that perplexes me to the point of distraction."

"Tell me about it," Verblioudovitch said, interested.

It was upon my tongue to relate to him the whole of the facts *sub silentio*, but a thought at that instant occurred to me that such a course would be unjust to Ella, therefore I evaded his invitation to make him my confidant. Returning quickly to the object for which I had sought him, I persuaded him to assist me by giving me a passport for Sonia.

"What will she do in return?" he again inquired, raising his eyebrows and shrugging his shoulders in a manner habitual to him when unduly excited. "She will concoct some idiotic, romantic story, in order that the woman you love shall suffer. I really cannot see, Geoffrey, what end can be attained in assisting a criminal to re-enter the country from which she is a fugitive. You don't know the real character of this apparently ingenuous girl, or I feel certain you would never ask me to imperil my reputation by rendering her assistance. If I had done my duty long ago, I should have allowed the extradition proceedings to go on. I'm sorry now I didn't, for if I had you would have been saved a world of worry, and we should have been rid of the pair for ever."

"You seem actuated by some spirit of animosity against her," I blurted forth.

"Not at all. I've never seen her in my life," he protested. "You apparently want confirmation of my words. Well, you shall have it at once," and he touched an electric button.

The summons was instantly obeyed by a messenger in uniform, and to this man Paul spoke some words. A few minutes later a short, middle-aged Russian entered.

His hair was grey, his clean-shaven face was rather red and slightly pimply, his small, jet black eyes were set too closely together, and his low brows met above his nose. Fashionably attired in frock coat of light grey, with a pink carnation in the lapel, he looked so spick and span that I regarded him with genuine surprise, when my friend, introducing us, said,—

"This, Geoffrey, is Ivan Renouf; I daresay you have heard of him. He is now chief of the section of Secret Police attached to our Embassies of London and Paris."

I nodded in acknowledgment of the bow of this expert detective who, at the time I had lived in St Petersburg, had been the terror of all criminals. The stories told of his amazing ingenuity in detecting crime were legion, though many of them were perhaps fabulous; yet there was no doubt that he was one of the most experienced police officers in Europe.

"Renouf," my friend exclaimed, "I want to ask you a question. What character does Sonia Korolénko bear?"

"Sonia?" answered the great detective, reflectively, in fairly good English. "Ah! you mean the daughter of Anton Korolénko who escaped from St Petersburg?—eh?"

"Yes. Tell my friend, Deedes," Paul said, with a slow gesture indicating me.

"Well," he answered, glancing quickly at me with his searching eyes, "for the past nine months we have kept her under strict surveillance, expecting that she intended to re-commence operations in London. Indeed, I have here in my pocket the report for the last forty-eight hours," and he took from his breast-pocket a long folded paper. "It shows among other things that she has had several visitors at her house in Kensington, one of whom was a gentleman who, according to the description, must have borne a strong resemblance to m'sieur. Two hours before this man had called a lady visited her, and remained with her about an hour." Then, reading from the report, he continued, "the description says, tall, good-looking, blue eyes, reddish-brown hair, straw hat trimmed with pale-blue, brown shoes, light blouse, black cycling skirt."

"By Heaven!" I cried excitedly, "that's Ella! Every word of that description tallies, even to the dress, boots and hat!"

"She is a frequent visitor," the detective observed. "She calls on her bicycle every day."

"Every day!" I echoed in astonishment. "I did not know they were friends."

"Did I not tell you that she was concealing the truth?" Paul observed, smiling at my dismay. "Tell m'sieur of the past, Ivan."

"Ah! her record is a very black one—very black," the officer of police answered gravely, again fixing his small dark eyes upon me. "Her swindling transactions extend over several years, and she has no doubt acquired quite a fortune, while at least one of her victims has lost his life. By one coup she accomplished in Moscow, with the aid of that soft-spoken old scoundrel, her father, they pocketed nearly one hundred thousand roubles between them."

"I really can't believe it," I exclaimed, dumbfounded.

"There is no doubt whatever about it," Renouf answered. "It was all in the papers at the time and made quite a stir throughout Europe. The story is a rather tragic one; sufficient to show what kind of woman she is. About three years ago she went with her father from St Petersburg to Moscow, where they took a handsome house, furnished it luxuriously, and gave a number of brilliant entertainments. At one of these the pretty Sonia, whose jewels were the admiration of half the city, met the young Prince Alexis Gazarin, a mere youth of twenty-two, who had only a few months before inherited a huge fortune from his father, the well-known promoter of the oil industry at Baku. Alexis fell violently in love with her, made her many costly presents, proposed marriage and was accepted, the parental consent being extracted only when he had deposited in the bank in Sonia's name one hundred thousand roubles as settlement upon her. A week before the marriage, the body of Alexis was discovered floating in the yellow Volga near Kostroma, but whether his death was due to accident, suicide or foul play has never been ascertained. The fact, however, remains that Anton Korolénko and his pretty daughter left Moscow a week later, carrying with them one hundred thousand roubles of the dead man's money."

"Do you allege that the pair actually murdered him?" I inquired, astounded at this story.

The detective smiled mysteriously, gave his shoulders a significant shrug, but did not reply.

"This," exclaimed Paul, "is the sort of woman you are trying to befriend! No doubt she has told you a most touching story of persecution, and all that; but can anyone be surprised if our police endeavour to arrest her? I tell you plainly she's a mere adventuress, with a plausible story ever upon her tongue."

"Do you refuse to do what I ask?" I inquired at last, when Renouf, pleading an appointment, had bowed and departed.

"I can really see no satisfactory reason why I should," he answered, standing in the centre of the Persian rug spread before the fireplace.

"You are my friend, Paul," I urged. "At all times I am, as you are aware, ready to perform you any personal service."

"It is not rendering you a personal service if, by giving the passport, I induce her to tell you a tissue of untruths."

"But it is evident, even from Renouf's report, that Ella visits her. It is to obtain an elucidation of a secret that I am striving, for I am convinced Sonia knows the truth."

"If she does, then you may rely upon it she will not tell it to you, but substitute some romantic fiction or other," he laughed. "It is really astounding to find you so confident in her honesty."

Paul Verblioudovitch's attack of ill-temper vanished as he threw himself back in his chair and showed all his white teeth in a hearty guffaw.

"I am not confident," I declared. "I have assisted the girl to obtain her freedom, therefore I cannot see that she can have any object in wilfully deceiving me. Her promise to reveal the truth regarding Ella in exchange for the passport is but a mere business arrangement."

"You apparently suspect the woman you love of some terrible crime or other," Paul said, after a pause. "I can't understand you, Geoffrey, I must confess."

"If you were in my place, fondly loving a woman who was enveloped in bewildering mystery, you would, I have no doubt, act quite as strangely as myself," I exclaimed, smiling grimly. "I only want to discover light in this chaos of perplexity; then only shall I be content."

"But if circumstances have so conspired to produce a problem, why not remain patient until its natural elucidation is effected? The police, when baffled, frequently adopt that course, and often very effectually, too."

"Truth to tell, old fellow," I said confidentially, "I am anxious to marry Ella, but cannot until I have ascertained some substantial truth."

"Of what do you suspect her—of a crime?" he inquired, smiling.

I paused.

"Yes," I answered gravely, "of a crime."

I fancied he started as I spoke, almost imperceptibly, perhaps, yet I could have sworn that my words produced within him some nervous apprehension.

"A crime!" he echoed. "Surely she cannot be guilty of anything more serious than some little indiscretion."

"It is more than mere indiscretion that I suspect," I said, in a low tone.

"Well," he observed mechanically, as, after a pause, he stood at the window, gazing fixedly into the street, "I certainly would never accept as truth anything whatever told me by Sonia Korolénko."

I was, however, inexorable in my demand, more than ever determined to hear Sonia's story. The strange, hesitating manner in which my friend had endeavoured to avoid complying with my request had aroused suspicion within me; of what, I could not tell. It struck me as curious that he should thus defend Ella so strenuously, although he knew her but slightly. He was, perhaps, acting in my interests as his friend, but if so, his intense hatred of Sonia was more than the mere official denunciation of an evil-doer. I did not believe his declaration that he had never met Sonia, but it seemed rather as if he had cause to well remember his meeting with her, and that its recollection still rankled bitterly within him.

The admission by Renouf was a little disconcerting. Sonia certainly did not dream that the Tzar's spies were even now watching her every action and carefully scrutinising each person who called at Pembroke Road. I saw that this knowledge I had acquired might prove extremely useful to her, for it was plain that even if she obtained the passport she would have to leave England secretly to avoid the vigilance of the secret agents of the Embassy. Again, why did Ella visit her? Instead of cycling in the Park she went to Pembroke Road, according to the report furnished to Renouf, nearly every day. For what purpose, I wondered. The more I reflected, the more deeply it became rooted within me that through Sonia I might ascertain the truth I sought.

Therefore I abandoned none of my efforts to persuade my friend to issue the document that would pass the sad-eyed girl across the frontier into the land she loved. For fully half-an-hour we discussed the situation, but he would not consent. She was an adventuress and a criminal, he said, and he was not prepared to risk the consequences if she were arrested in Russia with a false special permit issued by him.

"Besides," he added, "you have heard from Renouf how she is constantly kept under observation."

"But you could arrange that with him if you liked. A word from you and the vigilance of the police would be relaxed for an hour or two while she escaped," I observed.

"Ah, no," Verblioudovitch answered, "we have nothing whatever to do with Renouf and his subordinates, who are under the direct control of Sekerzhinski, the chief of the department in St Petersburg. They take no instructions from us."

"Renouf would, however, do you a personal favour," I hazarded.

"I fear not," was the reply. "We are not the best of friends. That is the reason I hesitate to issue a document that might implicate me. If he discovered the truth, my prospects in the diplomatic service might be ruined."

With all Paul's gay spirits and careless manner he possessed an eager enthusiasm, and an insatiable curiosity concerning humanity at large.

"But there is yet another way," I said.

"How?"

"Obtain the signature of His Excellency, the Ambassador. You can make an excuse that the permit is for a friend."

Paul remained silent, pacing the room with stolid face and automatic movement. At last he turned to me, saying,—

"I see, Deedes, it's quite useless to argue longer. I admit that I am exceedingly anxious to render you this service, but knowing as I do that the consequences must be disastrous either to you, or to the woman Korolénko, I have hesitated. Yet if you are determined to assist her I suppose I must obtain for you the necessary paper."

"Thanks, old fellow, thanks! I knew you would help me," I exclaimed enthusiastically.

"I cannot let you have it before this evening. If you will send Juckes round at seven you shall have it with the visé and everything complete."

"What a good fellow you are!" I cried joyfully, rising and shaking his hand. "Some day I hope to be able to perform a service for you."

"Let's hope so, old chap," he answered cheerily, but next second his face assumed a grave expression, as he added, "Take my advice now, and do not let any of Sonia's wild allegations disturb you. She certainly is too expert an adventuress to tell you anything to your own advantage, although whatever she does reveal will be to the detriment of the woman you love."

"Why are you so certain of this?" I inquired quickly, in genuine surprise.

"I have strong reasons for anticipating the course she will adopt," he answered ambiguously. "I therefore give you warning."

"It seems that she is acquainted with Ella," I observed.

"Yes, from Renouf's report. But remember my words, and don't be led away by any of her false statements. Do not forget that there is a very strong motive why she should denounce Miss Laing—a motive you will perhaps discover ere long," and he smiled mysteriously.

"Very well," I exclaimed, after a brief pause. Then again shaking his hand, I left, after expressing thanks and promising to send Juckes to the Embassy that evening.

Chapter Eighteen
Some Surprises

Several weeks passed uneventfully. In fulfilment of my promise to Sonia I had obtained the required permit and taken it personally to Pembroke Road on the same evening, but on arrival there discovered that the pretty Russian had been unexpectedly summoned to the bedside of a sick friend. She had, however, left a note with the English maid asking me to enclose the document in an envelope and leave it.

"I regret it is impossible for me to be at home to receive you," she wrote in French, "but I have every confidence that you will secure me what I require. If you leave it for me I will, in return, write down and send you the facts I promised to reveal. Time presses, therefore kindly excuse my haste. I shall always remember your kindness and be ready to render you any service in return."

This was disappointing. I had hoped to hear from her own lips her promised revelations, but this being impossible, I enclosed the special permit in an envelope, sealed it and left it, together with a brief note warning her that she was being carefully watched by police agents, and promising to call next day and bid her farewell.

When on the following morning I presented myself at her house, I was informed by the maid that mademoiselle had left early to visit her sick friend, and that she would not return till evening. Inquiry showed that she had received my letter, and when at eight o'clock that night I again called in the expectation of obtaining the fulfilment of her promise to tell me of Ella, I found her still absent, and gathered from the servant that she had taken a travelling-trunk with her. I concluded that she had left secretly for Russia.

From day to day I waited in the expectation of a letter from her, but although I remained in anxiety and doubt for more than a month, none came, and I was at last compelled to admit that I had actually been tricked, as Paul had predicted. He was right after all. Sonia, the innocent-looking girl with the sad, dark eyes and dimpled chin, was a woman internationally notorious, who, soft-voiced, had posed as my friend in order to attain her own ends, and had then departed without carrying out her part of the compact. As the weeks passed I gradually began to realise the force of Paul Verblioudovitch's words when he had tried to impress upon me the necessity of accepting her statements with caution. Without doubt she was a heartless adventuress, therefore I bitterly reproached myself for having allowed her libellous allegations against Ella to arouse suspicion within me, and at length determined upon regarding all her words as false, uttered merely for the purpose of enlisting my assistance to procure here re-entry into her own country. My anger that I should have allowed myself to fall into such a trap, and make such a demand upon a friend's goodwill, knew no bounds. I went to the Embassy, and to Paul admitted that my hopes had not been realised. In reply, he laughed heartily, saying,—

"I warned you, my dear fellow, of the kind of woman with whom you were dealing. Thank your stars that she has discarded you so easily, and be careful of pretty refugees in future. No harm has apparently been done, for inquiries I've made showed that she crossed the frontier at Verjbolovo without detection."

"I must confess I doubted the truth of your words before you issued the permit, but of course it is all plain now," I said.

"You don't believe her lies about Miss Laing, eh?" he inquired bluntly, but a trifle earnestly, I thought.

"No, I don't," I smiled; and then our conversation had drifted into a different channel. It was clear enough now, patent to everybody, that the girl I had fancied so pure, so unworldly—the goddess that sat in the clouds regarding all earth with clear, immaculate eyes—was simply an adventuress, a wretched creature, on the lookout for victims.

The popular excitement consequent from the belief that war was to be declared had died down, although in the Foreign Office the reason of the sudden abandonment of Russia's intentions remained an inscrutable mystery, while the panic on the Stock Exchange had enriched a few and ruined many. Parliament had risen for the recess, and Beck had taken a party in his yacht to the Norwegian fiords, Ella and Mrs Laing declining his invitation to join them. This course had been adopted at my suggestion. When Ella had spoken to me of their proposed cruise, I at once demurred, for although I had also been asked, I found absence from the Foreign Office impossible, owing to several delicate negotiations at that moment proceeding, and therefore urged her to remain in London. This she did at once, declining the invitation on behalf of both herself and her mother. The latter, who was not a good sailor, secretly thanked me for rescuing her from what she termed "three weeks of misery," and, truth to tell, although no longer jealous of Beck's attention to Ella, I was glad to have her remain in town.

Through the hot, stifling August days, when London was what is termed "empty," Mrs Laing and her daughter still lived in Pont Street. During the first three weeks following my visit to Sonia I called only twice, but meantime Ella was, I know, suffering tortures of doubt and anxiety. She had been trained in a school of self-repression, and it now stood her in good stead. She could not, however, prevent her cheeks being pale, neither could she help her eyes looking dilated and odd. Speech was difficult and smiles impossible; otherwise she held her own, and only I felt the difference, and knew that there lay a deep gulf of suspicion between us.

On the two occasions on which I had called we had no confidential chat, and the formal hours went by almost in silence. I had received positive proof from Renouf that she had been a constant visitor to Sonia, and it was impossible to talk with frivolity in that oppressive atmosphere of doubt. Mrs Laing, I noticed, hung her gold *pince-nez* high upon her nose in wonder. Ella was thus consuming herself with anxiety, while I, struggling along from day to day, saw my last hope growing thinner and yet more shadowy, and looming through it—despair.

Then at last, five weeks after Sonia's flight, I called at Pont Street and demanded of Ella the reason she had visited the house in Pembroke Road. Her reply was quite unexpected. She told me quite calmly that they had been schoolfellows at Neuilly, and that, finding Sonia had lost both her parents, she went to Pembroke Road each day to bear the bereaved girl company. She was in ignorance regarding Sonia's life since she had left the French school, and expressed surprise that she should have departed suddenly without telling her of her destination. Her replies to my inquiries set my mind at rest upon several points. It appeared quite plain that Ella herself had told Sonia of her engagement to me and had described the tragic incident at Staines, therefore the pretty refugee had been enabled to drop those ingenious hints at mystery that had so sorely puzzled me, and had cleverly secured my interests on her behalf.

When I realised how artfully I had been tricked, I ground my teeth, and Ella, standing statuesque on the opposite side of the drawing-room in strong relief against a background of dark, glossy palms and broad-leaved tropical plants, noticed my anger. The light fell upon her red-brown hair and upon her slightly upturned face, showing its delicate modelling in its almost childish roundness. Her profile was quite as charming as her full face, perhaps more so, as it had the advantage of the curl and sweep of the eyelashes and of the fine line of the upper lip.

She eyed me gravely, but spoke no word.

Yet in that instant I knew I had misjudged her, that through those long, anxious weeks while I had entertained dark suspicions she had nevertheless still loved me honestly and truly. I know not what words I uttered, but a few moments later I found her sobbing in my fond embrace. Her tears were tears of joy.

The silence was long. We had so much to think about that we forgot to speak, but presently, when she dried her blue eyes with her flimsy lace handkerchief and seated herself, I took the tiny hand lying idly in her lap and laid my cheek down on the tender, rosy palm.

"How I wish that this night could last for ever," I said, with a sigh of supreme contentment. "In my memory it will live always."

"Always?" she echoed, looking tenderly into my face; then for the first time she put her arms around me and held me tightly pressed against her heart.

"Yes, always," I said. "Until I die."

"Ah! Don't speak of death," she whispered. "If you died, I—I should die also, Geoffrey. I could not live without you. How I have endured these dark, weary weeks I scarcely know."

Together we remained a long time, while I reproached myself for entertaining suspicion that her friendliness with Dudley or with Beck was anything but platonic, declaring that my love had ever been unwavering, that my recent actions had been due to a mad and unjust jealousy for which I craved her forgiveness.

With her eyes still wet she told me how fondly she had always loved me, and urged me to think no more of the strange events that had led to Dudley's tragic end.

"It is my duty to ascertain the truth and clear up the mystery," she said. "I have promised you a solution of the enigma, and you shall have it some day."

"For the present, dearest, I am content to wait," I answered, and in the same breath repeated the question I had asked her months ago—whether she would be my wife.

"Alas! I fear you do not trust me sufficiently, Geoffrey," she answered in a low, intense tone, tears still welling in her blue eyes.

"I do," I cried. "I know that all the time I have been a jealously brutal fool you have loved me as truly as ever."

"I told you long ago that I loved you," she answered earnestly.

"Yes, I believe it now, darling," I said. "That is why I ask you to become my wife. Tell me once more that you will." In a whisper, as her handsome head pillowed itself upon, my arm, she repeated her promise, then burst into a torrent of tears, while I, in joyful ecstasy, still held her in my arms.

It was an idyllic evening, this first one of love and trust; a brief dream such as one has in the moment before waking. Bowing before my idol, I had humbly acknowledged myself wrong, and my well-beloved had frankly forgiven and forgotten. There was a long silence, deep and impressive, broken only by the confused sound from the street that came in through the open window. Then, when she stirred again and raised her head, I told her of my position at the Foreign Office, and the probability of my appointment to a diplomatic post abroad.

She listened, her clear, trusting eyes fixed upon me. She, too, was ambitious.

"It's a great responsibility for any woman," she said at last, "to think she is to be part of a career. I will help you, my darling," then she buried her face again in my coat-collar, protesting fervently, "I will never, never allow myself to hinder you; but will do my utmost to help you to success, only you must have patience with me." Suddenly she raised her head again, continuing, "I know there is one strange episode in my past that is a mystery to you, nay, to all. My misfortune is that I am unable yet to reveal the truth, because I fear the consequences of such disclosure. Some day you shall know everything, but until then think only of me as the woman who loves you with all her soul."

She spoke with a terrible earnestness, her slim fingers clutching my arm convulsively, and as I gave my promise to regard her always as a pure and upright woman, and forget the mystery surrounding her, I sealed our compact with a long, passionate kiss.

Mrs Laing, stiff and stately in black satin, entered the room a few moments later, and Ella, having whispered and obtained my consent, forthwith made a full and complete statement to her mother of the position of affairs. The old lady listened attentively in silence, inclining her head now and then with a gesture indicative of approbation, but when her daughter had concluded her face brightened.

"I am indeed glad to think that dear Ella is to marry you after all, Geoffrey," she said. "Once, not so very long ago, I feared that you two would never again be reconciled, for Ella moped day after day, crying, and quite spoiling her complexion. But the old saying about the course of true love contains much truth, and now that your little differences are readjusted, there can be no cause for any further regret. That Ella loves you dearly, I, as her mother, have had better opportunity for knowing than anyone else and were it not for the fact that I am convinced you both will be happy, I should never give my consent to your marriage. But I am absolutely sure that this marriage is one that Ella's father would have approved, therefore you have my entire consent and heartiest congratulations."

"Thank you, Mrs Laing," I answered. "I, too, am convinced that we love each other sufficiently well, and I can only promise to be a sympathetic and devoted husband."

Ella, who, standing beside her mother's chair, had entwined her arms affectionately around her neck, slowly released her, and walked across the room to turn the lamp higher. Then, deeming it but just that they both should know the reason of my recent coolness and suspicion, I told them in confidence of the mysterious theft of the secret convention, the strange and tragic events that followed, the discovery of the seal on the body of Dudley Ogle, and my absurd belief that Ella had, in some way, been implicated in the ingenious efforts of the spy.

"Do you actually suspect poor Dudley of having been in the pay of the Russian Government?" Mrs Laing asked, open-mouthed, in dismay.

"I do," I was constrained to reply. "There is no shadow of doubt that he was a spy. He tricked you as he did myself. I was his best friend, yet he nearly ruined all my prospects in the Service."

While we had been speaking the door had opened, and as I glanced from Ella across to Mrs Laing, I saw a grey-haired man-servant in the act of handing her a letter.

As he turned from her to leave he glanced at me suddenly. Our eyes met in mutual recognition, and I think I must have started perceptibly, for his brows suddenly contracted as if commanding me to silence; then he made his exit, closing the door noiselessly behind him.

"You haven't seen my new man Helmholtz before, Geoffrey," Mrs Laing exclaimed when he had gone. "He seems a perfect treasure, although he is a German. But, after all, German servants are more useful, and quite as trustworthy as English. I should certainly advise Ella to have one."

"Yes," I answered mechanically.

The man was none other than Ivan Renouf, the great Russian detective.

Chapter Nineteen
A Blade of Grass

Nearly three months had slipped away. It was mid-November. The cloud that had darkened my days had lifted, the sun shone out, and life and hope sprang up and ran riot in my heart. The long, anxious weeks were over, for Ella was now my wife, and our lives were full of joy and love. With utter contempt for the warning words of the ingenuous Russian who left so mysteriously without fulfilling her promise, I had taken the dearest other half of my soul, happy in the knowledge that I would be a solitary wretch no more.

After a quiet wedding at St Peter's, Eaton Square, at which, however, a large number of our friends were present, including Paul Verblioudovitch, the reception had been held at Pont Street, and we left to spend our honeymoon on the Continent while our house in Phillimore Gardens, Kensington, was being prepared. I loved my wife with the whole strength of my being. Her beauty was incomparable, her grace charming, and I could not doubt that she loved me with her whole soul, and that her vows came direct from her heart.

The reason of Renouf's presence in Mrs Laing's household was an enigma. Since the night when I had first seen him there I had visited Pont Street each day, and on several occasions had managed to speak with him alone. To all my inquiries, however, he remained dumb.

One night, when I had called and found Ella and her mother had gone to the theatre, I closed the door of the room into which I had been ushered, and asked him point-blank whether his presence there was not calculated to arouse suspicions in my mind. With an imperturbable smile he replied,—

"There is no allegation whatever against mother or daughter, therefore set your mind entirely at rest. We desire to ascertain something. That is all."

His manner angered me.

"If I were to denounce you as a spy you would be thrown out of this house very quickly," I said, indignant that this ill-featured man should, for some mysterious reason, watch every action of my well-beloved.

He glanced at me with an amused expression, as he answered in a half whisper, —

"By betraying me, m'sieur would betray one of his closest friends."

"Oh! How's that?"

"A word from you to either of these women," he exclaimed, with brows slightly knit, "and the department in St Petersburg will know the reason that Sonia Korolénko was enabled to pass the frontier at Verjbolovo; they will know that Paul Verblioudovitch, the Secretary of Embassy, has assisted a criminal to escape."

"You scoundrel!" I cried, facing him fiercely. "You listened to our conversation!"

He shrugged his shoulders, and with the same grim smile, answered, —

"My ears are trained, m'sieur. It is part of my profession."

"But why do you remain here, in a peaceable household?" I demanded. "Surely neither Mrs Laing nor Ella have incurred the Tzar's displeasure or the hatred of those in authority! They know nothing of Russia; they have never set foot in the country."

The man's features relaxed, and turning from me, he busied himself among some bottles on the sideboard.

"I desire an answer," I continued.

"I have my instructions," he replied, without looking towards me.

"From whom?"

"From headquarters."

"Well," I exclaimed. "We are not in Russia, therefore, when the ladies return, I shall explain who and what you are."

"You dare not," he said, regarding me suddenly with dark, penetrating gaze.

"Miss Ella will soon be my wife, and I will not allow her actions to be noted upon one of those formidable forms of yours that are too often the death-warrants of your victims."

"These ladies are not my victims, as you are pleased to term them," he protested, laughing at my anger.

"Victims or friends, they shall no longer remain under your accursed surveillance," I cried hotly. "You may practice your espionage upon your suspected compatriots; but I will never allow you to keep observation upon my friends here in England."

"Very well," he said, quite calmly, with that cynical expression that was so tantalising. "Act as you think fit. We, of the secret service, take no step before due consideration of its consequences, a policy it would be wise for you also to adopt." Then, with a show of mock politeness, he opened the door of the dining-room, and, bowing, exclaimed, "Madame is out, will m'sieur remain, or call again?"

Our eyes met, and I saw in his a look of triumph.

"I'll call again," I replied, and walked out into the hall, gaining the street a moment later.

The first passing hansom I hailed, and drove at once to Chesham House, where I was fortunate to find Paul. When we were closeted together, I told him of the police officer's threat, and my announcement caused him considerable astonishment.

"Curious," he repeated, as if to himself. "Very curious that Renouf should be installed in that family, above all others."

"Above all others," I echoed. "Why?"

"I—I mean that Mrs Laing could not possibly have done anything to offend our Government," he said, quickly correcting himself. "It is certainly very strange. Renouf is not a man to be trifled with," he added quickly. "There must be some very strong reason, known only to himself, that has induced him to act in this manner. If the motive were not a strong one, he would delegate the menial position he has had to assume to one of his subordinates. I know he has his hands full of important inquiries just now, and it therefore surprises me that he is calmly reposing as butler in Mrs Laing's service."

"But knowing him to be a spy, I cannot allow him to remain longer in daily contact with those two defenceless women," I exclaimed.

"Have they ever been in Russia?"

"Never!" I replied. "Only the other evening they were asking me about St Petersburg, and both expressed a wish to visit your country."

Paul, with his hands behind his back, and head bent in thought, paused for a moment, and then said,—

"From what I know of Ivan Renouf, I believe that were you to do him an evil turn, and obtain his dismissal from Pont Street, he would at once expose to the Ministry of the Interior how Sonia Korolénko obtained her passport. If he did so, the result would be disastrous to me, especially just at a time when our frontier regulations are extremely rigid."

"What, then, is the best course to pursue?" I asked.

He was silent, looking moodily into the fire. Then turning with a sudden movement, he said, with emphasis,—"You are my friend, Geoffrey. My future is in your hands."

"Which means that my silence is imperative," I observed reflectively.

Paul Verblioudovitch nodded, but uttered no word. If I denounced Renouf it was plain that my friend who had seriously imperilled his position at my urgent request, must undoubtedly suffer. In order to shield him I must therefore remain silent. With intense chagrin I saw myself ingeniously checkmated.

I dared not allow one single syllable of suspicion regarding the German servant, who was, according to Mrs Laing, "a treasure," to escape my lips, and thus, as the weeks passed preceding my marriage, I was compelled to watch and wait without any outward sign.

The reason of his vigilance was an inscrutable mystery. With Ella as my wife I had passed six blissful weeks, visiting many of the quaint, old-world towns in Central France. It had been Ella's fancy to do this. She hated the glare and glitter of Paris, and would only remain there the night on our outward and homeward journeys; indeed, cities had no charm for her, she preferred the lethargic provincial towns, from which we could make excursions into the country and spend the bright autumn days at old-fashioned inns. Fearing that she was becoming bored, I endeavoured to induce her to go to Biarritz or Pau, but to no avail. The crowded *table-d'hôte*, of the popular resort possessed no attraction, and I rejoiced in secret, for we spent a far happier time wandering through the country than if installed in some garish hotel in the neighbourhood of a casino.

Once, and only once since our marriage, had I made any mention of the death of Dudley Ogle. We were driving into the ancient town of Chateauroux, in the Indre, on the lumbering, dusty, old diligence that has performed the same daily journey for perhaps a century, when I chanced to incidentally utter his name, and express wonder when the mystery would be solved.

We were speaking in English, not a word of which could be understood by our driver, but instantly she turned to me with a look of reproach, and, placing her little gloved hand on my mouth in haste, exclaimed,—

"No, Geoffrey. Do not recall that terrible tragedy. Promise never again to mention his name; it only brings sadness to both of us, while the mystery surrounding the crime is irritating and puzzling. You have already told me that he was not your friend, although he posed as such, therefore forget him.

I have not forgotten; nor shall I ever cease to think and to strive towards the solution of the problem."

"But cannot I help you to search and investigate?" I suggested. "Why should you strive to elucidate this mystery alone, now that you are my wife?"

"Because it is my ambition," she answered, regarding me earnestly with clear, trusting eyes. "You will, I know, allow me to retain one object in life apart from you."

"Certainly," I answered, surreptitiously pressing her hand, although puzzled at her strange words. In the few weeks we had been together I had discovered that she was a woman of moods and curious fancies. Once or twice she had exhibited a strong desire to walk alone at night when the moon shone, and because I objected she had pouted prettily, scorning the idea that she was not able to take care of herself. Except when in this mood she was always eager to fulfil my every wish, and I had quickly arrived at the conclusion that her strange desires were but natural to one of a slightly hysterical temperament, and therefore troubled myself but little about them.

Thus after an enjoyable trip through one of the most beautiful districts of France, unknown to the average Briton, we returned and settled comfortably at our new home in Kensington. My duties at the Foreign Office took me away the greater part of the day, but Ella was not lonely, for she drove out frequently with her mother, who visited her almost daily. Of interference or maternal influence I had nothing whatever to complain, yet Ella's desire to wander about alone, aimless and absorbed, soon again seized her. We had been settled about a month when I made this discovery from the servants, who, on my arrival home earlier than usual on several occasions, told me, in answer to questions, that their mistress had gone out by herself. But on her return she betrayed no surprise, mentioning quite incidentally that she had been shopping in High Street, or that she had been to her milliner's in Bond Street, or elsewhere.

So frequently did this occur that at last I became puzzled, and on making further inquiries found that on many occasions she had been absent the whole day, returning only just in time to change her dress and receive me with that bright, winning smile that always held me entranced.

One bright December afternoon I returned at three o'clock, and found she had been absent since eleven that morning. I took a cab to Pont Street, but ascertaining she had not been there, returned home, and impatiently awaited her until nearly six. As soon as I heard her light footstep I seized a book that lay nearest and pretended to read. She burst in like a ray of sunshine, her face aglow with laughter, and in her hand an immense bunch of sweet-smelling violets.

The book chanced to be a Koran in Arabic. She came across to kiss me, but I waved her off with dignity, and went on translating the Word of the Prophet.

Ella stood back indignant, and with her flowers in front of her waited at the other side of the table.

After a pause I commenced, "You went out this morning ten minutes after I had gone; it is now six o'clock. You have been absent seven hours."

Ella nodded.

"And how have you employed your time?" I asked. "Have you been shopping, as usual?"

Ella again nodded.

"Seven hours is a long time. Where did you get those flowers?" I asked, sniffing contemptuously at the huge bunch of sweet-smelling blossoms she had let fall before me.

"I bought them at Scott's."

"That is a bunch specially made up for presentation," I said. "Someone gave them to you."

"Yes, the shopman," she laughed. "I gave him two shillings for them." Then she took off her hat and, impaling it with a long pin, cast it heedlessly upon the table.

"It has not occupied seven hours to buy a bunch of violets," I said ruthlessly. "Where have you been?"

Ella looked round laughing, and said in a quiet voice, "I have been to see a friend."

"Another aunt—eh?" I asked, suspiciously.

She took a chair and sat down opposite; then, with her head leaning upon her hands, she said demurely, "Yes, it was an aunt."

There was silence. Ella had picked up her bunch of violets, and every time I looked up she was watching me over them.

"Well," I exclaimed at last, "where does this aunt live—at Highgate?"

"No, not that one. She is poor. She lives in Camberwell."

"I don't believe it," I said, standing up suddenly.

Ella raised her eyebrows in interrogation. There was an ominous look in her blue eyes, and I put forth my hand to snatch the flowers and cast them into the fire. Instead, I sat down again and turned over another hundred pages of my Koran.

"Geoffrey," she said at length in a low, timid voice I perused my book with stolid indifference.

"Geoffrey," she repeated, "why are you angry with me without cause?"

Raising my head, I saw that her fine eyes were dimmed by tears, and almost unconsciously I reached, took her hand, and pressed it. Then Ella, rising slowly, came round and sat upon my knee.

"You see," she whispered, with her arms around my neck, "this is how it was. Last night I said to myself, —

"This poor, dear Geoffrey—he is so busy with his country's affairs, and works so hard—he will be away all day; therefore I will go over to call upon my aunt in Camberwell and take her a bottle of wine and some tea, for she is a great invalid and in poverty. Since my marriage I haven't seen her, and as she is in great straits I know dear Geoffrey will not object."

Here Ella stopped to nestle closer to me, and went on, —

"And to-day I took a cab down to Camberwell, to a dreary row of drab, mournful-looking houses, and all day long I have sat by her bedside trying to cheer her. Ah! she is so ill, and so sad. Then on my return I called at Scott's and bought these flowers for my darling, serious old boy who has been working all day in his dreary office with its window overlooking the dismal grey quadrangle. And I am so tired, and it was not at all amusing for me without him."

The flowers smelt so sweet in front of me; and Ella was so sweet, childlike and full of happiness, that I took her soft face between my hands, as was my habit, and kissed her.

But later that evening, on going to her room alone to fetch something for her, I noticed that her high-heeled French boots, thrown aside, as she had cast them off, were unusually muddy, although, strangely enough, it had been a dry day. I took them up, and upon examining the soles found them caked with damp clay in which were embedded some blades of grass.

I slowly descended the stairs engrossed by my own thoughts. Grass does not grow in the streets of Camberwell.

Chapter Twenty
Undercurrents of Diplomacy

A few nights later we went together to a ball at the Russian Embassy. Perhaps of all the functions in London a ball at Chesham House is one of the most brilliant and imposing, for it is always on a scale in keeping with the dignity of the representative of the Tzar.

The spacious state rooms with their great crystal chandeliers and heavy gilding, were filled to overflowing with pretty women and men in uniform of hues as varied as those of the ladies' dresses, from the black coat of the United States Minister to the bright yellow jacket of the Emperor of China's representative. All the diplomatic body were present, as well as many personages well-known in English society. At the head of the grand staircase Monsieur Grodekoff, the Russian Ambassador, a striking figure in his spotless white uniform, his breast glittering with orders set in brilliants, including the much-coveted ribbon of St Andrew, stood with his daughter receiving their guests, and as we advanced the courtly, white-haired old gentleman, whom I had met on many occasions in my official capacity, shook me heartily by the hand and congratulated us upon our marriage.

"I heard, Deedes, of your good fortune," he said, after greeting Ella. "I trust that you and your wife will have long life and every happiness."

"Thanks, your Excellency," I answered, smiling contentedly. "There is no doubt, I think, concerning our happiness."

"You should take madame to St Petersburg," the aged diplomatist laughed. "She would enjoy it, especially with you, who know our country."

"I hope to go very soon," Ella said. "I have heard so much about it, and am longing to see it."

"Go now," he urged. "This is just the season; plenty of snow, and skating and sledging and suchlike sports that delight us in the North."

We both laughed in chorus, while the representative of the White Tzar, dismissing us into the ballroom with a low bow, turned to greet the tall, full-bearded representative of his Imperial master's ally, the French Republic. In the corridor there was bustle everywhere. Gaily-uniformed servants hurried here and there, young attachés, their breasts decorated with crosses and ribbons of every combination of colour, lounged along with pretty women on their arms, while older diplomats of every shade of complexion from white to black, exchanged greetings as they met.

From the gay cosmopolitan throng in the ballroom rose the mingled odour of a thousand perfumes with the chatter of laughing women, and ere we had entered, Paul Verblioudovitch, erect, spruce and smart in his pale-blue uniform, and wearing many decorations, elbowed his way through the crush towards us.

We had not met since the wedding reception at Pont Street, and as we strolled through the brightly-lit *salons*, Ella, radiant and enthusiastic, began telling him of our idle days and explorations in the old-world French towns.

"Permit me, madame, to congratulate you," he exclaimed presently.

"Upon what?" asked Ella, in surprise.

"Upon being the prettiest woman it has ever been our honour to entertain here upon this small square of territory belonging to our Imperial Master," he said, bowing and smiling with that inborn *finesse* which was one of his chief characteristics.

"Ah, you diplomatists always flatter," she laughed lightly behind her fan. "Is it really wise of you to make a woman vain?" she asked, inclining her head slightly.

I felt compelled to admit that Paul had spoken the truth, for as we passed along I had not failed to notice that Ella's beauty was everywhere remarked. Her gown of cream satin, a trifle *décolleté*, with the corsage thickly embroidered with pearls and edged with flowers, suited her admirably, and the instant consciousness of success in that brilliant circle of society unfamiliar to her heightened the colour of her cheeks and added lustre to her eyes. ·

"The majority of the women who honour us with their presence on these occasions are vain enough," my friend admitted, adding in a low voice, "even though some of them are absolute hags."

"Mr Verblioudovitch is, I believe, past-master of the art of flattery," Ella observed, laughing, turning towards me. "He could make a dowager-duchess believe herself as youthful and attractive as a girl of eighteen."

"It is necessary sometimes, madame," he answered, amused. "Quite necessary, I assure you."

At that moment a quietly-dressed elderly lady of pronounced Teutonic type and matronly proportions was struggling to pass us, but, recognised by Paul, was introduced to Ella. It was a woman with whom I was well acquainted, the Countess Landsfeldt, wife of the German Ambassador. She at once joined our little group, and commenced to chat with a strong accent.

"We have not met, madame, for quite an age—three months, is it?" Paul exclaimed presently. "You have been away, I believe."

"Ah! yes. For a month I was in Berlin, and afterwards, just as I was returning to London, my youngest daughter fell ill, and I was compelled to spend two months with her in Ehrenburg, our schloss on the Mosel."

"The Ehrenburg!" exclaimed Ella, enthusiastically. "I know it quite well. How romantic and charming it looks perched high up upon its solitary rock. My mother and I drove from Brodenbach along the valley to see it last year."

"Ah, you did not enter?"

"No," my wife answered, smiling. "I had not then the honour of madame's acquaintance."

"Inside, we are back in mediaeval days, with dungeons, torture-chambers, and all sorts of relics of barbarism; while the legends connected with the place are legion. Some day, if you are interested in ancient castles, you and your husband must visit me in Germany."

"It is the most carefully preserved stronghold of the middle ages extant," Paul observed.

"Ah, yes," replied the Countess, "but it is gloomy and dull—ugh!" and, shrugging her shoulders, she pulled a little grimace. "I prefer Berlin—or even London."

"You say even London, Countess," exclaimed Paul. "I quite agree. London is *triste* after Vienna or St Petersburg. Is his Excellency with you this evening?"

"No. My husband is—oh, so busy. We only returned from Lord Maybury's this morning, and dispatches accumulate so fast in his absence."

"He has received another decoration from the Emperor, I hear," Verblioudovitch observed.

"Yes, the Iron Cross," replied the Countess, looking at him sharply. Then she added quickly,—

"But who told you? He only received His Majesty's intimation three days ago, and I thought for the present it was a profound secret."

Upon Paul's face there spread that imperturbable smile that he could assume at will, as he answered, —

"It is the object of a diplomatist to ascertain the nature of all secrets."

The Countess gave vent to a forced laugh as she exclaimed, "My husband, I think, fully deserved the honour."

"Certainly, madame," replied the Tzar's official, courteously, his hands clasped behind his back. "The completion of the secret convention with England was, I admit, a master-stroke, and even though directed against us, the rapidity and cleverness with which it was effected were worthy of reward." And he smiled at her mysteriously.

"Ah," she exclaimed, fanning herself slowly with a sudden hauteur; "no secret seems safe from you, m'sieur. Nothing escapes the Embassy of Russia." And bowing slightly, her stiff silks swept past us, and a moment later she became lost in the chattering, well-dressed crowd.

"You see, my dear Geoffrey," laughed Paul, when the Countess was out of hearing, "we are accredited with the omnipotence of the Evil One himself quite unduly. I particularly desired to learn whether her husband had been decorated by his Emperor for that convention which nearly cost Europe a war; therefore I hazarded a single remark. Whereupon she at once told me all about it, and having done so, in her next breath denounced us and all our works. But, there," and he gave his shoulders a shrug, "women are such strange creatures."

"How cleverly you managed to ascertain what you desired," observed Ella.

But the fine Viennese orchestra had struck up, and my wife, being engaged to him for a dance then commencing, he led her off, and I failed to overhear his reply.

For the next hour I did not dance, but wandering about the rooms I exchanged greetings and chatted with those I knew, until at length I came across Lady Farringford, the wife of Sir Henry Farringford, our Minister in Washington, sitting with her daughter Mabel. We were old friends, and Mabel quickly responded to my invitation to waltz. She was a smart girl, and rumour said that she had become engaged to a wealthy American, a statement which, in reply to my inquiry, she frankly confirmed. As we waltzed and lounged together I noticed Ella dancing first with Paul, and afterwards with several young attachés of my acquaintance. Once or twice we exchanged smiles, and I knew by the expression on her face how thoroughly she was enjoying her first night in the diplomatic circle. The scene was brilliant and full of colour, the music excellent, and the scent of exotics almost overpowering. Everyone seemed intoxicated with gaiety. In that cosmopolitan crowd hearts were lighter and talk more free than in the ordinary London ballroom, although experienced ones knew that here, amid this brilliant assembly, there were many strange undercurrents affecting the prestige of monarchs and the welfare of nations.

"So, you are to marry, Mabel," I observed when, after waltzing, I led her into an ante-room, and she sat down to eat an ice.

"Yes, at last," she sighed, looking up at me with a pair of mischievous dark eyes. She was about twenty-two, and rather pretty. "I'm to be married in June, and we are coming to Europe for a twelve months' tour. You are married already. I'd so much like to meet your wife. Since I've been here this evening I've heard nothing but admiration of her. You're the envy of all your male friends, Geoffrey."

I laughed. I confess that by the sensation Ella had caused I felt flattered.

"I'll introduce you when I have a chance," I said. "Our congratulations are mutual. You are to have a husband; I have already a wife."

"I hope you'll find the Biblical quotation correct," she laughed, peering at me over her gauzy fan. "Do you know the words?"

"No," I replied, "I'm not good at remembering quotations."

"Well, the Bible says, 'Whoso findeth a wife, findeth a good thing.' I hope you'll be no exception to that rule."

"Thanks," I replied. "I don't know what it says about husbands, but, however it may be worded, you have my heartiest wishes for long life and good luck."

At that instant Ella, on the arm of a young Italian marquis, possessed of a longer title than his rent-roll, entered. I sprang up at once and introduced her, and soon we all four were chatting merrily. When, a quarter of an hour later, we rose to return to the ballroom, Ella, radiant and happy, walked beside me. In reply to my question, she declared that she was enjoying herself immensely, but as we were re-entering the *salon* she clutched my arm, and in a half-frightened whisper exclaimed,—

"Look! Geoffrey. Look at that servant in uniform over there. Why, it's our man, Helmholtz!"

I glanced in the direction she had indicated, and sure enough there was the detective Renouf, who, in the Laing household, posed as Carl Helmholtz, in the handsome blue-and-gold livery of the Embassy, handing an ice to a lady. Instantly I grasped the situation.

"It is a striking resemblance, dearest," I said; "nothing more."

"But I'm certain it's Helmholtz," she declared excitedly. "Take me closer to him."

"When we were at Pont Street this afternoon, Helmholtz was there, wasn't he?"

"Yes. He brought tea into the drawing-room."

"Well, no doubt he is at home now. This fellow may be his brother, or something."

For a moment we stood watching, and saw him make a servile bow. Fortunately he turned his back upon us, hastening to execute some command, otherwise he must have come towards us and met us face to face.

"I'm certain it is Helmholtz," Ella exclaimed, in a tone of conviction.

"Without doubt it is a very striking resemblance," I admitted. "But the servants of an Embassy are not recruited from the nearest registry office. Besides, they would never employ a German here."

At that moment Paul approached and claimed her for the next dance, while I wandered on alone amid the crowd, my mind full of strange thoughts.

Presently, while watching the dancers, I chanced to glance aside and recognised a sparse, well-known figure approaching. It was the Earl of Warnham. Attired in plain evening dress of a rather antiquated cut, he wore no decorations, save the broad blue ribbon across his narrow strip of shirt-front, the highest honour his Sovereign had bestowed upon him. I was surprised to find him there, for I had believed him to be at Osborne in attendance on Her Majesty.

"Ah, Deedes," he exclaimed in a low voice, with a slight smile upon his colourless, wizened face. "In the enemy's camp—eh?"

"Yes, my wife wished to come," I explained.

"Of course. Women like this sort of thing. I have never met her. You must introduce her presently."

"She will esteem it an honour," I said, adding, "She is over there in a cream dress, dancing with Verblioudovitch."

He glanced in their direction, and started perceptibly. For some moments his keen eyes followed her. Then I noticed that his grey brows contracted, and his usually expressionless face wore a strange, ominous look such as I had never before detected upon it.

"Is that your wife?" he asked huskily, turning and eyeing me curiously.

"Yes."

"Was it she who alleged that your friend Ogle was the victim of foul play?" he inquired with emphasis, in a voice that betrayed dismay.

"It was," I replied.

The Foreign Minister sighed. As he again turned his eyes upon the pair at that moment gliding down the room to the strains of the latest fashionable refrain his brow darkened, and his teeth were firmly set. A silence fell between us.

Chapter Twenty One
In Kensington Gardens

On our return home in the early hours, Ella sat before the fire in her cosy boudoir, her opera-cape still about her shoulders, resting her tired head upon a cushion, and staring thoughtfully into the dying embers, while I lounged near, smoking a final cigarette. Times out of number I tried to account for the Earl's agitation when he had encountered her. It was evident they were not strangers, although when I had introduced them he treated her with studied courtesy. There were, I remembered, many suspicious incidents connected with her as yet unexplained, nevertheless, from that memorable evening when Dudley and I had dined at "The Nook" and we had become reconciled, I had never doubted that she loved me. Perhaps I had been foolish, I told myself. I ought to have obtained full explanation of the several circumstances that had caused me such uneasiness before marriage, yet I had abandoned all active effort to ascertain the truth, because of the intensity of my passion. Her beauty had captivated me; her voice held me spellbound, and because I loved her I could not bring myself to suspect her. For a long time she sat, reflecting gravely upon the events of the evening; then, shivering slightly, rose and went to her room, leaving me alone to ponder over her sudden seriousness.

Sometimes a slight shadow of suspicion would flit across my mind, as it often had on finding her absent, yet when she spoke caressingly to me I at once found myself laughing at the foolishness of my thoughts, basking in the sun of her brilliant beauty, heedless and content. Prior to our marriage, I had been madly jealous of every slight attention paid to her by one of my own sex, of whatever age, but now, recognising how marvellously fair she was, and that wherever she went she became the centre of attraction, I was no longer angry with any of our guests who paid court to her. Beck dined with us frequently, always gay and amusing, while once or twice Verblioudovitch had also accepted our invitation, and treated Ella with the courtliness of the polished diplomatist. I did not invite the latter often, because of her antipathy towards him. When, after his first visit, I had asked her what she thought of him, she had replied,—

"There is something about him I don't like, dearest. I cannot explain what it is. Perhaps it is his excessive politeness; or it may be his profuse flattery that bores me; nevertheless, I seem to have a feeling that I ought to avoid him."

"He's one of the best of fellows, darling," I said, laughing at her misgivings. "In my bachelor days we were very close friends."

"I don't like him," she answered frankly. "I hate all Russians."

"I thought you said once you would like to go to Russia?"

"Yes, I am anxious to see the country, but the Russians I have met I have always detested," she said, adding, with seriousness, "Now that I am your wife I may speak plainly, may I not?"

"Of course, darling."

"Then, in your own interests, promise me to avoid Paul Verblioudovitch as much as possible."

"Why?" I asked, surprised.

"Because—well," she answered in hesitation; "because I have some curious, inexplicable feeling that he is not your friend."

Then it occurred to me that they had been sitting together that evening in a cosy-corner in the drawing-room, deep in conversation, and it might be that Paul had uttered some compliments meant to be polite, but which she had misconstrued into flirtation. In that case, it was only natural that, loving me so deeply as she did, she should warn me that Paul was not my friend.

"In what way do you suspect him of being my enemy?" I inquired.

"He is untrustworthy," she replied, an answer that tended to confirm my supposition. On several other occasions I laughed at her fears, but she always made the same reply, that she believed he was not straightforward, and even went so far as to ask me not to invite him to our house in future. This caused me some little annoyance, for of all men Paul Verblioudovitch was one of my most valued friends; and, further, while she had conceived a violent dislike towards him, she nevertheless allowed herself to be flattered by the man of whom I had once been madly jealous—Andrew Beck.

Thus the early days of our married life proceeded, blissful and full of love, but with one tiny cloud of mystery that, although growing no larger, still cast its ominous shadow ever between us. Sometimes when alone I pondered deeply, wondering whether my confidence had after all been ill-placed, puzzled over one or two incidents such as I have already described. Trifling as they were in themselves, they nevertheless caused me much uneasiness, yet when Ella entered, bright and radiant, greeting me with an affectionate caress, I could not doubt her. I knew that, however suspicious her actions might appear in my eyes, she loved me honestly, with a passion as fierce and uncontrollable as my own.

Meanwhile Renouf, who explained his absence on the night of the Embassy ball to Ella's complete satisfaction, still continued to remain in service at Pont Street, and each time we dined there he hovered about us noiselessly and ever watchful, like a spirit of evil. When our eyes met, I saw in his a cold glance of contemptuous triumph, for he had already seen that I feared to denounce him for Paul's sake, and he was pursuing his mysterious investigations, whatever they were, without let or hindrance. Mrs Laing, sighing as stout ladies will, was always loud in his praise, declaring him to be the most steady and attentive servant that had ever been in her service, while Ella expressed a wish that we could meet with a man possessed of similar virtues. A dozen times I longed to take my wife and her mother into my confidence, but dared not, for the silence imposed upon me was absolutely imperative.

One day, early in January, I had received a message from Lord Warnham to call at his house in Berkeley Square, but when I arrived found a note stating that he had been compelled unexpectedly to go down to Lord Maybury's seat in Hertfordshire to consult him. Therefore I left, and it being a cold but invigorating afternoon I resolved to walk home. Proceeding along Piccadilly and Knightsbridge, I skirted the Park, and entering Kensington Gardens by the Alexandra Gate, strolled towards Kensington in the full enjoyment of a cigar. Ella had, I knew, gone to Pont Street, her mother being rather unwell, therefore I walked leisurely beneath the leafless, smoke-blackened trees. The short, gloomy day was now fast drawing to a close, and, with the falling gloom, a chill wind had sprung up, whistling mournfully through the bare branches, causing me to turn up my coat-collar and draw on my gloves. I fancied myself alone, for at four o'clock in winter the place is dismal and deserted. Having passed Queen's Gate, I was approaching the Broad Walk, when I was attracted by two figures strolling slowly together in front of me, a man and a woman. At first I took no heed, and would in a few moments have overtaken them, when it occurred to me that the silhouette of the woman was familiar even in the dusk. Again I looked, and noticed that she was fashionably dressed in a dark-brown tailor-made gown, a sealskin cape and close-fitting hat. Next second I realised the amazing truth.

The woman walking before me was Ella.

Her companion, a tall, broad-shouldered young man, wore a long drab overcoat of distinctly "horsey" cut, a silk hat of the latest shape, and displayed a good deal of shirt cuff. He was evidently a fop, and his whole exterior, from his varnished boots to the velvet cuffs of his overcoat, pronounced him to be a cad. Leisurely he strode by her side, smoking a cigarette, and earnest in conversation, now and then emphasising his words by striking the palm of one gloved hand with his fist.

Once, as I dogged their footsteps, my teeth clenched in fierce anger, I heard her give vent to a rippling peal of laughter that echoed among the black, gaunt tree trunks. I knew by that laugh she was tantalising him. My first impulse was to rush up to them and demand an explanation, but my second thought had been to hold my anger in control, and ascertain the true extent of her perfidy. Was not this the second time I had detected Ella walking alone with a man in lover-like attitude?

I loved her with all my heart, and had believed implicitly that she reciprocated my affection, yet here, in this single moment, the cup of happiness was dashed from my lips. I knew I had been the victim of base deception. While I, fool that I had been, had fondly imagined that she loved me; she had abandoned all self-respect and allowed herself to walk in a public garden with a chance-met acquaintance. Sonia's ominous words recurred to me, and I saw how I had been tricked and betrayed. The pretty refugee was right, notwithstanding the denunciations of the diplomatist and the spy, both of whom had some motive in discrediting her statements.

With eager eyes and heavy heart I followed the pair cautiously, fearing each moment lest either should turn and detect my presence. Apparently they were too deeply engrossed in each other's talk, which, although carried on in a tone so low that I could catch no single word, seemed scarcely of an amatory nature, judging from the man's gestures. To me it appeared rather as if he were urging her to do something from which she shrank. Once, while he spoke, she stopped short and stretched out both hands towards him in an attitude of supplication. But he did not heed her, for, giving vent to a low laugh, he continued, emphasising his words as before. Then, clenching her hands, she stamped her foot in anger, and tossing her head in contempt, walked forward again, heedless of her companion's threatening attitude.

From that moment both grew calmer, for the man, uttering words of forgiveness, snatched up her hand and imprinted a kiss upon it. For a brief second she allowed her hand to linger in his grasp, then withdrew it gently, but firmly, regarding him with earnestness the while. This action aroused my anger to a fierce, murderous hatred. With difficulty I managed to preserve an outward calm, because, in my state of mind, I felt compelled to watch and wait. Yet, if I had had a weapon ready to my hand at that moment, I verily believe that I must have thrown myself upon this arrogant cad, and mercilessly killed him.

The manner in which his hat was set upon his head, slightly askew, in the manner of the London "'Arry," and his over-burdening mannerism, were in themselves sufficient to show the type of lover my wife cultivated. As I stepped softly behind them in the gloom, I told myself that she must leave my house that night, or I should. I felt in my throat a choking sensation, for I had loved her so fervently that this discovery of her falseness had utterly unnerved me, and even in those moments of fierce anger and hatred I confess that tears welled in my eyes. Ella was the only woman I had ever loved, yet she who had taken her marriage vows only a few short months before had already discarded me for this overdressed idiot, who would be termed in vulgar parlance a "bounder."

Perhaps he did not know her to be married. This thought took possession of me. When their quarrel ended it became manifest that Ella herself was endeavouring to fascinate and hold him, just as she had charmed me, by the softness of her speech, her exquisite grace, and her wonderful beauty. She spoke quietly, with her dainty finger-tips laid lightly upon his arm, while he listened, gazing earnestly into her face, enchanted.

To-night, I told myself, the bonds uniting me to Ella should be for ever severed. I remembered the many occasions when she had been absent, visiting imaginary friends; I recollected the evening she brought home the violets and preserved them carefully in water until they smelt so faint that she was compelled to throw them away; I had not forgotten the fact that blades of grass did not grow in the squalid, overcrowded streets of modern Camberwell. I glanced around at the grass on every side. Perhaps she frequented that place, and took clandestine walks daily with her lover beneath those leafless trees. The thought provoked my bitter hatred, and I know not how I refrained from facing the pair. I managed, however, to hold myself back, watching them exchange a tender farewell at the gate that led into Kensington High Street, next the Palace Hotel, and while the man raised his hat politely and, turning, walked away in the direction of Knightsbridge,

Ella, her face radiant and happy, bowed and set out homeward in the opposite direction.

Beneath the lamp in the gateway I had, in those brief seconds, obtained a glimpse of his face. It was that of a young man of about two-and-twenty, with strongly marked features, fair-haired, and of quite a different type than I had conjectured. The features were rather refined, by no means those of a cad, but rather those of a well-bred young idler, who affected the dress and manners of that class of youths who frequent the Café Monico on Sunday evenings, the slaves of the counter.

Once he glanced back to Ella, but she did not turn; then he went on and was lost in the darkness, while I followed my wife's neat figure through the bustling throng of foot-passengers.

Chapter Twenty Two
To Err is Human

Instead of keeping behind her straight home, I turned from the main road, and with my mind full of gloomy thoughts, wandered about the dark, quiet thoroughfares in the neighbourhood of Campden Hill until, having walked for over an hour undecided how to act, I awoke to a consciousness that I was before my own house.

When I entered I opened a telegram lying on the hall table, and found it was from Lord Warnham, stating that he was leaving the Premier's suddenly, and asking me to call at Berkeley Square at six. It was then a quarter to six, and I saw that even by cab I must be ten minutes late for the appointment.

"Has my wife returned, Juckes?" I asked my faithful man, who stood ready to relieve me of hat and coat.

"Yes, sir. She returned an hour ago, and is now in the drawing-room."

My first impulse was to return to Berkeley Square without seeing her, but unable longer to bear the suspense, I allowed Juckes to take my things, and entered the room, where she awaited me.

"Ah! Geoffrey!" she exclaimed, jumping to her feet with an expression of joy, and coming forward to meet me. "I expected you home long ago, dearest." And she raised her face for the habitual kiss.

"Oh," I said coldly, placing her away from me without caressing her. "Have you been home long?"

"A long, long time," she answered, regarding my coldness with unfeigned surprise.

"Where have you been to-day?" I inquired, rather sharply, taking up a position on the hearthrug, with my back to the bright wood fire.

"This morning I went to Mr Praga's studio in Hornton Street, and gave him a sitting. He is painting my portrait for the Academy, you know."

"Yes," I answered. "He told me so at the club the other day. Where else have you been?"

"Why are you so anxious to have a complete record of my doings?" she asked, pouting. "You seem absurdly suspicious."

I smiled bitterly. Since her return she had exchanged her tailor-made gown for a handsome dinner-dress, and wore as her only ornament a string of pearls, my wedding gift. She stood gazing at me with her dark blue eyes wide-open, and brows arched in well-feigned reproach.

"You did not return to lunch," I said quietly.

"No, I went to Pont Street," she answered. "Mother was so fearfully upset."

"Why?"

"Last night she detected Helmholtz in the act of opening a letter he had taken from the postman. It contained a cheque, and she was compelled to discharge him at a moment's notice."

"I understood he was quite a model servant," I said, in genuine surprise at this latest development. To me it was astounding that a shrewd officer like Renouf should have thus allowed himself to be caught napping.

"Mother thought most highly of him," she went on. "But it now appears that for the past few weeks she has had suspicions that her letters were being tampered with, for two cheques sent by tenants for rent have been stolen."

"I never thought very much of him," I said.

"Neither did I," she declared. "He had such a silent, cunning way, and moved so softly, that dozens of times when I have turned suddenly I have been quite startled to find him standing close to me. I'm glad mother has got rid of him. She packed him off bag and baggage."

"Did he protest his innocence?"

"No. He treated her with cool indifference, placed his things in his portmanteau leisurely, hailed a cab, and went off without asking for his wages."

I was silent. The reason Renouf should descend to steal cheques was inexplicable. One thing, however, appeared clear, namely, that he had taken an unusual interest in the nature of Mrs Laing's correspondence. To me it was a matter for congratulation that as he had been detected by his mistress and discharged, he could not cast upon me the blame for his betrayal.

"What did you do after lunch?" I at last inquired, returning to my charge.

"I went shopping," she replied, smiling.

"With whom?"

"Alone."

"Were you alone the whole time?" I inquired, regarding her intently.

Her lips quivered slightly and her glance wavered. "Yes," she answered, "I did not meet anyone I knew."

"That is a lie, Ella!" I cried.

"It is not," she stammered, pale and agitated. "I have told you the truth."

"To prevaricate is utterly useless," I said angrily. "I followed you through Kensington Gardens, where you were walking with your lover. I—"

"My lover?" she cried hoarsely, in dismay. "He—he is not my lover. I had never seen him before!"

"Then by your own admission you have abandoned all respect for me and yourself. You are addicted to strolling alone with any idiot who flatters you."

"I swear I do not," she retorted. "You misjudge me entirely." And she placed her trembling hand upon my arm.

But I shook it off wrathfully, saying, "I have discovered the truth, alas! too late. While making pretence to love me you prefer the society of other men. I was a blind fool, or I should have discovered the fact, plain to everybody else, that Ogle was your lover, and that you mourned for him when he met the fate he so justly deserved."

"He never uttered one word of love to me, Geoffrey," she protested. "How can you make such horrible charges against me when I love you so dearly," she cried, bursting into a torrent of tears.

"Because!" I said, with emphasis, "because I have myself followed you this evening. Surely Kensington Gardens is not the spot where a wife should take recreation, unless clandestinely, as you have done! No, this is not the first occasion you have lied to me, Ella; but it shall be the last."

"The last!" she gasped, glancing up at me. "What do you mean?"

"I mean that I can have no further confidence in you, and that we are better apart."

"You don't intend to leave me. Surely you would never be so cruel, Geoffrey. It would kill me."

"I have loved you, Ella," I said hoarsely, after a pause, brief and full of suspense. "No man could have loved a woman with a passion more tender than I have done, but now that I have discovered how basely I have been deceived, my affection has turned to hatred."

"You hate me!" she wailed. "Ah, no, you cannot—you shall not," she cried, as, rushing towards me, she threw both arms around my neck, and, notwithstanding my efforts to avert her, pressed her tear-stained face to mine.

Roughly I unclasped her arms and cast her from me, saying,—

"I have resolved. Nothing will cause me to reconsider my decision. We must part."

"It is not like you, Geoffrey, to be cruel to a woman," she said reproachfully, standing before me. "I admit I have acted foolishly, but that man you saw was not my lover. I care for no one except your own dear self."

"Terms of endearment are unnecessary," I answered impatiently, turning from her. "Such expressions from one who has so grossly deceived me are absolutely nauseating. I have striven for your social advancement and have loved you dearly, but from this moment you are my wife only in name."

She buried her face in her hands and was seized by a fit of hysterical sobbing. All her self-control had vanished at the instant she realised that I know the truth, and she now stood before me bent and penitent.

"Forgive me," she whispered earnestly. "Forgive me, Geoffrey."

"No," I answered, with firmness. "I cannot trust you."

"Overlook this incident, and I will never again give you cause for jealousy," she exclaimed. "I will do anything you ask, only have patience with me."

"I have already had patience," I answered. "Yet, deceived as I am daily, we can live together no longer."

"But I love you," she declared, with fierce earnestness, fixing her fathomless eyes upon me. "If I lose you I shall kill myself."

"It is your own fault entirely," I said. "You have chosen to act in this manner, and whatever are the consequences they are of your own seeking. I suppose you will tell me next that this man who was with you compelled you to meet him."

"That is the absolute truth," she faltered.

"Ah, always the same lame tale," I observed in disgust. "I have not forgotten that night at 'The Nook' when I watched you walking with Beck.

No, Ella. There is some strange mystery about it all that I don't like. You pretend to love me; but you have some ulterior motive."

"There is a mystery, it is true," she admitted, her eyes dimmed with tears. "A mystery so strange and startling that when you know the truth you will stand aghast and dumbfounded. But with its elucidation you will have knowledge of how I have suffered and striven for your sake; therefore I can only pray that the revelations that must accrue may be hastened, for, although to-day you regard me as base and deceitful, you will then learn how much one woman has endured and sacrificed because she loved you."

"Then we must part until this mystery is cleared up," I said calmly, my heart full of grief. "You refuse to take me, your husband, into your confidence, therefore I can place no further reliance in your word."

"Think," she cried, clutching my arms convulsively. "Why should the happiness of both of us be wrecked by a mere misunderstanding?"

"A misunderstanding!" I echoed. "It is assuredly more than that."

"No," she answered, endeavouring to stifle her sobs. "You misunderstand me, believing me false to you, whereas I am acting solely in our mutual interests."

"To walk alone with a stranger is surely not acting in your husband's interests," I observed bitterly.

"Ah, you are mistaken," she said quickly. "When all is explained you will regret the cruel words you have uttered this evening."

"Have I, then, no cause to object to your acquaintance with this man?" I inquired, looking sharply at her.

"None whatever. He is neither my lover nor my friend."

"What is his name?"

"I do not know. He did not tell me," she replied.

"Was this the only occasion you had met?"

"It was."

"He spoke to you casually in the street, I suppose?"

"No, we met by appointment at Victoria Station," she answered quite frankly.

"By appointment! Then you knew him!"

"No, our meeting was arranged by a third person. It was by no means of an amatory character, I assure you."

"What was its object?" I asked.

Slowly she shook her head. "I cannot tell you without relating to you facts which I dare not yet divulge."

"Ah! as I thought," I cried in anger. "You refuse always to explain. As each week passes the mystery surrounding you increases."

"Unfortunately I cannot prevent it," she answered in a low, earnest tone. "Before we married I told you plainly that I intended to seek the truth of the conspiracy against Dudley's life, and you did not object."

"Why not leave that wretched affair to the police and secure our own happiness?" I urged.

"Because the police are powerless. They can have no clue."

"Is it then absolutely necessary that you should attain this end?" I inquired dubiously. "Are you ready to sacrifice your own home and husband in order to ascertain the truth regarding a crime?"

"Yes, it is absolutely imperative," she replied emphatically. "Before perfect happiness can be ours we must both be aware of the causes which led to Dudley's sudden death. Towards that end I am striving, and knowing what I do, I am regardless of your suspicions and your cruel words. If we part—well, it will be you who one day will be filled with bitter regret; and as for me, I shall not pause in my merciless quest."

Often she had told me that to ascertain the true cause of Dudley's death was, next to her duty as my wife, her main object in life, and these words, uttered with an earnestness that was genuine, bore out her most frequent declarations. Glancing at the facts as a whole, it was not surprising that I should have suspected Dudley of having been her lover, whose death she intended to avenge.

In silence and hesitation I paced the room that she had furnished with such exquisite taste. A dozen times she asked forgiveness, but no word passed my lips. She stood motionless, her head bent in submission, her hands clasped before her, awaiting my decision.

Her pale, tear-stained face betrayed signs of a terrible, breathless suspense, she fearing that I intended to cast her off, while I could not bring myself to any firm belief that her declarations of affection were genuine. Between us there yawned a gulf of darkness and mystery which hourly grew wider and more impassable.

"Tell me that you'll still be patient and wait," she implored at last. "Surely you can see how intensely I love you and how utterly aimless will be my life if we part."

"This mystery is, I confess, Ella, driving me to distraction," I said, halting at last before her. "Cannot you confide in me? I will preserve silence, I promise."

"No, no," she gasped in fear. "I dare not."

Her attitude was one of deep dejection, yet I could not fail to notice, even at this moment of her abject despair, how beautiful she was. But a look of unutterable terror was in her deep blue eyes, and upon her handsome features was an expression as though, dreading exposure, she were haunted by some terrible ghost of the past.

"You told me this once before," I said gravely, "and I trusted you. To-day I have discovered my confidence ill-placed."

"Trust me once again," she cried hoarsely. "Only once, and I will show you ere long that your suspicions are utterly without foundation."

I took another turn up and down the drawing-room, my hands clasped behind my back, my gaze fixed upon the carpet. I was still undecided.

With a sudden impulse she rushed forward, and flinging her warm arms about my neck, kissed me, next second bursting into tears and burying her face upon my shoulder. My hand unconsciously stroked her hair, and, bending, I pressed my lips upon her soft cheek.

Then she knew that I had forgiven, and holding back her sobs with difficulty, raised her face, and kissing me passionately, thanked me in a low, broken voice, assuring me that I should never regret the step I had taken.

During half-an-hour we remained together, she full of love and confidence, I admiring and hopeful. I was glad I had not acted rashly, nor left her as I had intended, and as we went in to dinner arm in arm, we laughed together, joyous in each other's love.

After we had eaten, I smoked a cigarette and lingered as long as possible, happy with my well-beloved; then kissing her fondly, I was compelled to take a hansom to Berkeley Square, promising her to return at the earliest possible moment, and expressing confidence that our love would last always.

The Earl, grumbling at my tardy arrival, was busy in his library with a number of important dispatches relating to our affairs in the East. When he had expressed displeasure that I had not been waiting to receive him, he added,—

"But there, I suppose now you are married, Deedes, your wife is exacting; they always are. She likes you to dine with her, eh?"

"Yes," I admitted, smiling. "I did dine at home."

"Ah, I thought so," snapped the shrewd old Minister. "A good dinner and your wife's smiles were of more consequence to you than England's prestige with the Sultan,—oh?"

I made no answer to this sarcasm, but began busying myself with the correspondence, packing it away in the dispatch-bag and sealing it for delivery to Hammerton, the messenger, who was waiting in an adjoining room ready to take it to Constantinople.

Not until eleven o'clock was I able to get away from Berkeley Square, and leaving the aged statesman alone, deeply immersed in the puzzling applications for advice of all sorts from Her Majesty's representatives at the various Courts of Europe, I drove back to Phillimore Gardens.

On arrival home my first question of Juckes was whether Ella was in the drawing-room.

"No, sir. Madame is out, sir."

"Out! When did she go out?"

"About an hour after you had left, sir," replied the man. "She has gone into the country, I believe."

"Into the country? What makes you think so?"

"Because she put on her travelling dress, and took two trunks with her," he answered. "Roberts, her maid, says she packed the boxes herself three days ago."

"Did she say where she was going?" I inquired breathlessly.

"No, sir. She left no message with anyone."

Entering the drawing-room with my overcoat still on, I noticed, lying upon her little rosewood escritoire, a note addressed to me.

Eagerly I took it up, tore it open, and read its contents. There were only a few hurriedly-scrawled words—a brief and formal farewell.

"You cannot trust me," she wrote, "therefore we are best apart. Do not attempt to follow me, for you cannot find me. Do not think ill of me, for even if I have wronged and deceived you, I have, nevertheless, been your friend." It commenced formally, without any endearing term, and concluded abruptly with the two words, "Your Wife."

For a few moments I stood with it in my hand, staring at it in blank amazement. Then it occurred to me that in that very escritoire she kept all her correspondence, and it was more than probable that I might learn the truth from some of the letters therein contained.

I endeavoured to open it, but it was, as usual, locked. She had taken the key. In my sudden excitement I called to Juckes to bring a hammer, and with a few sharp blows broke open the sloping, leather-covered top, finding a number of letters addressed in unfamiliar handwriting.

One, larger than the rest, crumpled, dirty and worn, as if it had reposed in someone's pocket for a long period, I took out, and eagerly opened beneath the soft-shaded lamp.

"My God!" I cried aloud, scarcely able to believe my own eyes, when next instant I realised the terrible truth. "My God! I had never suspected this!"

Chapter Twenty Three
A Terrible Truth

Ella's cold, formal adieu stunned me. I stood open-mouthed, petrified. We had parted on the best of terms, she kissing me affectionately, and with wifely solicitude bidding me hasten back; yet in my absence she had departed, evidently carrying out some pre-arranged plan. Her maid, Roberts, had noticed her packing her trunks three days before, therefore it was certain that she meant to desert me as soon as opportunity offered.

Unaccountable and astounding as was her sudden flight, the discovery I had made among the papers in her escritoire was even more amazing. It held me stupefied and aghast.

The paper I held in my hand was the original of the secret convention between England and Germany; the document which had been stolen from me, transmitted by telegraph to the Russian Foreign Office, and had nearly caused a terrible and disastrous European war.

When I took it from among the letters and saw its neat, formal writing and sprawly signatures, I gazed upon it in blank amazement, unable at first to realise the startling truth. There was, however, no room for doubt. It was the actual document which had been so ingeniously purloined, for it reposed in the escritoire still in its official envelope. The great black seal affixed by the Earl of Warnham had been broken, and both envelope and document had the appearance of having at some time or other been folded small, besides being sadly crumpled.

Beneath the shaded light I examined the envelope carefully, and detected a faint carmine streak upon it; then, placing it to my nostrils, found that it exuded a stale odour of sampaguita. In an instant the truth was plain. The pink discolouration had been caused by rouge; the scent was Ella's favourite perfume, which she always procured from Paris. No doubt the document had been carried for a considerable period in her pocket for safety, and become crumpled, as papers will if carried in a woman's dress. While the envelope might easily have absorbed the odour of that unmistakable perfume from her handkerchief, the streak of rouge puzzled me, for I had never suspected her of an artificial complexion, nor had I ever seen the hare's foot and carmine among her toilet articles.

"Tell Roberts I wish to speak to her," I said, turning to Juckes, who had stood by in silence, puzzled at my strange action of breaking the top of the escritoire.

He obeyed, and in a few moments the neat, dark-eyed maid entered.

"Roberts," I exclaimed, "I want you to tell me something. Does my wife use any carmine to give artificial colour to her cheeks?"

"Oh, no, sir," the girl assured me. "Madame is very averse to the use of such things. Once or twice, when she has been going out at night, and looked unusually pale, I have suggested a little additional colour, but she has always refused."

"Did she have any rouge or anything of that sort in her possession?" I inquired.

"No, sir, I am quite certain she hadn't."

"Why are you so confident?"

"Because only the other day, when I was ill with a sick headache, madame urged me to use some colour, as my face was so pale. Visitors were coming, she said, and she didn't want me to look like a ghost. I told her that I had no carmine, and she remarked that she had none, therefore nothing could be done."

"When did my wife pack those two trunks she took with her this evening?"

"Last Monday, sir," the girl answered, slowly twisting her befrilled apron in her hands. "She received a note by boy-messenger, and immediately set about packing the boxes."

"Did she tell you anything?" I asked, adding confidentially, "I have reason to believe that my wife has left us, therefore anything you tell me may assist me in tracing her."

The girl glanced at me in genuine surprise.

"Do you mean, sir, that madame has—has run away?" she gasped.

"No—well, not exactly," I stammered. "But did she tell you anything?"

With eyes downcast the girl paused in hesitation, answering at last, "She didn't actually tell me anything."

"But what do you know about her intentions?"

"Nothing," she answered. Then, after a pause, she added, "Well, to tell you the truth, sir, I had suspicions."

"Of what? Do not fear to speak because I am her husband," I said reassuringly. "I may as well know the worst at once."

"She used frequently to receive notes from a gentleman. They were brought by a commissionaire or by a man-servant, who waited for the answer. When they came I always knew that on the following day she would be absent many hours."

"You believe that she met this mysterious individual—eh?" I asked huskily.

"Yes, for she always told me never to admit to you that she had been long absent. Therefore I had suspicion that she met somebody clandestinely."

"What was his name?"

"I have never been able to ascertain. Once I glanced at a note lying on madame's dressing-table. It merely announced the writer's intention to attend Lady Pearson's 'at home,' and was signed 'X.'"

"Well," I said hoarsely, after a long silence. "What else?"

"Nothing," she replied. "That is all I know, sir."

"Has my wife taken her jewels?" I inquired.

"No. She has left her jewel-case unlocked, but everything is there. She has even left behind her wedding-ring."

"Her wedding-ring!" I echoed, astounded and dismayed. "Then she has discarded me completely."

"Unfortunately it appears so, sir," the girl observed gravely.

"Very well, Roberts," I said in a broken voice. "Thank you. You may go."

The girl glanced at me for an instant, with a sad, pitying look, then turned and left, closing the door noiselessly behind her.

Alone, I sank into the chair utterly broken down, still holding in my nervous, trembling fingers the secret document that secured the peace and welfare of the two most powerful nations on earth. I had at last discovered the hideous truth. Ella, the woman whose grace and beauty had held me enmeshed, and whom I had loved with an intensity of passion that was all-consuming, was, after all, base and worthless. Although making a hollow pretence to love me, she had cast me aside for this mysterious man who signed himself with an initial, and who met her secretly almost daily. I had been a blind, devoted idiot, I knew, but until I had watched her in Kensington Gardens I had never suspected her of infamy. It seemed, however, that she had no sense of shame, and cared nought for my dishonour or despair. Her perfidy was now revealed in all its painful reality. Ella, whom I had always regarded as pure, honest and trusting, was a woman of tarnished repute. The fact that she had the secret convention in her possession was, in itself, sufficient evidence that the mystery surrounding her was deep, and of no ordinary character. Sonia had warned me that she was my enemy, and this fact was now indeed vividly apparent.

How she had become possessed of the stolen treaty was inexplicable. Full well she knew all the terrible anxiety its loss had caused me, and the sensation that its revelation had created throughout Europe. Times without number I had mentioned to her how anxious my chief was to recover the original, so that our enterprising friends in St Petersburg could have no tangible proof that it had actually existed, yet she had given no sign that she knew anything of it, much less that it actually reposed in my own drawing-room. I did not fail, in those moments of my despair, to recollect that she had been on the most intimate terms with Dudley Ogle, the man suspected to have been in the service of the Tzar's Government, and as I sat in wonderment it became gradually impressed upon me that through those many months I had been basely tricked, and that Ella herself, charming and ingenuous as she seemed, was actually a secret agent of the enemies of England.

Several facts that I recollected combined to produce this startling belief. Because of my confidential position as secretary to the Earl of Warnham, it was apparent that Ella, with the assistance of my whilom friend Dudley and the encouragement of her mother, had conspired to hold me beneath her spell. She had become my wife, not because she had ever loved me, but because she could feign affection or hatred with equal impunity, and had some ulterior motive in obtaining my confidence. Her firm resolve to ascertain the true facts regarding Dudley's mysterious end showed plainly that if they were not lovers they had acted in complete accord, and what was more likely than that he, having stolen the secret convention, had on that memorable night at "The Nook" handed it to her, the instigator of the ingenious theft. Yet an hour or so later he died from some cause that neither doctors nor police had been able to determine.

To her, the tragic occurrence was a mystery, as to all, and her refusal to render me any explanation of her suspicious actions was, I now saw, quite natural. Held beneath the iron thraldom of her masters in St Petersburg, she dared not utter one word; hence I had remained in the outer darkness of doubt and ignorance.

However it might be, one thing was certain. She had been unexpectedly parted from me, either by choice or compulsion. Perhaps it was that to pose as my wife was no longer necessary; yet if she were actually a spy, was it not curious that in departing she should overlook this document, of which the Ministry at St Petersburg were so anxious to possess themselves.

Again, as I sat alone before the cheerless grate, I reflected that if she were in the pay of Russia, surely Monsieur Grodekoff, the Ambassador, would have been acquainted with her. Besides, what reason could Renouf have had in making such careful inquiries, or why did Paul Verblioudovitch discredit the truths uttered by Sonia and urge me to marry the woman I loved? Nevertheless if, as I supposed, my position in the Foreign Office had caused me to be the victim of a clever and deeply-conceived conspiracy, it was scarcely surprising that the Tzar's representative should disclaim all knowledge of the sweet-faced agent, or that Paul had praised her and cast obloquy upon Sonia in order that their plans, whatever they were, should be achieved. Of the actions of Renouf, and his strange disregard for detection, I could form no satisfactory conclusion. All I knew was that Ella's career had been an unscrupulous and inglorious one, and that she had cast me aside as soon as her infamous ends had been attained.

The only person who could elucidate the mystery was Sonia, the pretty girl who had been denounced by Renouf as a murderess, and who was now in hiding in far-off Russia, in some out-of-the-world place where I could never hope to find her. If she were clever enough to elude the combined vigilance of the detective force of Europe, as undoubtedly she had done, there was but little hope that I could ever run her to earth.

The mystery had, by Ella's flight, been increased rather than explained, for the more I pondered the more deeply-rooted became the conviction that she had decamped because she had cause to fear some strange development that would lead to her exposure and shame.

After a time I roused myself, and taking from the broken escritoire the other letters it contained, five in number, examined them eagerly beneath the light.

All were in the same hand, a heavy masculine one, written evidently with a quill. One by one I read them, finding that they contained appointments, which fully bore out her maid's suspicions.

"*My dear Ella,*" one ran, "*to-morrow I shall be on the departure platform at King's Cross Station at 11:30. I have good news for you. Come.—X.*"

Another regretted the writer's inability to keep an appointment, as he had been called unexpectedly to Paris, and was compelled to leave by the night mail from Charing Cross. He, however, promised to return in three days, and gave her the Grand Hotel as his address if she found it necessary to telegraph.

Strangely enough, the letters contained no endearing terms either at their commencement or conclusion. Formal and brief, they all related to appointments at various places in London where two persons might meet unnoticed by the crowd, and all were signed by the single mysterious initial. I stood with them in my hand for a long time, puzzled and hesitating, then placing them carefully in my pocket, together with the secret document I had so unexpectedly unearthed, I crammed on my hat and hastily drove to Pont Street.

The house was in darkness, save for a light in the basement, and in answer to my summons, after a lapse of some minutes a tall, gaunt, woman in rusty black appeared in the area below.

I was surprised at being thus met by a stranger, but inquired for Mrs Laing.

"Mrs Laing ain't at 'ome, sir," answered the woman, looking up and speaking with a strong Cockney twang.

"Not at home?" I exclaimed, surprised. "Where is she?"

"She's gone abroad somewheres, but I don't know where," the woman answered. "She's sold all her valuables, discharged the servants, and left me 'ere as 'ouse-keeper."

"When did she go?" I asked.

"This morning. I answered an advertisement in the *Chronicle* yesterday, and entered on my duties 'ere to-day. Quick, ain't it?"

The rapidity of her engagement I was compelled to admit, but proceeded to make further inquiry whether Mrs Laing's daughter had been there.

"No, sir. No one's been 'ere to-day, except a foreign-looking gentleman who asked if madame had left, and when I said that she had, he went away quite satisfied."

"What kind of man was he?"

"Tall and thin, with a longish dark beard."

The description did not correspond with anyone of my acquaintance; therefore, after some further questions regarding Mrs Laing's mysterious departure, I was compelled to wish the worthy woman good evening. She knew nothing of Mrs Laing's movements, not even the name of the terminus to which she had driven, such pains had Ella's mother taken to conceal the direction in which she intended to travel.

Some secret undoubtedly existed between mother and daughter; its nature held me perplexed and bewildered.

Chapter Twenty Four
Strictly Confidential

The early morning was dry, frosty, but starless. The clock of that fashionable temple of Hymen, St George's, Hanover Square, was slowly chiming three as I alighted from a cab at the corner of Mount Street, and walking along Berkeley Square, ascended the steps of the Earl of Warnham's great mansion, and rang its ponderous bell. The place was severe and gloomy enough by day, but in the silence and darkness of the night its exterior presented a forbidding, almost ghostly appearance. It was an unusual hour for a call, but, knowing that a porter was on duty always, and that dispatches frequently arrived during the night, I had no hesitation in seeking an interview.

In a few moments there was a grating sound of bolts drawn back, a clanking of chains, and the heavy door was slowly opened by the sleepy man, who, with a word of recognition, at once admitted me. Walking across the great square hall; warmed by a huge, roaring fire, I passed down the passage to the Earl's study and rapped at the door, receiving an impatient permission to enter.

The Minister for Foreign Affairs was sitting at his table where I had left him, with an empty tea-cup at his side, resting his pale, weary brow upon his hand and writing dispatches rapidly with his scratchy quill. His fire was nearly out, the pair of candles, in their heavy, old-fashioned silver candlesticks that stood upon his writing-table, had burned down almost to their sockets, and the strong smell of burnt paper that pervaded the book-lined den, showed that, with his innate cautiousness, he had destroyed documents that he did not desire should be seen by other eyes.

The world-renowned statesman raised his head as I entered, gave vent to a low grunt of dissatisfaction, and continued writing at topmost speed. I saw I was unwelcome, but, well acquainted with his mannerisms and eccentricities, walked to the fire, added more fuel, and waited in patience until he had finished.

"Well," he snarled, casting down his pen impatiently, and turning upon me at last. "I thought you, of all men, were aware that I do not desire interruption when at work."

"I should not have ventured to come at this hour," I said, "were it not that the news I bring is of extreme importance."

He sighed, as was his habit when expecting further complications.

"What is its nature?" he asked coldly, leaning back in his chair. "Abandon preliminaries, please, and come to the point. What is it?"

"I have recovered the original of our secret convention with Germany," I answered in as quiet a tone as I could assume.

"You have!" he cried excitedly, starting up. "You are quite right to seek me at once—quite right. Where did you obtain it?" he inquired.

Slowly I drew forth the precious document from my pocket, and handed it to him, still in the envelope that bore my own mark, with the remains of his broken seal. He took it eagerly and bent to the candles to examine it more closely. A few seconds sufficed to reassure him that the document was the genuine one.

"It is fortunate that this has returned into our possession," he observed, his thin blue lips quivering slightly. "I feared that it had already passed beyond our reach, and that one day or other in the near future our policy must be narrowed by the knowledge that it was preserved in the archives of the Foreign Office at St Petersburg, and could be used as a pretence for a declaration of war by Russia and France. Now, however, that the original is again in our possession we can disclaim all copies, and give assurances that no secret understanding exists between us and Berlin. The only fact that at present lends colour to the assertion of the boulevard journals is the ill-timed bestowal of the Iron Cross upon Count Landsfeldt. Such an action was characteristic of their impetuous Emperor." Then, after a second's reflection, he added, "Just sit down, Deedes, and write to Sir Philip Emden at Berlin, asking him to obtain audience immediately of the Kaiser, point out the harmful impression this decoration has occasioned, and get His Majesty to exhibit his marked displeasure towards Landsfeldt in some form or other. That will remove any suspicion that the convention is actually an accomplished fact. Besides, you may hint also that it may be well for the relations between the Kaiser and Sir Philip to appear slightly strained, and that this fact should be communicated indirectly to the Press. Sit down and write at once: it must be sent under flying seal."

I obeyed, and commenced writing a formal dispatch while, in answer to the electric bell rung by his Lordship, the sleepy night-porter appeared.

"Calvert," exclaimed the Minister, "telephone to the Foreign Office and say that I want a messenger to call here and proceed to Berlin by the morning mail."

"Yes, m'lord," answered the man, bowing and closing the door.

While I wrote, the Earl perused the document, the loss of which had caused the Cabinets of Europe so much apprehension, and taking his magnifying glass he examined the portions of the seal still remaining. Then carefully unlocking one of the small private drawers in the top of the great writing-table, he took therefrom some object, and gazed upon it long and earnestly. With a heavy sigh he again replaced it, and slowly locked the drawer. When I had finished and placed the instructions to Sir. Philip Emden before him, he took up his quill, corrected my letter, here and there adding an emphatic word or two, and then appended his signature. Obtaining one of the bags used for the transmission of single dispatches, I deposited it therein, sealed it, and placed upon it one of those labels with a cross drawn upon its face, the signification of that mark being that it is never to be lost sight of by the messenger. There are two kinds of bags sent out and received by the Foreign Office, one with this cross-marked label, and the other without it. The latter are generally larger and less important, and may be placed with the messenger's luggage. It is no pleasant life our messengers lead, liable as they are to be summoned at an hour's notice to "proceed at once" to anywhere, from Brussels to Teheran. Armed with a *laissez-passer*, they are constantly hurrying over the face of Europe as fast as the fastest expresses can carry them, passing through the frontier stations freed from the troublesome concomitant of ordinary travelling—the examination of luggage—known on all the great trunk lines from Paris to Constantinople and from Rome to St Petersburg, sometimes bearing epoch-making documents, sometimes a lady's hat of latest mode, or a parcel of foreign delicacies, but always on the alert, and generally sleeping on a layer of stiff dispatches and bulky "notes."

At last, having made up the bag, I rose slowly and faced my chief.

"Well," he exclaimed, raising his keen eyes from the document I had brought him and regarding me with that stony, sphinx-like expression he assumed when resolved upon cross-questioning, "how did you obtain possession of this?"

"I found it," I answered.

"Found it?" he growled, with a cynical curl of the lip. "I suppose you have some lame story that you picked it up in the street, or something—eh!" he exclaimed testily.

"No," I replied hoarsely. "Mine is no lame story, although a wretched one. The discovery has unnerved and bewildered me; it—"

"I have no desire to know how its discovery affected you mentally," he interrupted, with impatient sarcasm. "I asked where you found it," he observed coldly.

"I found it in my own house," I answered.

"Then you mean to tell me that it has been in your possession the whole time. The thing's impossible," he cried angrily. "Remember the dummy palmed off upon me, and the fact that an exact copy was transmitted to St Petersburg."

"No. It has not been in my possession," I answered, leaning against my writing-chair for support. "I found it among my wife's letters."

"Your wife!" he gasped, agitated. He had turned ghastly pale at mention of her name, and, trembling with agitation, swayed forward.

A moment later, however, he recovered his self-possession, clutched at the corner of his table, and regarding me sharply, asked, "What do you suspect?"

"I scarce know what to suspect," I answered gravely, striving to remain calm, but remembering at that instant the curious effect produced upon the Foreign Minister when he had first seen Ella dancing at the Embassy ball. My declaration that I had found this official bond of nations in her possession had produced a similar disquieting result which puzzled me.

"But surely she can have had no hand in the affair," he cried. "She certainly did not strike me as an adventuress, or an agent of the Tzar's secret service."

"It is a problem that I cannot solve," I exclaimed slowly, watching the strange, haggard look upon his usually imperturbable features. "After leaving you this evening I went home only to find a letter of farewell from her, and—"

"She has fled, then!" he exclaimed, with quick suspicion.

"Yes. Her flight was evidently pre-arranged, and curiously enough her mother, who lives in Pont Street, has discharged her servants, disposed of a good deal of her property, and also departed."

"Gone together, no doubt," the Earl observed, frowning reflectively.

"But is it not very strange that she should have left the stolen convention behind? Surely if my wife were actually a Russian agent she would never have been guilty of such indiscretion," I said.

"The mystery is inexplicable, Deedes," he declared, with a heavy look, half of pain, half of bewilderment. "Absolutely inexplicable."

This aged man, to whose firmness, clever statesmanship, and calm foresight England owed her place as foremost among the Powers, was trembling with an excitement he strove in vain to suppress. In manner that surprised me, his cold, cynical face relaxed, and placing his thin, bony hand upon my shoulder with fatherly tenderness, Her Majesty's most trusted Minister urged me to confide in him all my suspicions and my fears.

"You have, I believe, after all, been cruelly wronged, Deedes," he added in a low, harsh tone. "I sympathise with you because I myself once felt the loss of a wife deeply, and I know what feelings must be yours now that you suspect the woman you have trusted and loved to have been guilty of base treachery and espionage. She, or someone in association with her, has besmirched England's honour, and brought us to the very verge of a terrible national disaster. Providentially, this was averted; by what means we have not yet ascertained, although our diplomatic agents at the Court of the Tzar are striving day and night to ascertain; yet the fact remains that we were victimised by some daring secret agent who sacrificed everything in order to accomplish the master-stroke of espionage. I can but re-echo the thanks to Heaven uttered by my gracious Sovereign when she received the news that war had been averted; nevertheless it is my duty—nay, it is yours, Deedes, to strive on without resting, in order that this mystery may be satisfactorily unravelled."

For a moment we were silent. Then in a voice that I felt painfully conscious was broken by grief and emotion, I related to him the whole of the wretched story of my marriage, my suspicions, the discovery of Ella in Kensington Gardens, how I had taxed her with flirtation and frivolity, our peace-making, and her sudden and unexpected flight.

He heard me through to the end with bent head, sighing now and then sympathetically. Then he slowly asked,—"Did you ever refer to those earlier incidents, such as the death of that young man Ogle? Remember, whatever you tell me I shall regard as strictly confidential."

"I seldom mentioned it, as she desired me not to do so."

"When you referred to it, what was her attitude?" he inquired, in a pained tone, the furrows on his high white brow deep and clearly defined.

"She declared always that he had been murdered, and vowed to detect the author of the crime."

"Are you, in your own mind, convinced that there was anything really mysterious regarding her actions; or were they only everyday facts distorted by jealousy?" he asked gravely.

"There is, I believe, some deep mystery regarding her past," I answered.

He knit his grey, shaggy brows, and started perceptibly.

"Her past!" he echoed. "Were you aware of any—er—unpleasant fact prior to marriage?" he inquired quickly.

"Yes. She promised to explain everything ere long; therefore, loving her devotedly as I did, I resolved to make her my wife and await in patience her explanation."

"Love!" he cried cynically. "She did not love you. She only married you, it seems, to accomplish her own base and mysterious designs." Then, pacing the room from end to end, he added, "The more I reflect, the more apparent does it become that Ella Laing meant, by becoming your wife, to accomplish some great coup, but, prevented by some unforeseen circumstance, she has been compelled to fly, and in her haste overlooked this incriminating paper."

This, too, was my own opinion, and taking from my pocket the whole of the letters that were in the escritoire, I placed them before him.

"They are from your wife's mysterious lover," he observed, when a few moments later he had digested them. "Who he is there is no evidence to show. You suspect him, of course, to be the man she met in Kensington Gardens?"

I nodded. A sigh escaped me.

"Well," he went on. "Leave them with me. A calligraphic expert may possibly find some clue to the identity of their writer."

Afterwards, he took up the broken envelope that had contained the treaty, carefully re-examining its edges by the aid of his large magnifying glass.

"There is another curious fact that we must not overlook," he observed slowly. "While the seal has been broken this envelope has also passed through a 'cabinet noir.' See, this edge bears unmistakable traces after wear in the pocket," and he handed it to me, together with his glass.

The suggestion was startling, and one that I had entirely overlooked. The "cabinet noir" is a term well understood in diplomacy, but unfamiliar perhaps to the general public. Official documents of no great importance are often sent by post, and in most European countries this has led to the establishment of a "cabinet noir," in which the envelope is opened and its contents examined. The mode of procedure is interesting. The letter to be opened is first shaken well in such a way that the enclosure falls to one side of the envelope, leaving a space of about a quarter of an inch between it and the outer edge. This edge is then placed under an extremely sharp knife worked like a guillotine, care being taken to put it carefully at right angles to the knife, which is then brought down and cuts off a slip about one hundredth part of an inch wide. The envelope is now open, and the enclosure is extracted by a pair of pincers made for the purpose. After examination it is replaced, and the ticklish job of removing all trace of the opening has to be done. This is very ingenious. There are different pots of paper pulp mixed with a little gum, and each tinted a different colour to suit the various shades of paper that are operated upon. A very fine camel-hair brush is dipped into the pot containing the proper tint, and is then run carefully along the edges which have been cut open. They are then closed and left under a press for an hour or so, and after being smoothed with a flat steel instrument, it would take a very clever expert to notice that the envelope has passed through the "cabinet noir."

I saw, however, in this worn envelope the two edges were coming apart, and at once admitted the truth of the Earl's assertions. He was intensely shrewd; scarcely any minute detail escaped him.

"Well," he said reflectively, at last, "there is but one person from whom we may ascertain the truth."

"Who?"

"Your wife."

"But she has disappeared."

"We must trace her. She must not escape us," he cried fiercely, with set teeth. "She has wronged you and acted in collusion with a man who has betrayed his country and met with a tragic end, even if she herself did not actually sell the copy of the secret convention to our enemies—which appears to me more than likely."

"What causes you to believe this?" I inquired, surprised at his sudden assertion.

"I have a reason," he answered quickly, with an air of mystery. The cold manner of the expert diplomatist had again settled upon him. "If it is as I expect, I will show her no mercy, for it is upon me, as Foreign Minister of Her Majesty, that opprobrium has fallen."

"But she is still my wife," I observed, for even at that moment, when I had discovered her false and base, I had not ceased to regard her with a passionate affection.

"Wife!" he snarled angrily. "You would have been a thousand times better dead than married to such as she." Then he added, "Remain here. I am going to the telephone to apprise Scotland Yard of her flight. She only left to-night after the mails were gone, therefore if we have the ports watched we may yet find her."

And he left me, his quick footsteps echoing down the long corridor.

The moment he had gone I went to his table. Some sudden curiosity prompted me to endeavour to ascertain what he had been gazing upon so intently while my back had been turned in penning the instructions to Sir Philip Emden.

Quickly I took his keys, and, unlocking the tiny drawer, opened it.

Inside there reposed a highly-finished cabinet portrait of my wife.

Amazed to find this picture in the possession of my chief, I took it in my hands and stood agape. Its pose was unfamiliar, but the reason I had never before seen a copy of it was instantly made plain. It bore the name of a well-known St Petersburg photographer.

Ella had lied to me when she had denied ever having been in Russia.

Chapter Twenty Five
The Man of the Hour

Months of anxiety went wearily by, but no tidings of Ella could I glean. Time could never efface the bitter memories of the past. The police had, at Lord Warnham's instigation, exerted every effort to trace her, but without avail. She had disappeared with a rapidity that was astounding, for, apparently expecting that some attempt might be made to follow her, she had ingeniously taken every precaution to baffle her pursuers in the same manner as her mother had done. The cause of her sudden flight was an enigma only equalled by my discovery of her portrait in the Earl's possession. Although I had several times in conversation led up to the subject of photographs, and shown him Ella's picture, that had been taken by a firm in Regent Street, the astute old statesman made no sign that he already had her counterfeit presentment hidden among his most treasured possessions. When I recollected, as I often did, how on gazing upon it, while believing me engrossed in the writing of a dispatch, the sight of it had affected him, the new phase of the mystery perplexed me sorely. That they had been previously acquainted seemed more than probable, and his Lordship's earnest desire to secure knowledge of her whereabouts lent additional colour to this opinion.

Daily the aged statesman grew more gloomy and misanthropic. He lived alone, in an atmosphere of severe officialdom. His only recreation was a formal visit on rare occasions to a reception at one or other of the principal Embassies, or attendance on Her Majesty at Osborne or Balmoral; his brief, far-seeing suggestions at the Cabinet Council were always adopted unanimously, and his peremptory "notes" to the Powers incontrovertible marvels of diplomacy. He hated society, and never went anywhere without some strong motive by which he could further his country's interests. His eccentricities were proverbial, his caustic observations on men and things the delight of leader-writers on Government journals; and as director of England's foreign policy he was feared, yet admired, in every capital in Europe. He, however, cared not a jot for notoriety, but with an utter disregard for all else, served his country with a slavish devotion, that even the most scathing Opposition gutter-journal could not fail to recognise.

It was common talk that some strange, romantic incident had overshadowed his life, but with that innate secrecy that was part of his creed he never confided in anybody. Notwithstanding his frigid cynicism, however, he was nevertheless sympathetic, and at any mention of Ella's name he would rivet his searching eyes upon me, while across the white brow, furrowed by the heavy responsibilities of State through so many years, would spread an expression of regret, anxiety or pain. But he spoke seldom upon that subject. That he regarded my marriage as a deplorable fiasco I was well aware, but felt that in his cold heart, hardened as it was by the artful subterfuges of successful diplomacy, there yet remained a spark of pity, for he still regarded me as his *protégé*.

On the day after Ella had fled I called at Andrew Beck's office at Winchester House, Old Broad Street, but found he had sailed a few days before by the Union Liner *Scot* for Cape Town. Of late he had become connected with several South African gold ventures of enormous extent, and in the interests of some of the companies most prominently before the public, had undertaken the journey. His great wealth, in combination with that of his associates, had inspired public confidence, and there had commenced that feverish tendency in the city that quickly developed, and was later known as the "gold boom." The movements of the popular member for West Rutlandshire were cabled and chronicled in the newspapers as diligently as if he were a prince of a reigning house, and it was with extreme satisfaction that one morning in June I saw it announced that the mail had arrived at Southampton from the Cape bearing him on board, the same paper printing an account of an interview regarding gold prospects in South Africa which he had given its representative before he left the steamer. I was down at Warnham at the time, but three days later returned to London, and that same night sought Beck at the House of Commons.

I found him in the Members' Lobby, bustling about in his ill-fitting evening clothes and crumpled shirt-front, looking sun-tanned and well; a trifle more arrogant, perhaps, but nevertheless easy-going and good-natured as usual. He greeted me heartily, and the night being warm we lit cigars and walked out upon the Terrace beside the Thames. Big Ben was chiming the midnight hour. It was bright and star-lit above, but before us the river ran darkly beneath the arches of Westminster Bridge, its ripples glistening under the gas lamps. Across on the opposite bank, in the row of buildings comprising St Thomas's Hospital, lights glimmered faintly in the windows of the wards, while here and there on the face of the black, silent highway, lights, white, red and green, shone out in silent warning.

As we set foot upon the long, deserted Terrace, strolling slowly forward in the balmy, refreshing night air, my thoughts wandered back to the last occasion when we had spent an evening together beside the Thames, that memorable night at "The Nook," when we had afterwards discovered Dudley Ogle lying dead.

During the first half-hour we discussed the progress of several questions of foreign policy which had been pursued during his absence, and he, an enthusiast in politics, confided in me his intention to head a select circle of his party to demand a commission of inquiry into the working of our mobilisation scheme for home defence.

"One would think that you desired to obtain further notoriety," I laughed. "Surely you are popular enough; you are now the man of the hour."

"Well, I suppose I am," he answered, a trifle proudly, halting suddenly, leaning with his back to the stone parapet and puffing vigorously at his cigar. "But it isn't for the sake of notoriety that I'm pressing forward this inquiry. It is for the benefit of the country generally. The scheme for the mobilisation of our forces in case of invasion is utterly rotten, and had we been compelled to fight a little time ago, when France and Russia were upon the point of declaring war, we should have been in a wretched plight. The scheme is all very well on paper, but I and my friends are determined to ascertain whether it will act. It has never been tested, and no doubt it is utterly unworkable. What, indeed, can be said of a scheme which decrees that in case of an enemy landing on our shores a regiment of cavalry, now in London, must draw its horses from Dublin! Why, the thing's absurd. We don't mean to rest until the whole matter is thoroughly threshed out."

"You intend to worry up the War Office a little," I observed, smiling.

"Yes," he answered, ostentatiously. "We intend to bring public opinion to bear so heavily upon them that they will be absolutely bound to submit to the inquiry. This is, however, a secret for the present. It is best that the newspapers should not get hold of it yet. You understand?"

"Of course," I said.

We stood watching the dark, swirling waters and enjoying the cool night breeze that swept along the river, causing the lamps to flicker, when he suddenly asked, — "How is Ella? I quite forgot to ask after your wife."

"I don't know," I replied, after a brief pause.

"Don't know?" he echoed, looking at me, puzzled. "Why, what's the matter?"

"She has left me," I answered gravely.

"Left you!" he cried, removing his cigar and staring at me. "Have you quarrelled?"

"No. On my return home one night in January I found a note of farewell from her. I have heard nothing of her since. Mrs Laing disappeared on the same day."

"Disappeared!" he gasped. My announcement had caused him the greatest consternation, for he stood agape. "Have you no idea of the reason?"

"None whatever," I replied. Then confidentially I told him of Ella's mysterious absences, her walk in Kensington Gardens, and her letters from the unknown individual who had met her so frequently, omitting, however, all mention either of the theft or recovery of the secret convention, for it was Lord Warnham's wish that I should keep the existence of that instrument a profound secret.

"Have you no idea who this strange fellow is?" he inquired, sympathetically.

"Not the slightest," I said.

"Ella was not addicted to flirtation," he observed reflectively, a few moments later. "As you are aware, I have been acquainted with the family for some years, and have known your wife ever since she could toddle."

"Tell me of them," I urged impatiently. "I know scarcely anything beyond what Ella and her mother have told me. What do you know of Ella's past?"

"You speak as if you suspected her to be an adventuress," he said, and as the lamplight fell upon his face I saw that his lips relaxed into a good-humoured smile. "As far as I'm aware there is no incident of her life prior to marriage that will not bear the fullest investigation; and as for her mother, no more straightforward nor upright woman ever lived. Before poor Robert Laing died I was a frequent visitor at their country house, so I had ample opportunity of noticing what an affectionate family they were; and after his death it was I who succeeded in turning his great business into a limited liability concern."

To outsiders Beck was a swaggering parvenu, who delighted in exhibiting his wealth to others by giving expensive dinners and indulging in extravagances of speech and beverage; but towards me he had always been honestly outspoken and unassuming—in fact, a typical successful business man, with whose unruffled good humour I had, even when madly jealous of his attentions to Ella, found it impossible to quarrel. I had long ago grown to ridicule the suggestion that any secret had existed between them, and now felt instinctively that he was my friend.

"Do you think—" I asked him, after a long pause. "Candidly speaking, have you any suspicion that Dudley Ogle was her lover?"

He knit his brows. For an instant a hard expression played about his mouth, and he drew a long breath.

"I didn't, of course, know so much of Dudley as you did," he answered, slowly contemplating the end of his cigar. "But to tell you the honest truth, I always suspected that he loved her. In fact her own evidence at the inquest was sufficient proof of that."

"His death was an enigma," I observed.

"Entirely so," he acquiesced, sighing.

"She alleged that he had been murdered, and there is no room for doubt that she entertained certain very grave suspicions."

"Of what?"

"Of the identity of the murderer," I said. "She declared to me, times without number, that she would never rest until she had unravelled the mystery."

"Her theory was a very wild one," he laughed. "Personally, I do not entertain it for one moment. The medical opinion that he died from a sudden but natural cause is undoubtedly correct," he said, replacing his dead cigar between his lips, as, slowly striking a vesta, he re-lit it. Then he added, "Her anxiety to avenge Dudley's death certainly seems to bear out your suspicion that they were lovers."

"Then you entirely agree with me?" I cried.

"In a measure only," he answered, his voice suddenly harsh and cold. "I have no suspicion that she ever reciprocated his affection, although in seeking to learn the truth of your friend's tragic end she must have had some very strong motive."

"Another fact I also discovered was a trifle curious," I observed, after we had strolled along the deserted Terrace from end to end, discussing the details of Dudley's death, and the manner in which it had affected her.

"What was it?" he inquired, glancing towards me.

"I found that she was in the habit of visiting every day a pretty Russian girl with whom I was acquainted."

"Before marriage?" he asked, raising his eyebrows meaningly.

"Yes," I answered. "She was a refugee, and I had been enabled to render her father a service some time before; therefore we had become friends. I had lost sight of her for a long time, and when I again met her I discovered that she had not only been an intimate friend of poor Dudley, but that Ella visited her frequently on her bicycle when she was supposed by her mother to be riding in the Park."

"Was there anything remarkable in that fact?" he inquired, with a half-amused air, nevertheless regarding me with undue keenness, I thought.

"Nothing, except that the little Russian, who, having lost her father, was living a lonely life in a rather large house in Kensington, warned me against Ella, telling me she was my enemy. She, however, left without fulfilling her promise to reveal the details."

"Your enemy!" he cried, laughing jocosely. "She was evidently jealous of your attentions to her, my boy. A Russian, too! She was a Nihilist, I suppose, or some interestingly romantic person of that sort, eh? Surely you didn't heed what she said, did you?"

"Of course not," I replied, with a forced laugh. "I loved Ella too well; so I married her."

"And you now regret it," he added abruptly.

Without replying I walked on by his side, smoking furiously. My object in seeking him had been to learn what I could of Ella's past, but no mysterious incident had, to his knowledge, occurred. Her family were well-known in Yorkshire, respected throughout the county, and no breath of scandal had ever besmirched the fair fame of either Robert Laing's widow or his daughter. Beck, their intimate friend, concealed nothing from me, but frankly discussed my hopes and fears, expressing his heartfelt sympathy that I should have thus mysteriously lost my well-beloved, and offering me all the assistance that lay in his power.

"It certainly is extremely curious that Mrs Laing should have left Pont Street without sending me a letter to the club, giving me her new address," he said calmly, after reflection.

"You have not, then, heard from her?"

"No, I have had no letter. A week before I left for South Africa I dined there, and she then told me that she intended to remain in England throughout the year. She expressed the greatest gratification that Ella had married so happily, and seemed in the best of spirits. Yet a few days later, it appears, she fled as secretly as if she had been a criminal. It is really very extraordinary; I can't account for it in the least."

"All effort to trace Ella has failed," I observed gloomily, after a moment's reflection.

"Whose aid have you sought? A private inquiry agent?"

"No. The police," I answered.

"Police!" he exclaimed, surprised. "They have committed no crime, surely. I—I mean that the police do not trace missing friends."

"They will carry out the orders of any Government Department," I answered. "The request came from my chief."

"From Lord Warnham! Then you have told him!"

"Of course," I responded.

In contemplative silence he slowly blew a great cloud of smoke from his lips. Then he said, "There is one thing you haven't told me, Geoffrey. What was the name of this pretty Russian who made these mysterious allegations against Ella?"

"Her name was Sonia Korolénko."

"Sonia Korolénko!" he cried in a voice strangely hoarse, halting and glaring at me with wide-open, staring eyes. "Sonia! And she has gone, you say?"

"Yes. She has returned to Russia, I believe. But what do you know of her?" I quickly inquired.

"Nothing. I merely know her by repute as a notorious woman, that's all," he answered. "You were certainly wise to discard her allegations."

"Is she such a well-known person?" I asked.

"I should rather think so," he answered, elevating his eyebrows. "Her fame has spread all over the Continent. She was leader of a certain circle of questionable society in Vienna a year ago, and narrowly escaped falling into the hands of the police."

"But what can have induced Ella to associate with her?" I exclaimed in wonderment.

"Ah! That is more than we can tell," he answered, in a tone of sincere regret. "The ways of women of her type are ofttimes utterly incomprehensible."

"Were you aware that Ella was acquainted with her?" I inquired earnestly.

At that moment, however, the electric gongs along the Terrace commenced ringing sharply, announcing that the House was about to divide. The division was upon an important amendment, and had been expected at any moment since the dinner-hour. Turning back quickly he hurried through the tea-room along the corridor, and shaking hands with me in haste, promising to resume our conversation on another occasion, disappeared to record his vote.

For a single instant I stood alone in the Lobby, watching the receding figure of the portly man of the hour, and pondering deeply. Then, full of gloomy recollections of the past, I turned on my heel and went out through the long, echoing hall.

Chapter Twenty Six
A Mission and its Sequel

"You fully understand the position, Deedes?"

"Absolutely," I replied.

"Well, this is your first mission abroad—a secret one and most important—so do your best, and let me see how you shape towards being a diplomatist. Remember you have one main object to bear in mind, as I have already told you; and further, that the strictest secrecy is absolutely necessary."

It was the Earl of Warnham who thus spoke gravely as we stood opposite one another in the private room of the Minister in attendance at Osborne. Between us was a large table littered with state documents, each of which Her Majesty had carefully investigated before appending her firm, well-written signature. Late on the previous night I had travelled to the Isle of Wight in response to a telegram summoning me and my chief, who, after three rather protracted audiences of Her Majesty during the morning, had instructed me to proceed at once to Paris, entrusting me with a secret mission. Lord Gaysford, the Under Secretary, would undoubtedly have gone, but as he was away in Scotland attending some election meetings, and as time was pressing, I had, much to my gratification, been chosen. My mission was a rather curious one, not unconnected with Her Majesty's personal affairs, and the instructions I had to deliver to the Marquis of Worthorpe, our Ambassador to the French Republic, were of such a delicate nature that if written in a formal dispatch would, the Earl feared, cause that skilled and highly-valued diplomatist to send in his resignation.

I had therefore been chosen to put a suggestion politely to his Excellency, and at the same time deliver the Earl's instructions with deference, yet so firmly that they could not be disregarded. Mine was certainly a difficult task, nevertheless in my enthusiasm at being chosen to execute this secret mission abroad I was prepared to attempt anything, from the settlement of the Egyptian Question to the formation of a Quadruple Alliance.

"I shall carry out your instructions to the best of my ability," I assured him, after he had given me various valuable hints how to act.

"Yes," the aged Minister said, slowly gathering the tails of his black broadcloth frock coat over his arms and thrusting his hands into his pockets, "cross from Newhaven to-night, and you can see Worthorpe at noon to-morrow. Tell him to give you an interview alone; then explain what I have told you. He must obtain an audience of the President some time to-morrow."

"I shall act as discreetly as possible," I declared.

"I feel sure you will, Deedes," he exclaimed, with a look more kindly than usual. "This mission will, I hope, lead to others, further afield, perhaps. But remember that you were once victimised by a spy; therefore exercise the greatest care and caution in this and all matters."

"I certainly shall," I answered, smiling; then, after the further discussion of a point upon which I was not perfectly clear, I wished my chief adieu.

As I passed out of the room he said,—

"Put up at the Continental. If I have any further instructions, I'll wire in cypher."

"Very well," I replied, and as I went forth I met on the threshold a servant in the royal livery who had come to summon the trusted Minister to another audience with his Sovereign.

Eager to fulfil my mission to the satisfaction of the eccentric old statesman, who, if to others was a martinet, was to me a firm and sympathetic friend, I at once set out, crossed to Dieppe that night, and duly arrived in Paris next day. Shortly before noon I presented myself at the handsome official residence of the British Ambassador, and was quickly ushered into his presence. We were not strangers, having met on several occasions when he visited London and called to consult the chief; therefore he welcomed me cordially when I entered his private room. The Marquis was a tall, brown-bearded, pleasant-faced man, who had graduated in the Constantinople and Vienna schools of diplomacy before being appointed Ambassador in Paris, and who had achieved considerable reputation as a skilled negotiator of the most delicate points.

Seated opposite one another in softly-padded armchairs, we chatted affably for perhaps a quarter of an hour. First, he inquired after our chief's health, and then endeavoured to ascertain from me the policy about to be pursued towards Russia in view of our recent strained relations, but I strenuously avoided answering any of his artfully-concealed questions. A dozen times, with that consummate tact acquired by a lifetime of diplomacy, he endeavoured to get me to hazard an opinion or express a doubt, but I always refused. Lord Warnham's instructions were that I should say nothing of those affairs of State which, in my capacity of private secretary, were well-known to me, hence my determination to maintain silence.

Presently the Marquis smilingly exclaimed, "Lord Warnham has evidently taught you the first requisite of the successful diplomatist— namely, secrecy. You've borne well the test I have applied, Deedes. By the same questions I have just put to you I could have learnt just what I wanted from half the diplomatic circle here in Paris, yet you have fenced with me admirably. I shall not omit to mention the fact to Lord Warnham when next I call at the Foreign Office."

I thanked his Excellency, adding, with a smile, "One learns the value of silence with our chief."

"Yes," he answered, slowly tapping his table with a quill. "He's a curious man, extremely curious. His very eccentricity causes him to be feared by every Cabinet in Europe. Is he really as impetuous and strange in private life as he is in public?"

I paused, looking fixedly into my companions dark eyes.

"The object of my visit, your Excellency, is not to discuss the merits of my chief or the policy of the Home Government, but to make a suggestion which he has desired me to place before you with all deference to your wide experience as Ambassador, and your unequalled knowledge of the French people," I said gravely, and then, clearly and succinctly, I placed before him the Earl's ideas, together with the instructions he had entrusted me to deliver.

At first the Ambassador, resenting my interference with his actions, seemed disinclined to entertain the suggestions; but using the arguments my chief had advanced, I at length induced him to view the matter from the same standpoint. I even obtained from him what was practically an admission that the policy he had pursued in the past regarding the question under discussion was not altogether sound, and once having obtained that, I felt confident of gaining my point without any unpleasant incident. From that moment, indeed, he recognised that I bore a message from the chief, therefore he treated me pleasantly, and announced his intention of seeking an audience with the President of the Republic at the Elysée at four o'clock, to enter upon negotiations which Her Majesty earnestly desired should be carried forward without delay.

Although the Marquis treated me with calm, unruffled dignity, as befitted the Ambassador of the greatest nation on earth, I nevertheless congratulated myself that my efforts had been eminently successful. Aided by the promptings of the shrewd old Earl, I had, I flattered myself, exercised a careful and even delicate tact in dealing with this leader among diplomatists, and, as may be imagined, the knowledge that my mission was successful caused me the utmost satisfaction.

When I had first approached the subject he had been inclined to disregard my words, and grew so angry that I feared lest he might tender his resignation, as the Earl had apprehended. But the Minister's clever arguments, rather than my own tact, convinced him, for he saw that to act at once was imperative; hence the success of my first secret mission.

We sat together for nearly an hour calmly discussing the matter from various standpoints, and when we rose his Excellency again congratulated me upon the soundness of my views, laughingly declaring that, instead of penning the Earl's impatient and irritating dispatches, he ought to appoint me to a post abroad.

Full of elation, I descended the broad stairs, so thickly carpeted that my feet fell noiselessly, and met unexpectedly, a few moments later, my friend Captain Cargill, of the 2nd Life Guards, the junior Military Attaché, who greeted me with a hearty British hand-grip.

"Didn't expect to meet you here, old chap," he cried. "I thought you were tied up in the chief's private room always, and never allowed out of England."

"This is the first time I've been here officially," I replied, laughing.

"What's the trouble? Anything startling?" he inquired.

"No, nothing very extraordinary," I remarked, carelessly. "I've seen the Marquis, and concluded my mission."

Continuing, I extracted from him a promise to dine with me at the Continental that evening, as I intended to leave next day, and after a brief conversation we parted. Along the shady side of the Rue du Faubourg St Honoré I strolled leisurely, turning into the Rue Royale, passing the gloomy façade of the Madeleine, and continuing along the boulevard to the Grand Café. Paris possessed but little attraction for me in my gloomy frame of mind. Five years of my youth had been spent there, and I knew the city in every mood, but to-day, plunged as I was in a debauch of melancholy, its gay aspect under the warm sunshine jarred upon me.

On leaving the Embassy it had occurred to me to call upon an old friend, who, in my student days, had shared rooms with me, but who had been returned as Deputy at the last election, and now lived in the Rue des Petits-Champs. With that object I had walked along mechanically, and instead of turning down the Rue des Capucines, as I should have done, I had found myself in the Place de l'Opéra. Then, seating myself at one of the tables in front of the Grand Café, I ordered a "bock," and contemplatively watched the crowd of passers-by.

When last I had sat at that spot it was with Ella, on the night before we had returned to London from our honeymoon. Well I remembered how happy and content she had then been; how she had enjoyed the light, cosmopolitan chatter about her, and how fondly we had loved each other. In those days she had mingled tender words with her kisses, which seemed to bear my soul away. Yet how weary and full of terrible anxiety had been the nine months that had elapsed since that delightful autumn night, the last of our lazy tour through rural France. When I reflected upon all the remarkable occurrences, they seemed like some hideous nightmare, while she herself appeared striking, yet mysterious, as the fair vision in some half-remembered dream.

Thus was I sitting alone at the little marble-topped table, gazing into space, wondering, as I did daily, how my lost wife fared, and whether she ever gave a single passing thought to the man who, notwithstanding all her faults and follies, loved her better than his life, when before my eyes there arose for a second a face that in an instant was familiar.

A man, short of stature and well-dressed, had lounged leisurely by with a cigarette, but scarcely had he walked a dozen yards beyond the café when I jumped up, and rushing along, accosted him.

It was Ivan Renouf.

He turned sharply at mention of his name, regarding me with an inquiring glance, but next second expressed pleasure at our meeting. Together we returned to the café, and chatted amicably over a mazagran. Presently, after we had been speaking of our last interview at Mrs Laing's, I asked him the truth about his sudden dismissal from her service.

"What your wife told you was quite correct," he answered, with a mysterious smile; "I was detected."

"You are generally too wary to be caught by those upon whom you are keeping observation," I remarked.

Slowly he selected a fresh cigarette, and laughing carelessly, answered, —

"It was not by accident but by design that I was caught. My object was already attained, and I desired to be discharged at once from madame's service."

"She left London almost immediately," I said.

"Yes, I am quite aware of that. It was best for her," he observed, rather abruptly.

"My wife also fled on the same day," I exclaimed slowly. "I haven't seen her since."

At this announcement he betrayed no surprise, but merely remarked, "So I have heard."

"Tell me," I urged earnestly, "do you know anything of her movements? I am endeavouring to find her, and am in utter despair."

With a sharp glance at me, the great detective stirred his long glass, raised it to his lips, and took a deep draught. Then, slowly replacing it upon the table, he coldly answered, —

"I know nothing of your wife's whereabouts, m'sieur."

"Am I to understand that you refuse to tell me anything?" I asked, annoyed.

He shrugged his shoulders, but answered no word. I detested him instinctively.

"Is it not strange that they should both have fled in this extraordinary manner?" I suggested. "Can you assign any motive whatever for their flight?"

"I am really not good at conundrums," he replied indifferently. "But if you took my advice, m'sieur, you would abandon all thought of her, for at least one fact was quite plain, namely, that mademoiselle never loved you."

"How do you know that?" I cried, with sinking heart, as the ghastly truth was forced upon me for the thousandth time.

"From my own observations," he answered, looking straight at me across the table. "Your marriage was, I am fully aware, an unhappy one; therefore you should regard it entirely as of the past. She will never trouble you again, I can assure you."

"Why?" I demanded. "Your words indicate that you are fully aware of the true facts. Tell me all, Renouf, and set my mind at rest."

"I have told you all, m'sieur," he said, suddenly tossing his cigarette away, glancing at his watch and rising. "That is, I have told you all that I may. But I have an appointment," he added abruptly. "Adieu."

And before I could prevent him he had raised his hat with a show of politeness, and walked hurriedly off across the broad Place in the direction of the Boulevard des Italiens.

In chagrin I bit my lip, for instead of giving me any clue to the hiding-place of my errant wife, his words only tended to increase my mistrust and despair. Was not, however, his refusal only what I might have expected? I rose and slowly walked away down the Rue Auber, deeply reflecting upon his denunciation of Ella's faithlessness. What motive could he have, I wondered, in thus declaring that she had never loved me?

That night Cargill dined with me, and after taking our coffee and liqueurs in the courtyard of the Continental, watching the well-dressed crowd of idlers who assemble there nightly after dinner, we strolled out along the brightly-lit streets, where all Paris was enjoying the cool, star-lit evening after the heat and burden of the day.

Our footsteps led us unconsciously to that Mecca of the Briton or American resident in Paris, the Hôtel Chatham, and entering the American bar we found assembled there a number of mutual acquaintances. At one of the small wooden tables sat my old and valued friend, Henry Allender, counsel to the United States Embassy in Paris, a man universally liked in both British and American colonies of the French capital, and opposite him a short, stout, round-faced Frenchman, attired in grey, and wearing the Legion of Honour in his lapel—Monsieur Goron, the well-known Chief of Police. From both I received a cordial welcome, and as we sat down to chat over cocktails carefully mixed by the deft, loquacious bar-tender, Tommy, I took up Le Monde Illustré, lying upon the table, and opened it carelessly.

Several pages I had turned over, when suddenly my eyes fell upon a full-page illustration of a beautiful woman in evening dress, with a fine diamond tiara upon her head. The features were unmistakable. With an involuntary cry that startled my companions, I sat rigid and motionless, glaring at it in abject dismay.

The portrait itself did not surprise me so much as the amazing words printed beneath. The latter held me spellbound.

Chapter Twenty Seven
Cosmopolitans

"Why, what's the matter, old chap?" inquired Cargill, bending forward quickly to glance at the journal. "You look as if you've got an acute attack of the jim-jams."

"See!" I gasped hoarsely, pointing to the printed page upon which my strained eyes had riveted themselves.

"Deucedly pretty woman," declared the attaché, who was nothing if not a ladies' man. Few men were better known in Paris than Hugh Cargill.

"Yes, yes, I know," I exclaimed impatiently. I was sitting dumbfounded, the words beneath the picture dancing before my vision in letters of fire.

The portrait that seemed to smile mockingly at me was a reproduction of a photograph of Ella. The handsome, regular features were unmistakable. With the exception of the magnificent tiara, the ornaments she wore I recognised as belonging to her. All were now in my possession, alas! for on leaving me she had discarded them, and with ineffable sadness I had locked them away in a small cabinet. The jewel-case containing her wedding-ring was a veritable skeleton in my cupboard that I dare not gaze upon.

The picture was undoubtedly that of my lost wife, yet beneath was printed in French the words, —

"Her Imperial Highness the Grand Duchess Elizaveta Nicolayevna of Russia."

"Look!" I cried, my eye still upon the page. "Surely there's some mistake! That can't be the Grand Duchess!"

Allender and Cargill bent simultaneously over the little table, and both declared that there was no mistake.

"She's very well-known here," exclaimed the attaché. "I've seen her driving her Orloff ponies in the Bois dozens of times. Besides, one never forgets such a face as hers."

"Does she live here?" I inquired breathlessly.

"Sometimes," he answered; and smiling behind the veil of tobacco smoke, he added, "She's been away a long time now. I suppose you want an introduction to her—eh? Well, I don't expect you'll be successful, as her circle is the most select in Paris. She never invites any of the 'corps diplomatique.'"

"No," I answered huskily, "I desire no introduction." A sudden giddiness had seized me. The jingle of glasses, the incessant chatter, the loud laughter, and the heavy smoke of cigars had combined with this sudden and bewildering discovery to produce a slight faintness. I took up a glass of ice-water at my elbow and gulped it down.

"Do you know her?" inquired Allender, with a pronounced American accent, at the same time regarding me curiously.

"Yes," I answered, not without hesitation. "She is—I mean we have already met."

"Well, you're to be congratulated," he answered, smiling. "I reckon she's the finest looking woman in Paris, and that's a solid fact."

Without replying I slowly turned over the page, and there saw a brief article with the same heading as the legend beneath the portrait. Cargill and Allender were attracted at that moment by the entry of one of their friends, a wealthy young man who, with his wife, had forsaken Ohio for residence in the French capital, and while they chatted I eagerly scanned the article, which ran as follows,—

"Paris will welcome the return of Her Imperial Highness the Grand Duchess Elizaveta Nicolayevna of Russia, whose portrait we give on another page. For nearly nine months her great house in the Avenue des Champs Elysées, the scene of so many brilliant *fêtes* during her last residence there, has been closed, but she arrived in Paris about ten days ago, and has announced her intention of remaining among us until the end of the year. As our readers are no doubt aware, Her Imperial Highness, niece of the late Tzar Alexander, and cousin of the present Czar, is an excellent linguist, speaking English and French perfectly, in addition to her native Russian. She was born at Tzarskoïe-Selo, but her early days were spent in England. She, however, prefers Paris to either London or St Petersburg, although in the latter city her entertainments at the mansion on the English Quay are on a scale almost as brilliant as those at the Winter Palace itself. Her beauty is incomparable, and her diamonds among the finest in Europe.

Her munificence to the poor of Paris is well-known. Although moving in the highest circle, she does not fear to go herself into the very vilest slums, accompanied by her trusty Muscovite man-servant, and there distribute relief to the deserving from her own purse. Both the needy and the wealthy therefore welcome her on her return."

I re-read the article. Then I sat with the paper before me, staring at it in blank bewilderment. The surprising discovery held me petrified. This beautiful woman, who had masqueraded as Ella Laing, and had become my wife by law, was actually the daughter of a reigning house, the cousin of an Emperor.

The astounding truth seemed incredible.

"Well," asked Cargill, turning to me with a smile a moment later, "have you been reading all about her?"

"Yes," I answered, drawing a long breath.

"Come, don't sigh like that, old fellow," he cried, and glancing across to the bar, shouted, "Mix another dry Martini, Tommy, for my friend."

To affect indifference I strove vainly. Nevertheless, I listened with eager ears as my three companions commenced discussing the merits of the high-born woman who was my wife. To me she was no longer Ella. Her personality, so vivid and distinct, seemed in those moments of perplexity to fade like the memory of some half-remembered dream.

"Her beauty is simply marvellous," Allender acknowledged, smoking on in his dry, matter-of-fact way. He was not more than thirty-eight, but by sheer merit as a sound lawyer and a thorough good fellow, he had risen to the lucrative post he held, and had, in the course of five years, formed a large and valuable practice and a wide circle of friends among the English-speaking colonies in the French capital.

"I entirely agree with m'sieur," observed Monsieur Goron, in his broken English. "Her Highness is very beautiful, but, ah—cold as an icicle."

"Is there no scandal regarding her?" I inquired eagerly, well knowing that in Paris no woman is considered really *chic* without some story being whispered about her.

"None," replied the renowned investigator of Anarchist conspiracies. "I have the pleasure of knowing Her Highness, and I have always found her a most estimable young lady. There is, however," he added, "some curious romance, I believe, connected with her earlier life."

"A romance?" cried Cargill. "Do tell us all about it."

"Ah, unfortunately I do not know the details," answered the old Frenchman, suddenly exhibiting his palms. "It was alleged once by somebody I met officially—who it was, I really forget. She lived for years in England, and is a cosmopolitan thoroughly, besides being one of the richest women in Paris."

"Is it true that she sometimes goes into the low quarters of the city and gives money to the poor?" I asked him, for this love of midnight adventure accounted for Ella's strange penchant for rambling alone at night that had once caused me so much perturbation.

"Certainly. With her, philanthropy is a fad. I accompanied her on several occasions last year," he replied. "She attired herself in an old, worn-out dress of one of her maids, and disguised herself most effectually. On each night she distributed about five thousand francs with her own hands. Indeed, so well-known is she in certain quarters that I believe she might go there alone with perfect safety. However, when she is going we always know at the Préfecture, and take precautions. It would not do for us to allow anything to happen to an Imperial Highness," he added.

"Of course not," observed Cargill, adding with the diplomatic instinct, "Of course. Not in view of the Franco-Russian Alliance," an observation at which we all three laughed merrily.

"Has she a lover?" inquired Allender, turning to Monsieur Goron.

"I think not," the other replied. "I never heard of one. Indeed, I have never heard her accused of flirtation with anybody."

"Tell me, m'sieur," I asked, "are you acquainted with a Russian named Ivan Renouf, who is, I believe, in the secret service."

"Renouf!" he repeated, glancing quickly at me with his steel-blue eyes. "Yes, I have met him. He is in Paris at the present moment. Whether he is in the actual service of the Tzar's Government I don't know, but one thing is certain, namely, that he is a blackmailer and a scoundrel," he added frankly.

"What offence has he committed?" I asked, eager to learn some fact to his detriment.

"He keeps well within the bounds of the law," my companion answered. "Nevertheless he is utterly unscrupulous and most ingenious in his methods. He is reported to be chief of the section of Secret Police attached to the Russian Embassy, but they are a mysterious lot of spies, always coming and going. Sent here from St Petersburg, they remain a few months, watching the revolutionary refugees, and then go back, their places being taken by a fresh batch."

"Why is Renouf in Paris? Have you any idea?"

"None, m'sieur," Monsieur Goron answered. "He has been absent fully six months, and only last night I met him coming out of La Scala."

"Did you speak?"

"Yes. He did not, however, recognise me," smiled the Chief of Police. "I did not expect he would, as I chanced to be acting as a cabman, and was sitting upon my box outside the theatre. He hailed me, but I refused to drive him. I was waiting for a fare who was enjoying himself inside, and who, on coming out, I had the pleasure of driving straight to the Préfecture," added the man of a thousand disguises with a chuckle, swallowing his cocktail in one gulp.

"Where does the Grand Duchess live?" I inquired, after a slight pause.

"Deedes is simply gone on her," cried Cargill, with good-humoured banter. "He evidently wants to take her out to dinner."

"No," I protested, smiling grimly. "Nothing of the kind. I only want to know whereabouts in the Avenue des Champs Elysées she lives."

"It is a large white house, with green jalousies, on the left-hand side, just beyond the Avenue de l'Alma," explained the Chief of Police, laughing at Cargill's suggestion.

"But how did you become acquainted with her?" inquired the attaché, presently, after my companions had been praising her face and extolling her virtues.

"We met in London," I answered vaguely, for I was in no confidential mood.

"And she captivated you, eh?" my friend exclaimed. "Well, I'm not surprised. Half Paris goes mad over her beauty whenever she's here."

"It is said, and I believe there's a good deal of truth in it," exclaimed Goron, confidentially, "that young Max Duchanel, the well-known writer on the *Figaro*, committed suicide last year by shooting himself over at Le Pré St Gervais because she disregarded his attentions. At any rate an extravagant letter of reproach and farewell was discovered in his pocket. We hushed up the matter because of the position of the personage therein mentioned."

At least one man had paid with his life the penalty of his devotion to her. Did not this fact force home once again the truth of Sonia's disregarded denunciation that Ella was not my friend? It was now plain how neatly I had been tricked; and with what artful ingenuity she had masqueraded as my wife. Monsieur Grodekoff, the Russian Ambassador, Paul Verblioudovitch, and Ivan Renouf all knew her true position, yet feared to tell me. Indeed, my friend Paul had urged me to marry and forgot the past, and his Excellency had actually congratulated us both with outstretched hand. Because she was so well-known in Paris she had, while on our honeymoon, only remained in the capital the night, and had refused to go shopping or show herself unnecessarily. She had preferred a quiet, unfashionable hotel in a by-street to any of those well-known; and I now remembered how, even then, she had remained in her room, pleading fatigue and headache. From our first meeting to the moment of her flight her attitude had been that of a consummate actress.

"Did Her Highness pass under another name in London?" Goron asked me presently, appearing much interested.

"Yes," I replied.

"Ah!" he ejaculated. "She is perfectly charming, and so fond of concealing her real position beneath the most ordinary patronymic. To me, she is always so affable and so nice."

"Goron is sweet on her also, I believe," observed Allender, whereat we all laughed in chorus.

I struggled to preserve an outward show of indifference, but every word these men uttered stabbed my heart deeply. When I had ascertained the whereabouts of her house, my first impulse had been to rush out, drive there, and meet her face to face, but my nerves were, I knew, upset and unsteady, so I remained sitting with my light-hearted companions, endeavouring amid that jingle, popping of corks, and chatter of London, New York and Paris, to think deeply and decide upon the best course to pursue.

"Our chief sent her invitations to the Embassy balls on several occasions a year ago, but she declined each," I heard the attaché saying. "She's a royalty, so I suppose she thinks herself just a cut above us. But, after all, I don't blame her," he added, reflectively. "Diplomacy is but the art of lying artistically. She has no need to struggle for a foothold in society."

"Correct," observed Allender. "The women who flutter around at our Embassy are the gayest crowd I've ever struck. I reckon they're not of her set. But she's a very fine woman, even though she may be a Highness. She's simply beautiful. I've seen some fine women in my day, but for thrilling a man's soul and driving him to distraction, I never saw anyone to compare with her."

"That's so," Cargill acquiesced. "Yet her refusal to come to us has often been remarked by our chief, especially as we've entertained a crowd of other princesses and high nobilities at one time or another."

"She has a reason, I suppose," observed Goron, slowly twisting his eternal caporal.

"Goron appears to know all her secrets," said Cargill, winking at me knowingly. "He trots her about Paris at night, and she confides in him all her little anxieties and fears. A most charming arrangement."

The astute officer, who, by his energetic action, had succeeded in effectually stamping out the Anarchist activity, smiled and raised both his hands in protest, crying, —

"No, no, messieurs! It is in you younger men that the pretty women confide. As for me, I am old, fat and ugly."

"But you act as the protector of the philanthropic Elizaveta Nicolayevna," observed Cargill, "therefore, when you next see her, tell her how her portrait in Le Monde has been admired by an impressionable young Englishman, named Deedes, and present to her the compliments and profound admiration of all three of us."

"Don't do anything of the kind, Goron," I cried, rather angrily. "Remember I know the lady, and such words would be an insult."

"Very well, if you're really going to call on her, you might convey our message," exclaimed the attaché, nonchalantly. "You're not jealous, are you?"

"I don't think there's any need for jealousy," I responded.

Goron laughed heartily at this retort. He was more shrewd than the others, and I instinctively felt that he had guessed that Her Highness and myself were a little more than chance-met acquaintances. But the others continued their fooling, happy, careless, bubbling over with buoyant spirits. Many good fellows frequent the bar of the Chatham, one of the most cosmopolitan resorts in Europe. Many adventurers and "dead beats" make it their headquarters, but of all that merry, easy-going crowd of men with money, and those in want of it, to find two men more popular and more generous than Hugh Cargill and Henry Allender would have been difficult.

As we still sat together smoking and drinking, the pair directed their chaff continually in my direction. Evidently believing that the incomparable beauty of Her Highness had fascinated me, they urged me to go to her and suggest a drive in the Bois, a quiet little dinner somewhere, or a box at the opera. Little did they dream how every jesting word they uttered pained me, how each laugh at my expense caused me excruciating anguish, or how any detrimental allegation, spoken unthinkingly, sank deeply into my mind. But I had never worn my heart on my sleeve, therefore I treated their banter with good humour, determined that, at least for the present, they should remain in ignorance of the fact that I was the husband of the woman whose adorable face and charming manner had excited universal admiration in the gayest capital of the world.

Chapter Twenty Eight
Her Imperial Highness

Until we rose and separated I succeeded in hiding my sorrow beneath a smile, but when at length I had shaken hands with my companions at the corner of the Rue de la Paix, and to my relief found myself once more alone walking across the Place Vendôme, with the black column standing out before me in the bright moonlight, my outburst of grief became uncontrollable. My heart, lancinated by the careless words of my companions, had been burdened by a bitterness rendered the more poignant because I had been compelled to laugh with them. Now that I had proof that Ella was not what she had represented herself to be—an affectionate, unassuming woman of my own station—I felt crushed, bewildered and disconsolate, for with the knowledge of our difference of birth the iron had entered my soul.

The manner in which she had posed as daughter of the pleasant-faced widow of Robert Laing, and her calm, dignified bearing as my wife, had been a most perfect piece of acting. Never for one moment had I suspected her to be anything else than what she represented herself to be—plain Ella Laing, the only daughter of the deceased shipowner; yet she was actually a daughter of the Romanoffs, the most powerful and wealthy house in Europe. As I strolled slowly along the Rue Castiglione towards the hotel, I asked myself whether she had ever really loved me. At first I doubted her, because of the difference of our stations. Presently, however, when I recollected the perfect bliss of our honeymoon, when I remembered how childishly happy we had been together through those brief autumn days, in the sleepy old towns and villages of the Indre, content in each other's joys, I could not longer declare within myself that hers had been mere theatrical emotion. Yes, she had loved me then, this high-born woman, over whose beauty half Paris raved, and I, in my ignorance, had fondly imagined our love would last always. The experiment of the masquerade had amused her at first, perhaps, but soon, alas! she had grown tired of life in a ten-roomed house in a quiet road in Kensington, and with a brief, cruel farewell had returned to her jewel-case the ring I had placed upon her slim finger, and left me with ruthless disregard for all the love I had bestowed upon her. Yet after all, was it really surprising that she, the daughter of an Imperial House, should become weary of the humdrum life she had been compelled to lead with one whose private income, outside his salary, was a paltry nine hundred a year?

While we lived together, she had apparently exercised the greatest caution not to show herself possessed of money, for she always did her shopping in Kensington High Street, with due regard to economy, as became the wife of a man of limited means. Never once had she grumbled or sighed because she could not purchase higher-priced hats or dresses, but, always content, she had, I remembered, been proud to exhibit to me those odds-and-ends picked up in drapers' shops, so dear to the feminine heart, and known as bargains. When I had regretted my small income, as I had done more than once, she had fondly kissed me, declaring herself perfectly willing to wait until I had obtained a diplomatic and more lucrative appointment. "You have an excellent friend in the Earl," she would say, smiling sweetly. "He is certain to give you a post before long. Be patient."

I had been patient, and had lost her.

Plunged in deep despair, I turned into the courtyard of the hotel, and sat down to think. As I did so a servant handed me a telegram. It was from Lord Warnham at Osborne, requesting my return on the morrow.

The one thought that possessed me was that Ella—or the woman I had known and adored under that name—was in Paris. Could I leave without seeing her? She had deserted me, it was true, yet my passion was at that moment as intense even as it had been in those calm autumn days when we had wandered together along the peaceful lanes around old-world Chateauroux, hand-in-hand, in sweet contentment. In those never-to-be-forgotten hours we both possessed the delights of love and fever of happiness. To us everything was passion, ecstasy and delirium. We both felt as if we were living in a rose-coloured atmosphere; the heights of sentimentality glistened in our imaginations, and common everyday existence appeared to us to be far down below in the distance—in the shade between the gaps in these heights. I still felt the softness of that tiny hand I had so often pressed to my lips; I still felt the clasp of her arms about my neck; I still saw her deep blue eyes gazing into mine as we interchanged vows of eternal fidelity.

The cry of a man selling the *Soir* aroused me. I rose suddenly. Yes, I must see her again. I must see her, if for the last time.

Stepping into a cab, I directed the man to drive to her house, then, seating myself, glanced at my watch. It was already near midnight.

Soon, with the clip-clap of the horse's hoofs sounding upon the asphalte, we were crossing the Place de la Concorde, rendered bright by its myriad lights, then entering the broad avenue we passed the lines of illuminated cafés half-hidden by the trees surrounding them, and, driving on for some ten minutes, at last pulled up among a number of private carriages that were setting down guests before a great mansion, where I alighted.

One of those brilliant *fêtes* that were the talk of Paris was apparently about to commence, for many notabilities were arriving, and as I went forward to the spacious portico I was preceded by two pretty laughing girls attended by a tall and distinguished-looking man of military appearance. I drew back while they entered the great, brilliantly-lit hall with its fine marble staircase and profusion of exotics; then, when they had passed on, I inquired in French of the gigantic Russian concierge whether Her Highness was at home.

"Yes, m'sieur," answered the man, gruffly, scanning me closely, noticing that I was attired in a suit of dark tweed, for so suddenly had I left England that I had had no time to take with me a claw-hammer coat. "Her Highness is at home, m'sieur, but she is engaged," he said, when he had thoroughly inspected me.

I half drew my card-case from my pocket, but fearing lest she might not see me if she knew my name, I said,—

"Go to her, and say that a friend craves one moment of her time upon an important matter."

"M'sieur gives no card?" he inquired, with a quick, interrogative look of suspicion.

"No," I answered.

He led me across the hall wherein hung an elaborate Russian ikon, down one long well-carpeted corridor and then along another, at last ushering me into a great apartment resplendent with mirrors, statuary and gilt furniture, the latter bearing embroidered upon the crimson backs of the chairs her monogram, "EN", surmounted by a Russian coronet. In the costly inlaid cabinets were arranged many pieces of priceless china, the carpet was of rich turquoise blue, the tables of ebony were inlaid with silver, and over all electric lamps, dotted here and there, shaded by coral silk, shed a warm, subdued light. Near the four long windows that occupied one end of the great room was a grand piano, upon which two photographs in ormolu frames stood conspicuously. I crossed to look at them and discovered that one was my own, that she had evidently taken with her when she had so suddenly left my house, and the other a portrait of the man who had betrayed me—Dudley Ogle.

Slowly my eyes wandered around the elegant apartment, unable to realise that this handsome, luxurious abode could actually be my wife's home. How mean and paltry indeed must our small drawing-room in Phillimore Gardens have appeared to her after all this stately magnificence and rigid etiquette. As I passed through the great mansion, one of the largest private residences in Paris, my nostrils had been greeted by the subtle odours of exotics, and upon my ears there had fallen the strains of an orchestra somewhere in the opposite wing of the building. Guests were evidently not shown to the side of the house where I had been conducted, for not a sound penetrated there. All was quiet, peaceful and stately.

Suddenly, just as I bent to more closely examine Dudley's portrait, and had distinguished that it was a copy similar to the one I had seen in Sonia's possession, the door was thrown wide-open by a tall, liveried servant, who entered, and, bowing low, announced in stentorian tones,—"Her Imperial Highness Elizaveta Nicolayevna."

The rapid frou-frou of silk sounded outside, and next second my wife and I stood face to face.

In an instant the colour left her cheeks. She staggered as if she had been dealt a blow, but managing to regain her self-possession, she turned quickly to the servant, and in a frigid tone said,—

"Go, Anton. And see that I am not disturbed."

The man, glancing at me for a moment in unfeigned surprise, bowed, and withdrew in silence.

I stood motionless, gazing upon her, noting the beauty of her costume, the brilliance of her diamonds, and the deathly pallor of her adorable face.

"Geoffrey!" she gasped at last. In a half-fearful whisper she repeated my name, adding, "So you have found me!"

With a quick, impetuous movement she walked unevenly towards me, with rustling skirts and outstretched hands. It seemed to me, as I looked at her, as if my soul flew towards her, spreading at first like a wave around the outline of her head, and then, attracted by the whiteness of her breast, descended into her.

"Yes," I said, slowly and gravely. "I have found you, Ella."

"Ah, no!" she cried, advancing so close to me that the well-remembered odour of sampaguita intoxicated me. I felt her warm, passionate breath upon my cheek. "Do not call me longer by that false name. Forget it—forget it all, and call me by my right name—Elizaveta."

"It is impossible," I answered.

"No, do not say that," she cried hoarsely. "I—I know I have deceived you, Geoffrey. I lied to you. But forgive me. Tell me that you will some day forget."

"Think," I said, in a low, reproachful tone, my heart filled with grief to overflowing—"think how you have wrecked my life," I urged. "You masqueraded before me as a plain English girl; you married me and allowed me to adore you—ah! better than all the world besides—until you grew tired and left our poor, matter-of-fact home to reassume your true station—that of a Grand Duchess. You never loved me; but it amused you, I suppose, to become the wife of a man who was compelled to earn his livelihood. The economy you practised while with me was a new sensation to you, and your—"

"Stop!" she cried vehemently, putting up her tiny hand to my mouth, as had been her habit long ago when she wished to arrest the flow of my words. "Stop! I cannot bear it! I tell you I did love you, Geoffrey. I love you now, dearer than life."

"Then why did you practise such base deception?" I demanded. "Why did you leave me and cast aside my wedding-ring?"

"I—I was compelled," she faltered.

"Compelled!" I echoed, in a voice full of bitter sarcasm. "I do not—indeed I cannot blame you for regretting the false step you took when you consented to become my wife, yet why you should have done this is to me utterly incomprehensible."

"It will all be plain ere long," she assured me, in a low, intense voice. "If I had not loved you, I should never have become your wife."

"But you were cruel to deceive me thus," I retorted.

"It is my misfortune, Geoffrey, that I was born a Grand Duchess," she answered, looking straight at me with her deep blue eyes full of intense anxiety and sorrow. "It is not my fault. I swear I still love you with a love as honest and pure as ever a woman entertained towards a man."

"But after deceiving me in every particular regarding both the past and the present, you thought fit to leave me," I went on ruthlessly.

"Ah!" she exclaimed, as if reflecting, "I admit that I wronged you cruelly; yes, I admit it all, everything. Nevertheless, since we have parted, Geoffrey, I have recollected daily, with a thousand heartfelt regrets, the supreme joy of our married life. Ah! it was happiness, indeed, with you, the man I so dearly loved. But now," and she shrugged her shoulders, half-hidden in their pale blue chiffon, the movement causing her diamonds to gleam with fiery iridescence. "Now, without your love, I have happiness no longer. All is despair."

"I have not forgotten. Every detail of our brief, joyous life together is still fresh in my memory," I declared sorrowfully.

"Forgotten! How can either of us forget?" she cried impetuously, pushing back from her white brow her gold-brown hair, with its scintillating star. "Only in those few months spent by your side, Geoffrey, have I known what it is to really live and to love. Although I have been absent from you I have, nevertheless, known from time to time how you have fared, yet I dared not give you any sign as to my whereabouts, fearing that you would brand me as base and heartless. To you I must appear so, I know; yet, although we are separated, I am still your wife and you my husband. I still love you. Forgive me."

And she stood before me with bent head in penitent attitude, her slight frame shaken by tremulous emotion.

A lump rose in my throat. I felt choked by the intoxication of her love, for I idolised her. Yet I knew that, although my wife, she could never be the same to me as in those blissful days in Kensington before the shadow of suspicion fell between us.

"You are silent, Geoffrey," she whispered hoarsely at last, starting at the sound of her own voice. Then, throwing her soft arms about my neck, she clung to me passionately, as she was wont to do in those bygone days of happiness, saying, "You cannot deny that you still care for me—that I am yours. Yet you are thinking of the past; of what you regard as my base faithlessness! My actions were, I admit, full of apparent ingratitude. Yes, I cast your great love beneath my feet and trampled it in the mire, not because

I am what I am, I swear, but because such action was imperative—because I was striving for my emancipation."

"Your emancipation?" I exclaimed, with a touch of anger. "From your marriage vows, it seems."

"Ah, no!" cried the Grand Duchess, throwing back her white neck, which rose with her hot, panting breath. "No, no, not that! I struggled to free myself from a tie so hateful that I believe I should have killed myself were it not that I loved you so fondly, and hoped that some day happiness would again be ours. But, alas! I strove in vain; for, when within an ace of success, you became filled with suspicion and accused me of unfaithfulness, while it became imperative, almost at the same moment, that I should return to the position I had sought to relinquish. Since I fled from you I have lived on from day to day full of bitter regrets and in constant fear lest you should discover that I was not what I represented myself to be, and come here to demand an explanation. Well, at last you have come, and—and all I can now do is to assure you that I acted in our mutual interests, and to implore your forgiveness."

I still gazed at her without replying.

"Forgive me, Geoffrey," she repeated. "One cannot get accustomed to the loss of happiness, and I cannot live without you; indeed, I cannot. Say that we may begin again, that, even though we must for the present be parted, we may still love and live for each other. See! I am laughing and am happy," she cried hysterically. "Speak! Do speak to me?"

Tears were trembling in her deep, wonderful eyes like dewdrops in the calix of a blue flower, and without knowing what I did, I stroked her silky hair. Slowly she bent her head, and at last I softly kissed her eyelids.

"Yes," I said huskily, "I love you, Ella—for I can call you by no other name, and cannot think of you other than as the woman I believed you to be. I can see that although we are man and wife in the eyes of the law, that you were right to end the folly, even though you were unable to do it without some pangs of conscience. You are my wife, it is true, but our lives lie apart, for your position precludes you from acknowledging me to the world as your husband. You—"

"Yes, I will. I will, Geoffrey! Soon I shall be freed from this terrible yoke that crushes me beneath its burden," she exclaimed eagerly. "Be patient, and ere long we may again live together and enjoy our happiness to the full. You still doubt that I really love you. You believe that my marriage was a mere freak, of which I afterwards repented, and then strove to hide my identity. What can I do?" she cried, dismayed. "What can I do to give you proof that I love no other man?"

"One very small action," I answered gravely, still holding her slight, trembling form in my arms.

"What is it?" she inquired quickly, glancing up into my face. "I am ready to do it, whatever it is."

For a moment I paused in hesitation.

"Answer me a single question, Ella," I said. "Remember you are my wife, and should have no secrets from me. Tell me, truthfully and honestly, how there came into your possession the secret document that was stolen from me on the day of Dudley's death."

The colour left her face, her lips moved, and a slight shiver ran over her shoulders as she gazed at me. Never before had her eyes seemed so large, nor had there been such depths in them. Some subtle influence seemed in an instant to have transfigured her whole being.

Chapter Twenty Nine
The Seal of Silence

"No, you must not ask me, for I cannot tell you," she faltered, after I had gravely repeated my earnest inquiry. She shrank from my embrace, and as she stood before me, her handsome head was bent in an attitude of utter dejection.

"Ah, the same lame story?" I cried impatiently. "You refuse."

She raised her sad eyes. I saw in their clear depths a yearning for pity.

"I dare not tell you yet, Geoffrey," she whispered, in a strained, terrified voice.

"You know well how much keen anxiety the loss of that document caused me," I said. "Why did you not tell me that it was in your keeping?"

"It was not in my keeping," she protested. "I recovered it only a few days before we parted."

"But you knew something of its whereabouts?" I argued.

"I was not certain," she vaguely replied, her slim fingers picking at the bands of pearl passementerie across the flimsy chiffon of her bodice.

With an expression of disbelief I turned from her.

"Ah, Geoffrey," she cried wildly, "I am fully conscious of what your thoughts must be. Now that you have discovered my true position, that I am a Russian, you believe I had a hand in the theft of the Anglo-German Convention; that by my machinations its text was transmitted to St Petersburg—eh?"

No answer passed my lips, but I think I bowed my head in confirmation of her fevered words.

"Well, it is untrue, as you will learn some day. It is untrue, I swear," she exclaimed with terrible earnestness. "Instead of endeavouring to bring suspicion and opprobrium upon you, and disaster upon the nations of Europe, I have striven both night and day to clear away the ill effect produced by the dastard revelations made to our Ministry in St Petersburg.

Remember that the single spark required to fire the mine and convulse the world from Calais to Pekin was not applied; the Tzar refrained from declaring war. Some day you, and through you, the British Government, will know the reason a recourse to arms was averted. When you are made aware of the truth, then no longer will you misjudge me."

She spoke with a fervency that was entirely unfeigned; her bright eyes met mine with unwavering glance, and with a quick movement she had placed one hand upon her breast as if to allay the palpitation there. Her heart was full; upon her fair face was an expression of mingled anxiety and dread, and her bejewelled hands trembled.

"I am your husband," I said calmly. "If I promise you not to divulge—surely I may know your secret whatever it may be."

"No," she answered, speaking almost mechanically, "I dare not tell you anything at present. It would be fatal to all my plans—fatal to me, and to you."

"You speak so strangely," I observed, with some warmth. "Mystery seems one of your idiosyncrasies."

"Ah," she sighed, advancing a step towards me, her head sunk upon her breast, "it is imperative. You cannot know how I have suffered, Geoffrey, ever since we met. Long ago at 'The Nook,' fearing that I should bring you unhappiness, I strove to tear myself from you and return here to this life, but was unable. I loved you, and hated all the strict etiquette and theatrical display with which I am bound to surround myself, merely because I chance to be born of an Imperial family. I married you, and, content in the knowledge that you loved me devotedly, I was prepared to renounce my name and live quietly with you always. But, alas! we of the Romanoffs are ruled by the head of our House, and our actions are ofttimes in obedience to the will of the Emperor. I was compelled to depart without revealing to you the secret of my birth."

"But why did you masquerade in that manner?" I inquired.

"At first I did so in order to avoid all the trammels of Court life in St Petersburg, the eternal gaiety of la Ville Lumière, and to be free to do what I liked and go where I chose," she answered. "Soon, however, my life as Ella Laing became a stern reality, for I met and loved you."

"Then you regretted?"

"I regretted only because I feared that I cared for you too much—that one day we should be compelled to part."

"You knew that it was impossible for you to renounce both title and position," I hazarded, looking at her gravely.

"I feared that my family would not allow me to do so," she answered frankly. "Yet you proposed marriage; we became man and wife, and the first weeks of our new life were full of joy and happiness. Soon, however, the Nemesis that I dreaded fell upon me, crushing all desire for life from my heart. I was compelled to fly and leave you in ignorance."

"And you forgot that in your escritoire there remained the stolen agreement?" I said slowly, looking straight into her pale face.

"Yes, I admit it," she replied, in a voice almost inaudible, her dry lips moving convulsively. "So full was my mind of thoughts of you that I did not remember it until too late to return and secure it."

"The woman who passed as Mrs Laing was not, of course, your mother?"

"She was no relation whatever. I paid her to pose as my maternal relative and keep house for me."

"Where is she now?"

"I have no idea," my wife answered. "She was a curious woman, and, strangely enough, she left London suddenly, on the very morning of the day of my departure."

"And what of Beck?" I asked. "Did he know who you really were?"

"Scarcely," she exclaimed. "Do you think he could have kept to himself the knowledge that I was a relative of the Tzar. Why, such a man would have related the fact that he knew me, and dined at our house, to every member of his club within twenty-four hours. You know, as well as I do, how he simply adores anybody with a title. It is the same with all the newly-wealthy crowd who are struggling to get into society."

It was upon my tongue to explain to her the truth regarding the man-servant who passed as Helmholtz; nevertheless, I hesitated to do so at present because of my promise to Paul Verblioudovitch. The silence between us was protracted. She had covered her tear-stained face with her hands, and was sobbing.

Nevertheless, I was not moved with pity. Her determination to preserve her secret filled me with annoyance. I had expected her to make confession, but I plainly saw she had no intention of revealing the truth.

"Why did you associate with a woman of such doubtful reputation as Sonia Korolénko?" I asked abruptly at last.

"Because I wished to ascertain something," she replied, in a harsh voice.

"She is scarcely your friend," I observed.

"She is," she declared. "I have known her for several years."

"And you were actually aware of her true character while associating with her!" I exclaimed, rather surprised.

"Of course," she sighed. "She is an adventuress, I know; nevertheless, she has proved my friend on many occasions."

"That's curious," I remarked.

"Why?"

"Because she made certain allegations against you," I answered.

"Yes," she said, without betraying either anger or surprise. "I am fully aware of that. Strange though it may appear, her statements were made with a definite object."

"Why did she utter such unfounded calumnies?"

"Because I wished to see whether you really loved me," she answered, drawing herself up and regarding me with sudden calmness. At that moment she assumed the air of the Grand Duchess.

"I did love you," I declared, "and I took no heed of her assertions. I notice, however," I added, turning and pointing towards the piano, "I notice that you have placed in a position of conspicuousness the portrait of the man she declared was your lover. Side by side you have placed the pictures of betrayer and betrayed."

She held her breath, gazing across to the spot I had indicated. Then, in a voice full of emotion, she said, —

"You were foully betrayed, Geoffrey, it is true, but the evil that was done has now been eradicated."

"In other words, Ogle has paid the death penalty, eh?" I observed, with a grim expression of satisfaction.

"No, no, not that," she protested seriously. "I mean that the strained relations between your country and mine have now been readjusted, and that a feeling more amicable than before prevails. Even the Earl of Warnham must admit the plain truth that no Power joins another in war unless it sees its own interest in so doing. Russia now, as before the effusion of hearts here in Paris, will attend to her own business, and will not send her Black Sea and Baltic Fleets flying out unless her interests bring her into collision with your British Government — and then it may happen it will not be the interest of France to fight. In the latter days of Louis Philippe there was talk of a Franco-Russian alliance, and there were people who knew—they did not think they knew on the best authority—that the two would be one next spring. Yet Louis Philippe went over to your England an exile by the useful name of Smith, and before long France and England were allied in war against my country. No, good counsel has prevailed, and by the very revelation of the secret alliance contracted between England and Germany, European peace has been secured."

"You talk like a diplomatist," I observed reflectively.

She shrugged her shoulders, and with a forced laugh said,—

"It is but natural that I should take an interest in the affairs of nations, I suppose."

"Let us put them aside," I said. "We are not rival diplomatists, but husband and wife; we—"

"Yes, yes," she cried, interrupting. "I am happy because you are here with me; you, whose presence I have been fearing for so long. See! I smile and am happy;" and she gave vent to a hollow, discordant laugh.

"Happy because you have so successfully mystified me," I sighed.

"No. Happy because I love you, Geoffrey," she exclaimed, again throwing her arms affectionately about my neck, and raising her full red lips to mine. "Forgive me; do say you will forgive me," she implored.

"How can I ever forget the ingenuity and deep cunning with which you deceived me," I said. "I cannot but recollect how, on that night at Chesham House, Grodekoff congratulated you upon your marriage, yet how careful he was not to disclose to me your identity. Again, even my friend Verblioudovitch must have known who you really were. Why did he not tell me?"

"Because the staff of the Embassy had already received strict orders from St Petersburg not to acknowledge me," she exclaimed, with a smile. "Lord Warnham fancied he recognised me, and spoke to the Ambassador; but the latter succeeded in assuring him that before marriage I was Ella Laing, and that the Grand Duchess Elizaveta Nicolayevna was at that moment with the Tzarina at Tzarskoïe-Selo. He believed it, and afterwards M'sieur Grodekoff assured me that was the first occasion he had been enabled to successfully deceive your lynx-eyed Foreign Minister."

"You feared that the Earl might recognise you," I exclaimed, surprised, for I now remembered the effect produced on my chief when his eyes had first fallen upon my wife. "You knew him, then?"

"Ah, no," she faltered; "well, we were not exactly acquainted," and she appeared rather confused, I thought, for her cheeks were suffused by the faintest suspicion of a blush.

"Did you expect he would be there?"

"No; you told me distinctly that he was not going, otherwise I should never have accompanied you," she said frankly.

"Why?"

"Because I did not desire to meet him," she replied, adding, with a laugh, "As it was, however, he was satisfied, and went away marvelling, no doubt, at the striking resemblance."

"Yet you told me nothing," I observed reproachfully.

"No; I was afraid," she replied, in a serious voice. "With you I lived on from day to day, fearing detection, dreading lest you should discover some facts regarding my past, and by their light believe me to be an adventuress. Yet, at the same time, I worked on to achieve my freedom from a yoke which had become so galling that, now I loved you, I could endure it no longer."

"And did you not succeed in breaking asunder this mysterious bond?" I inquired, half doubtfully.

"No," she answered, shaking her head sorrowfully. "By an untoward circumstance, against which I had not provided, I was prevented, and compelled to flee."

"If you will divulge absolutely nothing regarding the manner in which you became possessed of the stolen convention, or the reason you have masqueraded as my wife, you can at least tell me why you received so many communications regarding clandestine meetings, and explain who was your mysterious correspondent who signed himself 'X.'"

Her heart beat quickly; she sighed, and lowered her gaze. She strove to preserve a demeanour of calm hauteur as befitted her station, but in vain.

"You have also found those letters," she remarked, her voice trembling.

"Yes. Tell me the truth and put my mind at ease."

"I can put your mind entirely at ease by assuring you, as I did after you detected me walking in Kensington Gardens, that I have had no lover besides yourself, Geoffrey," she cried vehemently. "I have told you already that I worked to secure freedom of action in the future. Those letters were from one who rendered me considerable assistance."

"What was his name?" I demanded quickly.

"I may not tell you that," was her answer, uttered in a quiet, firm tone.

"Then, speaking plainly, you refuse, even now, to give me any elucidation whatever of this irritating mystery, or to allow me to obtain any corroboration of your remarkable story," I said, with a sudden coldness.

She noticed my change of manner, and clung to me with uplifted face, pale and agitated. Her attempt to treat me as other than her husband had utterly failed.

"Ah! do not speak so cruelly," she exclaimed, panting. "I—I really cannot bear it, Geoffrey—indeed I can't. You must have seen that I loved you. I was, when I married, prepared to sacrifice all for your sake; nay, I did sacrifice everything until—until I was forced from you, and thrust back here to this place, that to me is little else than a gilded prison. Ah?" she cried, sobbing bitterly, and gazing around her in despair, "you cannot know how deeply I have sorrowed, how poignant has been the grief in the secret and inmost recesses of my heart; or how, through these months, while I have been travelling, I have longed to see you once again, and hear your voice telling me of your love. But, alas! without knowledge of the strange secret that seals my lips, you can know nothing—nothing!"

"I only know that I still adore you," I said, with heartfelt fervency.

"Ah! I knew you did," she exclaimed, raising her eager lips to mine in ecstasy. "I knew you would pity me when you came, yet I feared—I feared because I had lied to you, and deceived you so completely." Then she kissed my lips, but I did not return her hot, passionate caress, although I confess it made my head reel.

"You have not forgiven," she exclaimed, in a voice quivering with emotion, as she drew back. "You have not yet promised that you will still regard me as your wife."

I hesitated. The startling fact of her true station, and the revelation of how ingeniously I had been tricked, caused me a slight revulsion of feeling. Somehow, as Grand Duchess she seemed an entirely different being to the plain, unassuming woman I had known as Ella. From the crown of her well-dressed hair to the point of her tiny, white kid shoe with its pearl embroidery, she was a patrician; the magnificence of her dress and jewels dazzled me, yet in her declarations of devotion her voice seemed to be marred by some indefinable but spurious ring.

Even now she was deceiving me. She would allow no word of her mysterious secret to pass her lips. It had always been the same. She would tell me absolutely nothing, vaguely asserting that to utter the truth would be to invoke an avenging power that she dreaded. I remembered how she had seemed terrorised on more than one occasion when I had demanded the truth, yet what I had learned that night increased my suspicions.

"If I forgive and seek no explanation of the past," I said at last, "we must, I suppose, remain parted."

"Ah, yes!" she gasped. "But only for a few short weeks. Then we will come together again never to part—never."

"I can forgive on one condition only," I said—"that you tell me the truth regarding the dastardly theft from me on the day of Dudley's death."

For an instant she was silent. Then, burying her face on my shoulder, sobbing, she answered in a tone so low as to be almost inaudible,—

"I cannot!"

Gently but firmly I put her from me, although she clung about my neck, urging me to pity her.

"I cannot pity you if you refuse to repose confidence in me," I answered.

"I do not refuse," she cried. "It is because my secret is of such a nature that, if divulged, it would wreck both your own happiness and mine."

"Then to argue further is absolutely useless," I answered coldly. "We must part."

"You intend to leave me without forgiveness," she wailed. "Ah, you will not be so cruel, Geoffrey. Surely you can see how passionately I love you."

"You do not, however, love me sufficiently well to risk all consequences of divulging your mysterious secret," I retorted, with almost brutal indifference, turning slowly from her.

"Then kiss me, Geoffrey," she cried wildly, springing towards me and again entwining her soft arms about my neck. "Kiss me once again—if for the last time."

Our lips met for an instant, then slowly I disengaged myself and strode towards the door. In her refusal to throw light upon the incidents that had so long held me perplexed and bewildered, I fancied she was shielding someone. Although crushed and downcast, I had resolved to go forth into the world again with my terrible burden of sorrow concealed beneath a smiling countenance. I regretted deeply that I had sought her, now that I was aware of the gulf that lay between us.

"Stay, Geoffrey! Stay. I cannot bear that you should go," she wailed.

Halting, I turned towards her, saying,—

"When I have learnt the truth, then only will I return. Till then, I can have no faith in you."

"But you are my husband, Geoffrey. I love you."

She tottered forward unevenly, as if to follow me, but ere I could save her she staggered and fell forward upon the carpet in a dead faint.

I rang the bell violently, then, with a final glance at the blanched features of the woman I so dearly loved, I passed out, struggling through the brilliant, laughing throng of guests in the great hall, and was soon alone in utter dejection beneath the trees in the long, gas-lit avenue.

Chapter Thirty
Honour among Thieves

In brilliant sunshine, with the larks singing merrily in the cloudless vault of blue, and the air heavy with the scent of hay, I drove from Horsham station along the old turnpike road to Warnham Hall. A carriage had been sent for me, as usual, and as I sat back moodily, I fear I saw little of interest in the typical English landscape. The joys of the world were dead to me, consumed as I was by the one great sorrow of my life. My mind was full of the tristful past. I had reached London from Paris on the previous night, and in response to a telegram from the Earl, saying he had left Osborne and gone to the Hall, I had travelled down by the morning train.

As we entered the park and drove up the broad, well-kept drive, the startled deer bounded away, and the emus raised their small heads with resentful, inquiring glance, but dashing along, the pair of spanking bays quickly brought me up to the great grey portico. As soon as I alighted I handed over my traps to one of the servants and walked straight to the great oak-panelled dining-room.

As I paused at the door, it suddenly opened, and a man emerged so quickly that he almost stumbled over me. Our eyes met. I stood aghast, staring as if I had seen an apparition. In the semi-darkness of the corridor I doubt whether my face was quite distinguishable, but upon his there shone the slanting rays of light from an old diamond-paned window. In a instant I recognised the features, although I had only seen them once before.

It was the foppish young man who had been Ella's companion on that lonely walk in Kensington Gardens.

Why he had visited the Earl was an inscrutable mystery. He regarded me in surprise for a single instant, then, thrusting both hands negligently into his trousers pockets, strode leisurely away along the corridor, a straw hat with black and white band placed jauntily at the back of his head. I watched him until he had turned the corner and disappeared, then I entered the great old-fashioned apartment.

"Well, Deedes!" exclaimed the Earl, in a voice that was unusually cheerful. He was standing at the window gazing across the park, but my presence caused him to turn sharply. "Back again, then?"

"Yes. I think I have fulfilled the mission," I managed to exclaim. Truth to tell, this extraordinary encounter had caused me considerable perplexity and annoyance.

"You have done excellently," he said. "A telegram this morning from Lord Worthorpe shows with what tact you put matters to him, and I am glad to tell you that his interview with the President proved entirely satisfactory. I wired the news to Her Majesty only half-an-hour ago."

"I did my best," I observed, perhaps a trifle carelessly, for there was another matter upon which I was anxious to consult my eccentric benefactor.

"The task was one of unusual difficulty, I admit, Deedes, and you have shown yourself fully qualified for a post abroad. You shall have one before long."

At other times I should have warmly welcomed the enthusiasm of this speech, and thanked him heartily for the promise of a more lucrative position, but now, crushed and hopeless, I felt that joy had left my soul for ever, and merely replied,—

"I am quite satisfied to be as I am. I do not care for the Continent."

"Why?" he inquired, surprised. "If you remain in the Service here you will have but little chance of distinguishing yourself, whereas in Rome, Constantinople or Berlin, you might obtain chances of promotion."

"I have been already in St Petersburg, you remember," I said.

"Ah, of course. But you didn't get on very well there," he said. "It is a difficult staff for younger men to work amongst. You'd be more comfortable in Vienna, perhaps. Viennese society would suit you, wouldn't it?"

"No," I replied, very gravely. "I fear that henceforward I shall be, like yourself, a hater of society and all its ways."

"Oh?" he exclaimed, placing his hands beneath his coat-tails, a habit of his when about to enter any earnest consultation. "Why?"

"Well, if you desire to know the truth," I said, "it concerns my marriage."

"Ah, of course!" he observed, with deep sorrow. "I had quite forgotten that unfortunate affair. Yet time will cause you to forget. You are young, remember, Deedes—very young, compared with an old stager like myself."

"It is scarcely likely that I shall forget so easily," I said, after a slight pause. "Since I have been in Paris I have made a discovery that has bewildered me.

I confide in you because you are the only person who knows the secret of my wife's flight."

"Quite right," he said, regarding me with those piercing eyes shaded by their grey shaggy, brows. "If I can assist you or give you advice I am always pleased, for the romance of your marriage is the strangest I have ever known."

"Yes," I acquiesced, "and the truth I have accidentally learnt still stranger. I have discovered that my wife was never Ella Laing, as I had believed, but that she really is the Grand Duchess Elizaveta Nicolayevna of Russia."

"The Grand Duchess!" he cried, amazed, his eyes aflame in an instant. "Are you certain of this; have you absolute proof?"

"Absolute. I have seen her, and she has admitted it, and told me that she masqueraded in England as Ella Laing because she desired to avoid Court etiquette for a time," I said.

"Grodekoff lied," he growled in an ebullition of anger. "I recognised her at the Embassy ball when you pointed her out, yet the Ambassador assured me that Her Highness was at that moment in Russia. We have both been tricked, Deedes. But he who laughs last laughs longest."

He had folded his arms and was standing resolutely before me, gazing upon the dead green carpet deep in thought.

"The mystery becomes daily more puzzling," he said at length, seating himself. "Tell me all that transpired between you."

I sank into a chair opposite the renowned chief of the Foreign Office and repeated the conversation that had taken place at our interview, while he listened attentively without hazarding a single remark.

"Then again she would tell you nothing," exclaimed the Earl, when I had concluded. "She refused absolutely to divulge her secret."

"Yes," I said. "I promised to forgive if she would only tell me the truth. She refused; so we have parted."

"And what do you intend doing?"

"I intend to seek the truth for myself," I answered with fierce resolve.

"How?"

"I have not yet decided," I said. "The reason she took such infinite pains to conceal her identity is incomprehensible, but her firm resolution to preserve her secret at all hazards appears as though she is in deadly fear of exposure by some person or other who can only be conciliated by absolute silence."

"Then we must discover who that person is."

I nodded, answering:—"I intend to do so."

Presently, after he had crossed and recrossed the room several times with hands behind his back, murmuring to himself in apparent discontent, but in tones that were undistinguishable, I turned to him saying,—

"As I entered, a visitor left you. Who is he?"

"Cecil Bingham. He is staying with me for a few days."

"A friend?"

"Well—yes," answered his Lordship, halting, and regarding me with no little surprise. "What do you know of him?"

At first I hesitated, but on reflection resolved to explain the circumstances in which we had met, and slowly related to him how I had encountered him with my wife in Kensington Gardens on that well-remembered wintry afternoon.

The Earl grew grave, and after observing that Bingham had arrived on the previous day to spend a week, he for some moments stood looking aimlessly out of the window upon the broad park and the great sheet of water glistening in the sunlight beyond. Then, muttering something I could not catch, he walked quickly back to the fireplace, and touched the electric bell.

"Ask Mr Bingham to see me for a moment," he exclaimed, when the man answered the summons, and in a few minutes the Earl's guest came in with that affected jaunty air that had caused me to class him as a cad.

When he had entered, the Earl himself walked to the door and softly closed it, then, turning, said in a hard, dry voice,—

"This, Cecil, is my secretary, Deedes, the husband of the woman known as Ella Laing, with whom you have, I understand, been in correspondence, and have met clandestinely on many occasions."

"What do you mean?" he cried, resentfully, glancing from the Earl to myself. "I know no one of that name. You are mistaken."

"There is no mistake," answered the great statesman, coldly, at the same time taking from an old oak bureau a large linen-lined envelope of the kind used in our Department. From a drawer he took one of his visitor's letters, while from the envelope he drew forth a second letter. At a glance I saw that the latter was one of those mysterious missives signed "X" that had been received by my wife. Opening both, he placed them together and handed them to me without comment.

They were in the same handwriting.

"Do you deny having written that letter?" asked the Minister, sternly, at the same time showing him the note. He made a motion to take it, but suddenly drew away his hand. His lips contracted, his face grew pale, and with a gesture of feigned contempt he waved the Earl's hand aside.

"Do you deny it?" repeated my chief.

He was still silent—his face a sufficient index to the agitation within him.

"You have endeavoured to deceive me," continued the Earl, harshly. "You have some fixed purpose in accepting my invitation, and coming here to visit me, but you were unaware that already I had knowledge of facts you have endeavoured so cunningly to conceal. It is useless to deny that you are acquainted with Deedes's wife, for he recognises you as having walked with her in Kensington Gardens, while I have ascertained at last who she really is—that her name was never Ella Laing."

He started at this announcement. His lips moved, but no word escaped him.

That the Earl should have learned the true name and station of my wife apparently disconcerted him. His complexion was of ashen hue; all his arrogance had left him, for he saw himself cornered. I stood glaring at him fiercely, for was not I face to face with the man whom my wife had met times without number, concealing from me all motive or duration of her absences? Some secret had existed between them—he was the man whom she apparently feared, and whose will she had obeyed. I felt that now, at last, I should ascertain the truth, and obtain a key to the strange perplexing enigma that had held me in doubt and suspicion through so many weary months.

His shifty gaze met mine; I detected a fierce glint in his eyes.

"Well?" exclaimed his Lordship, as determined as myself upon seeking a solution of the problem. "Now that you admit these mysterious meetings with Her Highness, perhaps you will explain their object."

"I admit nothing," he answered in anger, knitting his brows. "Neither have I anything to explain."

"See!" the Earl said, drawing Ella's photograph from the envelope. "Perhaps you will recognise this picture?" and his bony hand trembled with suppressed excitement as he placed it before him.

At sight of it my wife's strange friend drew a long breath. He was white to the lips. Never before had I witnessed such a complete change in any man in so short a period, and especially curious, it seemed, when I reflected that he had been charged with no very serious crime.

"You may allege whatever it may please you," he said at last, with affected sarcasm. "But a woman's honour is safe in my hands."

"My wife's honour!" I cried, with fierce indignation, walking towards him threateningly. I could no longer stand by in silence when I recollected what Ella had said about being compelled to act according to the will of another. She had, no doubt, been under the thrall of this overdressed dandy. "Now that we have met," I exclaimed, "you shall explain to me, her husband."

With a quick movement he strode forward as if to escape us, but in an instant I had gripped him by the shoulder with fierce determination, while the Earl himself, apprehending his intention, placed his back against the door.

"Speak!" I cried wildly, shaking him in my anger. "You shall tell us the true nature of the secret between you and my wife, and prove your statement to our satisfaction, or, by heaven, I'll thrash you as a cunning, cowardly cur!"

Chapter Thirty One
Due East

"Bah!" retorted the Earl's visitor, contemptuously, shaking himself free with a sudden twist, and standing before me in defiance. "I understand," he cried, glancing towards the elder man before the door. "You believe, gentlemen, that from me you can ascertain a key to certain curious occurrences that have puzzled you. But I may as well undeceive you at once. I can tell you absolutely nothing."

"But you shall tell us!" I cried, angrily. "I found you walking with my wife in Kensington Gardens, and followed you. It was apparent from her demeanour that she feared you."

He smiled sarcastically, and answered with a flippant air:

"Perhaps she did. If so, she certainly had cause."

"Why? What power do you hold over her, pray?" I demanded.

In his eyes was a mysterious glance. He was scarcely the brainless young dandy that I had imagined.

"It is hardly likely that I shall divulge to you a secret. Remember that your wife comes of one of the highest families in Europe, and the slightest breath of scandal must reflect upon them."

"At what scandal do you hint?" I asked, in fierce, breathless eagerness.

"At what is best kept quiet," he answered, gravely.

His enigmatical words maddened me. I felt that I could spring upon him and strangle him, for I knew instinctively that he was my wife's enemy—the man of whom she lived in deadly fear. If only I could silence him, she might then relate to me those long-promised facts.

"Then if you decline to prove that there is a concealed scandal, utter no more of your lying allegations," I blurted forth.

He bowed deeply with mock politeness, and smiled grimly.

"Come," exclaimed the Earl at last, in a conciliatory tone, advancing towards him and laying his hand upon his shoulder. "Let us get at once to the point. It is useless to quarrel. You decline to reveal to us the nature of your curious friendship with the Grand Duchess—eh?"

"I do," he answered, firmly.

"Well," said the tactful old Minister. "First carefully review the situation, and you will, I think, admit that I have been your friend. And how have you shown your gratitude?"

"By concealing from you a truth both hideous and terrible," he replied, with apparent unconcern.

"But you can, if you will, give us some clue to this remarkable chain of circumstances. I appeal to you on behalf of Deedes, her husband," the old man said.

"I am well aware of the reason you yourself desire to know the absolute truth, Lord Warnham," he answered, after a brief pause, "but, unfortunately, I am unable to tell you, because of certain promises having been extracted from me."

"At least you can tell us from whom I may ascertain the true facts," I cried.

He looked at me for an instant gravely, then answered in all seriousness:

"The only person who knows the truth is Sonia Korolénko, the refugee."

"Sonia!" gasped the Earl. "That woman is not in England, surely?"

"I think not," Bingham replied. "But if you would ascertain the key to the enigma, seek her, and she may explain everything. That is as far as I can assist you. Remember, I myself have revealed nothing."

"She has returned to Russia," I observed. "Have you any knowledge where she is?"

"No, there are reasons why her whereabouts should remain unknown," he answered, hesitatingly. "She is in fear of the police."

"Do her friends know of her hiding-place?"

"No. A short time ago I desired to communicate with her, but was unable. The last I heard of her was that she was living at Skerstymone, a little town somewhere in Poland."

"If she can successfully elude the vigilance of the Russian police, I can have but little hope of finding her," I said, doubtfully.

"Make the attempt, Deedes," the Earl suggested. "I will give you leave of absence."

"I intend to do so," I replied; and remembering my wife, lonely amid all her splendour, I added, "The elucidation of the mystery is, as it has long since been, the main object of my life."

In consultation we sat a long time. This caddish young man of whom I had been so madly jealous had now grown quite calm and communicative, apparently ready to render me all assistance; yet to my questions regarding my wife he was as dumb as others had been. Now, more than ever, the Earl seemed anxious to solve the strange problem. With that object he obtained from the library a section of the large ordnance map of the Russian Empire, and with it spread before us we discovered that Skerstymone was a little place remotely situated on the bank of the Niemen river, within a short distance of the German frontier. I had long ago learned from Paul Verblioudovitch that my friend, the well-known adventuress, had crossed the frontier at Wirballen, or Verjbolovo, as it is called in Russian; but after that I knew nothing of her movements. Bingham seemed anxious to lead me indirectly towards the truth, and after assuring me with a firm hand-grasp that the secret that existed between himself and my wife was of a purely platonic nature, and that he had throughout acted on her behalf, I ate a hasty luncheon and again left the Hall on the first stage of my long, tedious journey across Europe. As I entered the carriage the old Earl and his guest stood out upon the gravelled drive and heartily wished me "Bon voyage," and, waving them farewell, I was whirled away through the great park that lay silent and breathless beneath the scorching sun.

At the bookstall at Horsham station I bought an early edition of the *Globe*, and on opening it in the train my eyes fell upon the following announcement in its "Court and Personal" column, —

"A marriage is arranged, and will shortly take place between Mr Andrew Beck, the Member for West Rutlandshire, who is well-known in connection with African mines, and Miss Gertrude Millard, only daughter of Sir Maynard Millard, Bart, of Spennythorpe Park, Montgomeryshire."

This was not exactly unexpected, for I had already heard vague rumours that news of Beck's engagement would shortly be made public, therefore I tore out the paragraph and placed it in my pocket-book, with the reflection that my friend's marriage might be more happy than mine.

That evening about six o'clock I called at Chesham House, the Russian Embassy, and obtained the signature of the Ambassador, Monsieur Grodekoff, to my passport. I did not, however, see Verblioudovitch, he being absent at Brighton, therefore I left the same evening for Flushing, and after a long and wearisome ride across Germany duly arrived at Verjbolovo, one of the principal gates of the great Russian Empire. The formalities troubled me but little, for I had passed the frontier on several occasions when stationed in St Petersburg. After getting my passport stamped I strolled up and down the platform gazing about over the flat, uninteresting country, contemplatively smoking a cigarette, and watching the crowd of tired, worried travellers experiencing the ways of Russian officialdom for the first time. Among them was an elderly Russian lady who, travelling with her three daughters, good-looking girls, ranging from eighteen to twenty-three, had omitted to have her passport viséd by a Russian Consul outside the Empire. So stringent were the regulations that, although they were subjects of the Tzar returning to their own country, the officer would not allow them to proceed, and all four were detained while the passport was sent back to the nearest Russian consul in Germany to be "treated."

At first it had occurred to me to travel on to St Petersburg, and there endeavour to learn from a police official of my acquaintance whether Sonia Korolénko had been heard of lately, but on reflection I saw that every precaution would no doubt be taken by her in order that the police should not be made aware of her presence in Russian territory. A strange vagary of Fate it seemed that through my own action in obtaining for her a false passport she had been enabled to escape, and that my own endeavours had actually thwarted my own ends. As I paced the railway platform, with the brilliant afterglow shedding a welcome light across that dead level country so zealously-guarded by the green-coated sentries in their black and white striped boxes, and Cossack pickets, each with his "nagaika" stuck in his boot, I remembered with failing heart how this woman, whose fame was notorious throughout Europe, had told me that once past this portal of the Tzar's huge domain all traces of her would be obliterated completely. This fact in itself convinced me that she had never intended to travel direct to St Petersburg, and it became impressed upon me that in order to trace her it would be necessary to first visit the little out-of-the-world town of Skerstymone, that was situated a long way to the north along the frontier. With that object I allowed the St Petersburg express to proceed, and after an hour's wait entered a local train, alighting at a small town euphoniously termed Pilwiszki, where I spent the night in an exceedingly uncomfortable inn.

Next day I learnt with satisfaction that this town was situated on the main post-road between Maryampol and Rossieny, and that about thirty miles due north along this road was Skerstymone. The innkeeper, at an exorbitant figure, provided me with a rickety old cart and a pair of shaggy horses, driven by an uncouth-looking lad, wearing an old peaked cap so large that his brow and eyes were hidden. An hour before noon I set out upon my expedition. Our way lay across the boundless Nawa steppe, a plain which stretched away as far as the eye could reach without a single tree to break its monotony, until at a wretched little village called Katyle we forded a shallow stream, the Penta, and presently passed through the town of Szaki. Soon afterwards the road became full of deep ruts that jolted us terribly, and for many miles we travelled through a pine forest until at last we found ourselves at the ferry before Skerstymone.

In the mystic light of evening the place, standing on the opposite bank of the Niemen, presented a novel and rather picturesque aspect, with its wooden houses, their green and brown roofs of painted sheet-iron, but when landing from the ferry I was soon undeceived. It was one of those towns best seen from a distance. The dirt and squalor were horrible. For a fortnight I remained at the wretched little inn making inquiries in all quarters, but could hear nothing of the pretty dark-eyed girl who had earned such unenviable notoriety, and who in Vienna spent such an enormous sum in a single year that her extravagance had become proverbial, even in that most reckless of cities. That she had been here was certain from what Bingham had told us, and somehow I had an instinctive feeling that here the dainty-handed refugee had assumed a fresh identity, it being dangerous for her to proceed further into Russia, so well-known was she. Therefore, with fixed determination, I still prosecuted my inquiries everywhere, until I found the police regarding me with considerable mistrust, for the officers of public order are everywhere ubiquitous in the giant empire of the Tzar.

The hot July sun shone on the dusty streets; through the open windows of the white-washed barrack-like Government office the scratching of pens could be heard; the "factors," agents who offer their services to strangers, lolled in the shade, keeping a watchful eye upon any stranger who might happen to pass by, and looking out eagerly for a "geschäft," or stroke of business. The townspeople eyed me distrustfully as I wandered aimlessly about the streets, where tumble-down hovels alternated with endless expanses of grey moss-grown wood fences and plots of waste ground heaped with rubbish and offal. The place was full of horrible smells, filth, rags, and dirty children, who enjoyed themselves by rolling in the soft white dust. At either end of the noisy, evil-smelling place, a post-road led out along the bank of the sluggish yellow stream, and at the entrance to the town on the German side was a "schlagbaum," a pole painted with the national colours that served as toll-bar, in charge of a sleepy invalided soldier in a dingy old uniform with a tarnished eagle on his cap, who looked the very incarnation of undisturbed slumber.

Life in Kovno was by no means diverting. Truly Skerstymone was a wretched, half-starved, miserable little place of terribly depressing aspect, notwithstanding the brilliant sunshine and blue sky.

The long, gloomy days dragged by, but no tidings could I glean of Sonia Korolénko. It was evident that if she had ever been there she had passed under some other name, and that her identity had been lost before arrival there.

One warm morning, while seated outside a "kabák" moodily watch·ng the old women in the market selling their twisted rolls of bread called "kalách," an ill-dressed man approached me, and, touching his shabby cap respectfully, pronounced my name with strong Russian accent, at the same time slowly sinking upon the wooden bench beside me. He was tall and square-built, with coarse but expressive features. His long grey hair was matted and unkempt; his low brow, protruding jaws, and the constant twitching of his facial muscles reminded me of a monkey, but the stern eyes shining from beneath a pair of bushy, overhanging brows, spoke of indomitable energy, cleverness, and cunning. They never changed; and while the rest of his face was a perfect kaleidoscope whenever he spoke, the expression of his eyes remained ever the same.

His confidence surprised me, and I immediately asked him how he had ascertained my patronymic, to which he replied, not without hesitation,—

"I am fully aware of your high nobility's object in visiting Skerstymone. You are seeking Sonia Korolénko."

"Yes," I replied, in the best Russian I could remember. "Do you know her whereabouts? If you take me to her you shall have a handsome reward."

He smiled mysteriously, and glanced so wistfully at my vodka that I at once ordered for him a second glass of the spirit so beloved of the Muscovite palate.

"Is your high nobility well acquainted with Sonia!"

I replied in the affirmative, offering him a cigarette from my case. At last I had found one who had met the dark-eyed girl of whom I was in search.

"You know her," I said. "Where is she?"

"In hiding."

"Far from here?"

"Well, not very," he answered. "I could take you to her this very night— if you made it worth my while."

"Why not in daylight?" I inquired.

"Because the frontier-guards are here in swarms."

Then, in reply to my questions, he admitted that he was one of those who obtained his living by smuggling contraband goods and persons without passports across the frontier into and out of Germany. Along the whole of the Russo-German frontier there are bands of peasantry who live by smuggling emigrants, Jews, malefactors, and others who have no permit to leave the country, across into Germany by certain by-paths that remain unguarded, notwithstanding the constant vigilance of the military.

"And what is Sonia doing at present?" I inquired, after he had frankly related to me his position in a low tone so that we might not be overheard by any eavesdropper or police spy.

"She has always been a leader," he answered, laughing gaily. "She is so still."

"A leader of smugglers!" I exclaimed, surprised that the pretty girl who had been admired in every capital in Europe should adopt such a hazardous, reckless life.

"Well, yes, if you choose to call it so," he said, rather resentfully, I thought. "We merely assist our countrymen to escape the police, and they pay toll for our aid," he added. "She heard you were inquiring for her, here in Skerstymone, and has sent me as messenger to take you to her. She fears to come herself."

I looked steadily at the man, and saw for the first time that, although a moujik, he was nevertheless a sturdy adventurer, whose brow was deeply furrowed by hardship.

"And you wish me to pay toll like the others?" I exclaimed with a smile.

"If we act as guide we are surely entitled to something. There are many risks," he answered, puffing at his cigarette, afterwards examining it with the air of a connoisseur.

"How much?"

"The high nobility is rich," he replied. "He was once at the English Embassy in St Petersburg. Let us say two hundred roubles."

"Two hundred, to be paid only in Sonia's presence," I acquiesced eagerly. Truth to tell, I would have paid five hundred, or even a thousand for safe conduct to her.

"It's a bargain," he answered, draining his glass. "Meet me to-night at ten o'clock at this place. I hope you are a good walker, for we must travel by the secret paths. The post-road would mean arrest for me; it might also go rather hard with you to be found in my company."

"I can walk well," I answered. "To-night at ten."

Then I ordered more vodka, and after drinking success to our midnight journey, he rose and left me, bending a good deal as he shuffled along the street in his old frieze overcoat many sizes too large for him.

In any other circumstances I should have looked upon this devil-may-care, shock-headed adventurer with gravest suspicion, for his face was of distinctly criminal physiognomy, and his speech was that of one utterly unscrupulous. Yet when I remembered the allegations that Sonia, the woman who lured the young Prince Alexis Gazarin to his death, was an associate of the most desperate thieves in Europe, the fact that she had sent him as messenger seemed by no means remarkable. From what he had told me it was apparent that this girl, whose beauty had brought her renown and held her victims fascinated, had returned to her own country and become leader of a desperate band of nomads who drove a thriving trade by guiding fugitives from justice out of the Tzar's dominions, and importing from Germany dutiable articles of every description.

Sonia's offences against the law did not, however, trouble me much. I only desired to ascertain from her the truth regarding my wife, the Grand Duchess, and in order to meet her was prepared for any risk.

Thus I placed myself in the hands of this villainous-looking rascal whose name I did not know, and who had come to me entirely without credentials. My natural caution warned me that from every point of view my midnight expedition was fraught with considerable danger, yet thoughts of my sad-eyed wife whom I so dearly loved aroused within me a determination to ascertain some key to the enigma, and I was therefore resolved to accompany the unkempt stranger in face of any peril.

Chapter Thirty Two
On the Frontier

The first hour of our walk in the bright balmy night proved fresh and pleasant after the stifling malodorous town. My unknown guide was, I soon discovered, a typical gaol-bird, the fact being made plain by the scanty growth of hair on one side of his head revealed when he inadvertently removed his cap to wipe his brow with his dirty hand. His strong knee-boots were well-patched, but he was out at elbow, and his moustache and matted beard sadly wanted trimming. He kept his appointment to the moment, and declining my invitation to drink, we set off together, ascending the low hill behind the town, and taking a circuitous route back to the river bank. By no means devoid of a sense of humour, he strode along jauntily, laughing, joking, and making light of any risk of capture, until I began to regard him with less suspicion. That he was no ordinary moujik was certain, for he spoke of life and people in Moscow, in Nijni, and even in Petersburg, his conversation showing a more intimate acquaintance than could be acquired by mere hearsay. Our way at first was through narrow lanes of dirty wooden houses, where the foetid odours of decaying refuse greeted our nostrils; then, leaving the town, we ascended through some cornfields until, suddenly descending again, we came to where the Niemen flowed onward between its sedgy banks, its placid bosom a sheet of silver beneath the light of the full moon.

Fully three miles we trudged along the post-road beside the river, passing a solitary little hamlet. Not a soul stirred, not a dog barked. The place seemed uninhabited. Now and then we passed a country cart driven by some sleepy peasant who had imbibed too freely of vodka, until we came to where a striped verst-post stood at the junction of another narrower highway.

"That's the road to Jurburg, and to the frontier at Poswentg," my companion remarked, in reply to my enquiry. "It's too dangerous for us."

"Why?"

"It swarms with frontier-guards," he answered, with a low laugh. "We have no desire to encounter any of these gentlemen this evening, therefore we must presently take to the paths. See!" and he nodded upward to the sky, "The tail of the Great Bear points downwards. We shall have luck to-night."

"Is this the route you take with the fugitives?" I asked, pausing to take breath, and gazing around upon the lovely scene, for here the moonlit river flowed among its osiers and rushes, across the great grass-covered steppe.

"Yes," he answered. "This is the only portion of our journey where there are serious risks of detection, so let us hurry. On a bright night like this, a man can be seen a long way off. The guards are too fond of hiding along the banks, fearing that any German boats from Endruszen may creep up the river."

I started forward again, and we both quickened our pace. I now saw from his demeanour that he feared an encounter, for at each unusual sound he paused, his hand uplifted in silence. At last, at a point where the stream made a sudden bend, we left the river road and plunged into a great marsh, where the reeds grew almost as high as ourselves, and where our feet ever and anon sank deep into chill, slimy mud. As soon as we had left the river, my strange guide became as jovial as before, and spoke entirely without restraint. Fear of detection no longer troubled him, for as we held on our way over the soft clay, the silence of the calm night was now and then broken by his coarse laughter. On that flat, marshy land, each step became hampered by huge cakes of yellow mud that clung to our boots, while often I sank with a splash ankle-deep in water, much to my companion's amusement. Whistling softly to himself, he laughed at all misfortunes, assuring me that we should very soon find drier ground, and that before dawn I should meet Sonia Korolénko, who was awaiting me.

"She is your leader—eh?" I asked.

"Well, of course," he answered, with a grim smile. In the moonlight he looked a shaggy, evil-faced ruffian, and more than once, when I remembered that I had upon me a good round sum in notes and gold, I regretted that I had trusted myself with him unarmed. "The police drove her from Vienna, from Paris, from London; so she has come to us."

"And is yours a paying profession?" I asked interested.

"Generally," he answered, with that frankness that characterised all his conversation. "You'd be surprised how many people seek our assistance. Some of our party are in St Petersburg, Moscow, and Warsaw, and make the contracts with the fugitives; then they hand them over to us, and we do the rest."

"You guarantee to put them on German soil, or bring foreigners into Russia for a fixed sum?"

"Yes. You would open your eyes if you knew some of the people I've guided over this very path. Sometimes it is a Jew peasant who has no permit, and desires to emigrate to London, or to America; at others, an escaped prisoner, a murderer, or a revolutionist, who is being tracked down by the Security Section. We always know why they are leaving Russia, and make them pay accordingly. Not long ago I brought a young titled lady across here; accompanied her into Germany, and put her into the train for Berlin. We had a narrow shave of being captured, but she gave me a thousand roubles when we parted."

"Why did she want to leave secretly?" I asked.

"She had poisoned her husband somewhere down in Minsk, and the police were in search of her," he laughed. "Never a night passes, but one or other of us cross the frontier."

"And you find it an adventurous game—eh?"

"Well, it is pleasant after ten years of Siberia," he answered grimly. "I let loose the red rooster and burned down the barin's house in a village in Tver. He well deserved it. I and two friends got away with his money and jewels to Moscow, but one night, a week later, I had an appointment to meet my companions opposite the fountain in the Lubyansky Square, and was arrested."

"And you got ten years?"

"They made out that the barin got burned to death, so I was packed off for life to Kara. After ten years I managed to escape and become a 'cuckoo.' Then after a year's wandering I succeeded in returning to Moscow, where I found one or two old friends, and we started together in this business. We don't intend to fall into the drag-net of the police again," he added with a sardonic grin, at the same moment drawing from his trousers pocket a big army revolver.

"Do the frontier-guards ever trouble you?"

"Sometimes," he laughed. "When we meet we always show fight. Three were killed in a brush with some of our party not long ago. It will teach them not to interfere with us for a little time."

Long ago I had heard of a gang of desperate characters who made the strip of zealously-guarded territory between Germany and Russia a terror to travellers, and the utter loneliness of the dismal place, and the swaggering demeanour of my evil-faced companion increased my mistrust.

We left the swamp shortly afterwards, and strode out again across the boundless undulating steppe that stretched away as far as the eye could reach. The moon had sunk lower in the sky, and a whitish cloud appeared in the zenith which seemed to shine with a phosphorescent light. Our trackless path wound between low shrubs, and then, after another hour's weary, lonely plodding across the grass-covered plain, we came to a clump of trees where the underwood was thick and tangled.

I paused for a moment to gaze behind at the great expanse of flat, uncultivated, uninhabited country we had traversed. A mystery seemed to plane over the boundless steppe. The night wind played among the dry grasses, and sad thoughts awakened in my soul.

Hist!... there was a slight rustling! A reddish fur gleamed in the moonlight so close to me that I could see the ears of a fox and its bushy tail sweeping the ground. It disappeared between the trees, and my heart beat faster as together we went forward, bursting through the underwood. The twigs struck me in the face; I stumbled, gasped for breath, and halted. The wail of a night bird broke the silence.

At that moment I saw my companion bending at the foot of a solitary tree that stood alone amid the tangled undergrowth. There was a hole in its trunk from which he drew forth something and placed it hastily in his pocket. Then, turning towards me, he took out a cigarette and calmly lit it, saying, —

"We have nothing now to fear."

He allowed the match to burn much longer than was absolutely necessary. Instantly the thought flashed upon me that this light might be a signal to some of his nefarious companions.

But together we went forward again; he jovial and amusing, I moody and thoughtful. His actions had aroused my suspicions. I glanced at my watch, and in the dim light distinguished that it was just past two o'clock. We had already been walking four hours.

Presently, chattering and laughing as we proceeded, we left the wide rolling steppe and plunged into a great wood. The forest was still as death. The moss-grown fir trees stretched out their huge arms as they waved slowly to and fro like funeral plumes. Little light penetrated there, but now and then we could see the bright stars between the branches as we went along a narrow winding track, the intricacies of which were apparently well-known to my guide, for he went onward with the firm, confidential tread of one who know the path, while I followed him closely, the dead branches crackling beneath our feet.

Once or twice a noise fell upon his quick ear, and we halted, he standing revolver in hand in an attitude of defence. Each time, however, we ascertained that we had no occasion for alarm, the noise being made by some animal or bird startled by our sudden intrusion. Then we resumed our midnight journey in single file.

During half an hour we proceeded, he leading the way, directing his footsteps by marks upon the trunks of the trees, so near the ground that they would have escaped the notice of any but those who knew of their whereabouts.

Once I thought I detected a dark figure between the trees, and fearing that it might be one of the sentries, whispered a word of warning to my guide, but he reassured me by telling me that we were skirting the frontier outside guarded territory, therefore there could be no danger. Nevertheless, as he turned to me, I thought his furrowed face looked darker, and his teeth gleamed whiter than usual.

We walked on. The forest was silent, save for the soft whisper of the pines. Without uttering any word I was following closely the footsteps of my guide, when suddenly, how it occurred I know not, I was conscious of being stopped dead by my evil-faced companion, who, with a quick movement, brought up his ready revolver to a level with my head.

Fate had played me an ugly trick. One thought remained uppermost in the chaos of wild, feverish fancies that seized me—the thought of the woman who was my wife.

Chapter Thirty Three
Bad Company

"Well," I managed to ejaculate, standing quite still, without moving a muscle. I saw that his attitude was one of determination, and that he had been joined by a ruffianly-looking companion who had emerged from the undergrowth as if by magic.

My only thought was of my past life. How had I been able to bear the suspicion and suspense so long? I had borne it because the star of hope had glimmered in the darkness. And now the star had vanished, and the hope was dead. Darkness had fallen upon my soul, and a storm arose within it like the chill whirling wind that swept across the steppe at dead of night. I could not think; I forgot where I was, forgot everything except my anger. My heart was full of blind despair.

I was conscious that the gaol-bird spoke. He was demanding my money, and threatening to put a bullet through my head if I refused.

"I promised you money on condition that you took me to Sonia Korolénko," I answered. "I am ready to pay when you have fulfilled your part of the contract."

Both men laughed heartily.

"We have no knowledge of her," declared the man who had been my guide. "All we know is that you have money; if you don't hand it to us quietly your grave will be in yonder heap of dead leaves."

"He'll be company for the others," observed the man with a fox-like countenance, who had joined us, and was leaning upon an old Berdan rifle.

"Then I understand you have brought me here, to this spot, on a false pretence. You mean to rob me?" I said. "You assured me that you were Sonia's messenger, and so implicitly did I trust you, that I left my revolver behind at the inn."

"That is no affair of ours," answered the old scoundrel, shrugging his shoulders unconcernedly. "Hand us over your money, and we are ready to guarantee you safe conduct, either on into Germany or back to Skerstymone."

"I'll pay you nothing, not even a rouble, na vódkou, until you take me to your leader," I answered defiantly, for somehow I had from the first been convinced of the truth of the man's assertion that Sonia was in that neighbourhood.

"As we are unable to conduct you to the lady, whoever she is, we shall therefore be compelled to use violence," observed my guide, glancing at his companion, who nodded approvingly. Then, still holding the muzzle of his weapon to my face, he added with brutal frankness: "You'd better make the sign of the cross now, if you want to. It will be the last chance you'll get. When a man's dead and buried he can tell the police nothing."

Well I knew the desperate character of these brigandish nomads, and fully recognised that they were not to be trifled with.

"The people who come to us for aid never get across the frontier unless they part with their money first," he continued. "If they don't—well, we put them to rest quietly and unceremoniously, and give them decent burial. A good many of all sorts, rich and poor, lie buried in these woods. You asked me whether it was a paying profession," he laughed. "Judge for yourself."

He still spoke with that unaffected carelessness that had impressed me when we had first met outside the dingy little "tractir" in Skerstymone.

"Come," cried the ragged, fox-faced man, impatiently, with an accent of South Russia. "We have no time to waste; we have many versts before us ere dawn."

"Then you'd better be off, and leave me to find my way back as best I can," I said, endeavouring to preserve an outward show of calmness.

Some noise, so faint that I did not distinguish it, caused both outlaws to hold their breath and listen. They exchanged quick glances. They had wandered thousands of versts across the "taiga" and the steppe, and constantly on the alert to evade Cossack patrols and police, knew every sound of the forest. They had learnt to know the voice of the wood; the speech of every tree. The great firs rustle with their thick boughs, the dark, gloomy pines whisper to one another in mystery, the bright green leafy trees wave their dewy branches, and the mountain-ash trembles with a noise like a faintly rippling brook. They knew, to their disgust, too, how those spies of the frontier, the magpies, hover in crowds over the track of the man who tries in daylight to creep unseen across the bare open steppe.

It was evident that the noise had for an instant puzzled them; yet, after listening a moment, both became reassured, and re-demanded with many violent threats whatever money I had upon me.

"I tell you I refuse," I answered. "If you take me to Sonia you shall have two hundred roubles each, with twenty more na vódkou."

"Then you do not wish to live?" exclaimed the man who had so cunningly entrapped me.

"I will give you nothing," I said resolutely.

"Then take that!" he cried, wildly, and at the same time his revolver flashed close to my face.

The shot echoed far away among the myriad tree trunks, but the bullet passed harmlessly by my ear.

Ere he could fire a second time I sprang upon him, and clutching him by the throat with one hand, with the other grasped the wrist of the sinewy hand that held the revolver. It was a struggle for life.

Again my antagonist drew the trigger, but the weapon was exploded in mid-air. Then his companion flung himself upon me in an endeavour to drag me off. This he was unable to do, and, apparently, fearing lest I should succeed in wresting the weapon from his accomplice's grasp and use it against him, he sought to stun me by raining blows with his clenched fist upon my head.

A third time the ruffianly assassin's revolver went off with loud report, but doing no harm. At that moment, however, I was conscious that my strength was failing me. I was muscular, but against this pair of hulking brutes I had no chance in a contest of mere physical power.

The repeated blows upon my skull dazed me, but hearing shouts resounding in the darkness, I held on with grim, dogged courage, with the faint hope that they might be Cossacks. In the dim light I could distinguish figures moving rapidly beneath the trees. The forest seemed suddenly alive with men, but at that instant the fox-faced ruffian, finding his efforts unavailing, stepped back a pace or two, and lowering his rifle, took deliberate aim at my breast.

I closed my eyes tightly and held my breath.

A shot rang out, followed by a burst of wild shouting, but finding myself unharmed, I opened my eyes again. In terror I glanced up, and saw my fox-faced assailant lying face downward. The cowardly villain had evidently been shot at the very instant he had covered me with his Berdan.

Half-a-dozen men sprang forward, and wrenching the revolver from the scoundrel who had attempted to take my life, seized him in their strong grasp, while I, breathless and exhausted, struggled up from my knees, amazed at my sudden and unexpected delivery.

Some twenty men, an ill-dressed, ruffianly crowd, in patched cloaks and dirty grey caps covering their long hair, surrounded me, talking excitedly, bestowing opprobrious epithets upon the man who lay wounded and groaning, and as I turned suddenly in wonder, I was confronted by a peasant woman in a short skirt of some dark stuff, an ill-fitting striped bodice, with a handkerchief tied about her head.

She uttered my name. In an instant I recognised her. It was Sonia.

"I arrived only just in time to save you," she explained, half breathlessly, in English. "The shots attracted us. That villain, Stepanovitch, whom I sent into Skerstymone to bring you here, no doubt intended to take your money and decamp, but, fortunately, we caught him redhanded. He has long been suspected of doing away with people entrusted to his care for conduct across the frontier, but I never believed him capable of treating any of our friends as victims."

"He fired at me point-blank," I said, "although I was unarmed."

"What shall we do with him, little mother?" cried the excited crowd of burly malefactors, dragging the man before the notorious woman, with pleasant countenance, sonorous voice, and lively manners, whom they acknowledged as leader.

"Tie him up to yonder tree and let him be shot," answered Sonia, pointing out a lofty pine. "Pick a marksman from among yourselves, and do not shout so loudly. Only one shot must be fired, for I believe the guards are lurking about to-night, and more may attract them."

With yells of execration the crowd hurried away the unfortunate wretch who had so treacherously treated the friend of their leader, and ere a couple of minutes had elapsed he had been secured to the tree. Then they commenced haggling among themselves as to who should fire the fatal shot. It was a weird scene, this summary justice directed by a woman. The choice fell at last upon a tall hulking fellow in ragged coat and a hat of dirty sheepskin, who, addressed by the nickname of "The Goat," on account of the shape of his beard, lifted his gun with a jeering remark at the cowering wretch, and stepped back to take more deliberate aim.

"No," I cried, "don't let him be shot on my account, Sonia. Give him his life."

She shook her head, saying simply: "He betrayed my trust."

"I ask you to forgive him," I urged. "At least grant me this favour."

She was undecided, and the outlaws hearing us speak in English, called to their tall champion to stay his hand.

"Very well," she said, at last. "I forgive him because you plead."

Without a word I pushed past the men surrounding us, and, taking out my pocket-knife, severed the cord holding the terrified wretch. The old scoundrel, dropping upon his knee, kissed my hand amid the loud jeers of his rough, brutal companions, then regaining his feet, took off his cap, and looking towards heaven, made the sign of the cross.

"This, I hope, will be a lesson, Stepanovitch," exclaimed Sonia, sternly, in Russian, advancing towards him. "I forgive you only because of the request of this Englishman. Remember in future that the person of any friend of mine, or any of our brothers, is sacred."

"Yes, I will, matóushka," answered the old villain, penitently. "That I will. I owe my life to his high nobility's intercession. I will not again offend, little mother."

"Very well," she answered, abruptly; then, briefly explaining how they had just returned from a hazardous trip across the frontier, during which they were detected and followed by a Cossack picket, she gave the order to return home, and we moved forward in single file along the narrow secret paths which wound with so many intricacies through the dark, gloomy forest. As I walked behind her we chatted in English, she telling me how she had been compelled to leave London unexpectedly, and relating how she had fared since we had last met. She, however, made no mention of the nefarious trade she had adopted, and I hesitated to refer to it.

When at length we emerged from the forest, the wounded man being assisted along by his companions, it was near morning. The darkness had gradually become less intense, the stars shone more faintly, and a streak of dawn showed on the far-off horizon. The pale light revealed grassy plains as far as the eye could reach, and the fresh morning breeze swept softly over the thick, green grass that promised an abundant hay crop, such as the dwellers on the broad Kovno plains had longed for for many years. Soon after leaving the forest, however, the party separated, arranging as meeting-place, when the moon rose on the morrow, the third verst-post out of Wezajce, a small village five miles distant. All her associates, Sonia explained, lived in villages in the vicinity, scattering themselves in order to avoid detection by the authorities. The villagers themselves, although well aware of their doings, said nothing. To all inquiries by Cossack frontier-guards or police spies they remained dumb, for the simple reason that while contraband trade could be transacted the village thrived, each of these small, wretched little places receiving indirectly a portion of the outlaws' profit. In summer there were no empty barns or thistle-grown threshing floors, and in winter the stoves in the huts were always burning, and the "borstch," or soup, was never without its proper proportion of buck-wheat gruel.

Many were the rumours of missing travellers and violent deaths in that neighbourhood, but the villagers feared nothing from this adventurous gang, who had grown more bold now that they were led by their "little mother." From what I gathered from my fair companion as we pushed forward together towards the dim line of trees that bounded the steppe in the direction of the sunrise, it appeared that the band had been in existence for several years, but that a few months before, the leader, a well-known escaped convict, was shot dead by a picket while creeping by day across the Zury steppe, and that a proposal had been sent to her at Skerstymone, where she was hiding, that she should become their head. She admitted, with a smile, that the men who had just left us to return to their various occupations were all of bad character, and that, almost without exception, all had served long terms of imprisonment for robbery or murder.

"But is not the assassination of those who have paid for guidance into Germany quite unjustifiable?" I exclaimed, reproachfully, as we walked side by side across the long, dewy grass.

"How can I prevent it!" she asked. "I do all I can to preserve the lives of our clients, but with men of their stamp it is impossible to stop it. Nearly every one of the brotherhood would slit a throat with as little compunction as lighting his cigarette: first, because it avoids the risk of crossing the boundary, and secondly, because of the money the victim has in his pockets. Again, persons who accept our escort are not those persons after whom any inquiry is made. When they are missed, their friends naturally conclude they've fallen into the hands of the police, or have escaped abroad and fear to write. Stepanovitch, for instance, does not obtain the rolls of notes he sometimes has by importing contraband goods, neither could he afford to keep a snug house down in Ludwinow, where he spends the winter, and is regarded as a highly respectable member of the Mir."

"He is an assassin, then?"

Sonia smiled and shrugged her shoulders.

We were approaching a small village with a background of high pine trees, situated on the edge of the great treeless plain. Its name was Sokolini, she told me. Once, in the days of serfdom, it had been the property of a landowner, but now, enjoying liberty, its emancipation was attested by its half-ruined huts, whose bulging walls and smoke-blackened timbers were supported by wooden props. There were not more than thirty houses, all of a similarly squalid, miserable character, and as we entered the tiny place the cocks were crowing in the yards, for the sun had by this time fully risen.

"Five miles through yonder forest as the crow flies brings us into German territory," she said, indicating the dense wood behind the houses, then pausing before the door of one of the tumble-down huts, pushed it open, and invited me to enter.

The interior was one square room, with huge brick stove, the flat top of which served as bed in winter, a low sloping ceiling and two small windows with uneven panes of greenish glass that imparted to the rays of light a melancholy greyish tint. The bare miserable place was poorly furnished with wooden chairs, a rickety table, and a very old moth-eaten sofa covered with velvet that was once red, but now of faded brown. Over the door was nailed a cheap, gaudy ikon, and on the opposite wall was pasted a crude woodcut of his Majesty the Tzar.

The room was, indeed, in strange contrast to the dainty little drawing-room in Pembroke Road.

While I threw myself into a chair worn-out by fatigue, she removed the ugly wrapper from her head, and disappearing into a little inner den, the only other room in the house, soon reappeared with a steaming samovar, afterwards handing me tea with lemon.

The pale yellow sun struggling in through the thick green panes, fell in slanting rays across the carpetless room, and as we sat opposite one another sipping our cups we exchanged curious glances. Ours had, indeed, been a strange meeting.

She burst out laughing at last.

"Well," she said, "I see you are surprised."

"I am. I did not expect you had exchanged your life in London for this," I exclaimed.

"Ah! I was horribly tired of inactivity there. I had spent all my money, and could do nothing in your country. It is a drawback to be too well-known," she laughed.

"But surely this life is attended by very serious risks," I observed, noticing, as the sunlight fell across her hair, that she was still as handsome as ever, notwithstanding her ugly peasant costume and clumsy boots.

"Yes," she answered reflectively. "Perhaps, in a little while, when I have made more money I shall leave here and return to London. One cannot live without money."

"True," I answered. "Yet life here must be terribly dull and monotonous after Vienna and Paris."

"Ah!" she cried, with the slightest suspicion of a sigh. "All that I have forgotten long, long ago."

Her eyes were downcast, and I thought I detected tears in them. I gazed at her, this woman who was known in nearly every capital in Europe as one of the most daring and enterprising adventuresses of the century, half-fearing that she might still refuse to disclose her secret.

Chapter Thirty Four
Outcast

She moved slightly, raised her cup to her lips with a coquettish air, and on setting it down her dark bright eyes again met mine with inquiring glance.

"Well," she exclaimed. "Is it not strange that you, of all men, should be in Skerstymone?"

"I came to seek you," I said, looking earnestly into her pretty face.

"For what reason?"

"Because by your aid alone can I regain my lost happiness," I answered in deep earnestness. "Once, before you left London, you made certain allegations against Ella; but you failed to substantiate them, or to fulfil your promise in exchange for your passport."

"Yes, I remember."

"She is now my wife, and I have come to hear the truth from your own lips, Sonia."

"Your wife!" she gasped, glaring at me. "Has—has she actually dared to marry you?"

"Yes," I answered. "She has dared, because she loves me."

She remained silent, with knit brows, for a long time engrossed in thought.

Then briefly I told her how, after her departure, we had married, and related how suspicion had been aroused within me by her clandestine meetings with Cecil Bingham, her flight, and my subsequent discovery of her true position.

"Then you are aware who she really is," she observed slowly at last. "That she has dared to enter into a matrimonial alliance with you is certainly astounding. Indeed, it is incredible."

"Why?" I inquired in surprise.

"There are the strongest reasons why she should never have become your wife," she replied ambiguously.

"She lives apart from me. She has returned to her house in Paris," I said.

"Ah! it is best," she answered mechanically. "It is best for both of you."

"But we love one another, and although she fears to tell me the truth regarding all this mystery that has enveloped her for so long, you, nevertheless, are in a position to explain everything. Therefore I have come to you. You were my wife's friend, Sonia," I went on. "Tell me why she has acted with all this secrecy."

"Her friend," she echoed blankly. "Yes, you are right," she sighed. "It was a strange friendship, ours; she, a Grand Duchess against whom never a word of scandal had been uttered, and I—well I was notorious. The people in Vienna and Paris pointed at me in the streets, and fashionable women copied my manners and my dress. Yet there was, nay there still is, a strong tie between us, a tie that can never be severed."

"Tell me of it," I urged, when, pausing, she turned her pale agitated face away from me towards the small grimy window that overlooked the great sunlit steppe.

"Once I believed that she was your enemy, and told you so. I feared that because of her position she would never marry you. Yet it seems she was really in earnest, therefore I now withdraw that allegation. She evidently loves you."

"Yes, but we are living apart because she fears the revelation of some terrible secret if she acknowledges me as her husband."

"And that is why you have come here—to learn of her past!" she cried in a hoarse hollow voice, as if the truth had suddenly dawned upon her.

I nodded gravely in the affirmative, then told her of our meeting in Paris, and her refusal to make any satisfactory explanation.

"I envied Elizaveta once," she said reflectively at last. "I envied her because she was so supremely happy in your love. Yet it now seems as if I, degraded outcast that I am, have even more happiness and freedom."

"You were once her friend—she visited you every day. You can be her friend now; and by telling me the truth, bring joy and confidence to both of us. You can make our lives happy, if you only will."

"No," she answered coldly, her face hard and set. There was a cruel look in her eyes. "Why should I? Why should I strive for the happiness of one to whom I owe all my grief and despair?"

"Surely no misfortune of yours is due to her?" I protested quickly.

"Misfortune!" she wailed, her eyes flashing. "Would you not call the loss of the man you love, misfortune?" Then, in quieter tones, she added with a sigh, "Ah, you don't know, Geoffrey, how intensely bitter my strange, adventurous life has been. You believe, no doubt, that a woman of my character cannot love. Well, I thought so once. But I tell you that in London I loved one man; the only man I ever met that I could marry. I had renounced my past, and sought to lead a new life when I knew that he cared for me, and was preparing to make me his wife. But she, the Grand Duchess who tricked you so cleverly, came between us, and we were parted. Then I came here, to Russia, sought solace among my former companions, the scum of the gaols and ghettos, and have now descended in despair to what I am. By her, the woman you ask me to free from a terrible thraldom, I have been thrust back into hopelessness, and have lost for ever the one chance I had of joy and love."

Then, covering her handsome face with her hands, she burst into a torrent of tears.

"Come," I said, rising, and stroking her soft, silky hair. Her arms were upon the table, and she had buried her head in them, sobbing as if her heart would break. "Come, do not give way," I urged. "Who was the man you loved?"

"That concerns no one but myself," she murmured. "Even she has never had proof that we loved one another. Yet to her is due all this grief, that has fallen upon me."

Raising her head, she strove to suppress her emotion, and her brilliant tear-bedewed eyes fixed themselves steadily upon mine.

"I may perhaps be able to assist you," I said. "I did on a former occasion."

"No," she answered, in a voice of intense sorrow. "I have now grown careless of myself, careless of life, careless of everything since I left London. With the man I loved so truly I could have been happy always, yet she knew my past, and would allow me no chance to redeem myself. It is but what I deserve, I suppose, therefore I must suffer. But can you wonder that, hating the world as I do, I entertain a certain grim satisfaction in being leader of this ragged, ruffianly band of frontier free-lances?"

"No," I answered, echoing her sigh; "I am scarcely surprised, yet I cannot think that my wife, who was your friend, would willingly serve you as you believe."

"She did," Sonia answered, again raising her sad, dark eyes. "She alone I have to thank for the sorrow that has wrecked my life."

"What was the name of the man you loved?" I asked. "Do I know him?"

"Yes, you know him; but his name is of no consequence," she answered evasively, in a faint voice, lowering her eyes. "My secret is best kept in my own heart."

"If my wife did it unintentionally, without knowing you were lovers, there is some excuse," I said, half apologetically.

"No," she answered, with sudden harshness. "No excuse is possible. There were other circumstances which rendered her conduct unpardonable."

"I really can't believe it," I said. "I feel certain that she would never have exposed you willingly."

"Alas!" she said at last, "the evil is now done, and the stigma cannot be removed. But you asked me to reveal certain facts that would place her mind at rest, restore her confidence, and give her freedom. I have told you. I have made a confession to you that no other person has had from my lips."

"Ah, do not be pitiless," I cried imploringly, feeling assured that she alone knew the truth. Her assertion that she could restore my wife to freedom meant, I knew, the removal of that dark cloud of suspicion and dread that, overshadowing her, held her spellbound by fear. "Think," I urged, standing close to her, my hand resting upon the bare, unpolished table. "Once when you came to me, a stranger, and I rendered you a service, you promised to perform one for me in return when I desired it. I am now sorely in need of your friendship, and have come to you for aid."

"We shall be friends always, I hope, Geoffrey," she answered quietly, pushing back her dark hair from her brow. Her head was untidy and her hair tangled, for so callous had she grown that she took no heed either of attire or personal appearance.

"Then you will, at least, fulfil your promise," I said.

"No," she replied, with dogged firmness. "In this matter I absolutely refuse. I know how weary and wretched your life must be, with mystery surrounding you as it does, and being compelled to live apart from the woman you love; but, frankly, the fact that her cold, proud Highness fears to acknowledge you, or tell you the truth, is a source of satisfaction to me. She has sown dissension, and is now reaping her harvest of tears."

The cankerworm of care was eating out my heart, and I resolved to make one final appeal to her better nature, albeit I saw from her demeanour how embittered she was against Ella.

"No effort have I left unattempted to seek some solution of the problem," I said. "Yet all is unavailing. I have sought the truth from Cecil Bingham, but he refused to utter one word, and referred me to you. He said you knew all."

"Cecil Bingham!" she cried, suddenly starting. "Do you know him? He was your wife's friend."

"Yes," I answered. "I know that, although I am unaware of the true character of their relationship."

"Ah!" she ejaculated, and I thought she winced beneath my words. "He sent you here?"

"Yes," I said. "But before seeing him I had endeavoured to obtain some facts from another of Ella's acquaintances, Andrew Beck."

"Andrew Beck?" she repeated in a low, hollow voice, her brows contracting as if mention of his name were unpleasant to her ears. "You were jealous of him once," she added in a hard, dry tone.

"Yea," I smiled. "But I am so no longer."

"Why? I thought from what Ella told me long ago that you had some cause. He certainly was one of her admirers."

"Yes. But he's about to be married."

"Married!" she cried wildly, starting to her feet, her lips moving convulsively. "Andrew Beck?"

I nodded, for a moment surprised; but, suddenly remembering, I took from my pocket-book the newspaper cutting announcing the engagement.

Eagerly her strained eyes read the three formal lines of print, then hastily crushing the piece of paper in her hand she cast it from her with a gesture of anger. Her face was pale and determined, her thin hands, no longer loaded with rings as they once had been, twitched nervously, and I could plainly see the strange convulsion that the unexpected intelligence had caused within her.

"Do you know the—the girl who is to be his wife?" she stammered presently.

"No, we have never met," I answered. "His marriage does not, however, concern us for the moment. It is of Ella and her strange secret that I seek knowledge. Tell me the truth, Sonia, so that I may be able to place within her hand a weapon wherewith to combat this mysterious enemy she fears."

There was a long pause. Her breath came and went quickly in hot convulsive gasps. Her hands were so tightly clenched that their nails were driven into the palms; her mouth was firmly set, and in her eyes was a cold, stony stare. The knowledge of Beck's intended marriage had aroused within her a veritable tumult of passion.

"The truth!" she cried hoarsely at last, her hand upon her throbbing breast. "You ask me to clear suspicion from the woman whose whim it has been to marry you and I refuse, because I should bring her happiness, and remove from her the terror that now holds her enthralled. But I have reconsidered my decision. I—"

"Ah, tell me!" I exclaimed, interrupting her in my eagerness.

"I will speak because my disclosures, remarkable though they may be, will not only bring peace to you and your wife, but will also prove a trifle disconcerting to her companions. Once they hunted me from town to town as a criminal; they will now beg to me for mercy upon their knees."

"Tell me. Do not conceal the truth longer," I cried anxiously.

"No. Only in Elizaveta's presence will I speak," she answered, in a strained voice quivering with violent emotion. "Let us start for Paris to-night. When the moon rises I will guide you through the forest into Germany; we can cross the Jura by the bridge beyond Absteinen, and from Tilsit take train to Berlin. In two days we can be in Paris. Take me to her," she said with sudden eagerness, "and you shall both learn facts that will astound you."

"I am quite ready," I said; "I knew you alone would prove my friend."

"No," she answered, regarding me gravely. "No, Geoffrey. It is a secret full of grim realities and ugly revelations, which, when disclosed, will, I fear, cause you to hate me, and count me among your enemies. But you seek the truth; you shall therefore be satisfied."

Chapter Thirty Five
Confession

"Her Highness has this moment returned from driving, m'sieur," answered the big Russian concierge, when, accompanied by Sonia, I entered the hall of the great house in the Avenue des Champs Elysées, and handed him a card.

Then a second servant, in the blue-and-gold livery of the Romanoffs, conducted us ceremoniously along the wide, soft-carpeted corridor to the well-remembered room wherein I had taken leave of the woman I loved. My companion, in her neat, tailor-made travelling gown of dark grey cloth, looked a very different person to the dirty, unkempt peasant woman who led that band of desperate gaol-birds on the frontier, and as she glanced around the fine apartment on entering, she observed, with a slight sigh, that this was not her first visit.

The afternoon was breathless. All Paris had left for the plages of Arcachon, Dieppe, or Trouville, or the baths of Royat, Vichy or Luchon, and the boulevards were given over to unhappy business men, *café* loungers, and soft-hatted, gaping tourists in check tweeds. The green jalousies of the room were closed, the senses were suffused with a tender and restful twilight, for the glare had been tempered to suit the dreamy languor of that great mansion's world-weary mistress. The open windows admitted, with air, the faint sound of traffic from the Avenue. A lad passing somewhere outside whistled a few bars from the gay chansonette, "Si qu'on leur-z-y, f'rait ça," which Judic was singing nightly with enormous success at the Summer Alcazar. I noticed that upon the piano there still stood my own photograph, while that of my betrayer had been replaced by a picture of my wife.

With my back to the great tiled hearth, filled with ferns and flowers, and surrounded by its wonderful mantel of Italian sculptured marble, I waited, while Sonia, fatigued after our long and dusty journey, sank into one of the silken armchairs, unloosened her coat, and sniffed at her little silver bottle of smelling-salts. Scarce a word had she uttered during our drive across the city from the Gare de Lyon, so full she seemed of unutterable sadness.

During several minutes we remained in silence, when, without warning, the long doors of white-and-gold were flung open by the flunkey who, advancing into the room, announced his mistress.

Next instant we were face to face.

"Ah! Geoffrey. At last!" she cried, with flushed cheeks, a smile of glad welcome lighting up her pale countenance as she rushed towards me with both hands outstretched. A second later, noticing Sonia, she suddenly halted. Instantly a change passed over her face. She was unlike the gay, light-hearted girl who loved to idle up the quiet Thames backwaters, or punt along the banks at sundown. She was different from the happy, trustful bride who had wandered with me during those autumn days in quaint old Chateauroux. She had none of the flush of joyous youth, and the harder lines of resolve and determination were softened by an expression for which there is no better word than consecration. There were signs of endurance in her face, but it was the endurance of the martyr, not of the champion.

Facing Sonia, she drew herself up haughtily, and demanded in French in a harsh, angry voice,—

"To what, pray, do I owe this intrusion? I should have thought that after what has passed you would not dare to come here. But I suppose cool audacity is a characteristic which must be cultivated by a woman of your character."

Sonia rose slowly from her chair, her features haggard and blanched, her head bent slightly, as if in penitence. No effort did she make to resent the bitter, angry words my wife had uttered, but in a low tone simply replied,—

"I have come here with Geoffrey, to tell you the truth."

"The truth!" echoed the Grand Duchess, with withering contempt. "The truth from such as you! Who would believe it?"

"Wait! Hear me before you denounce me," Sonia urged, in a strange, hollow voice, that sounded like one speaking in the far distance. "I do not deny that my presence may seem unwarrantable. I admit that between us there can no longer be friendship, yet strange it is that, although you are honest, upright and respected, while I am a social outcast, spurned and degraded by all, there nevertheless exists a common bond between us—the bond of love. You love Geoffrey, the man who by law is your husband; while I love another, a man you also know;" and her voice faltered, "the man to whom you denounced me as base and worthless."

"Well?" asked Ella, standing stern, upright, full of calm, unruffled dignity. She still wore the cool-looking summer gown in which she had been driving in the Bois, and had not removed her large black hat with its long ostrich plumes.

"You are quite right, quite right," Sonia admitted in a voice trembling with emotion. "You were justified to undeceive him as you did. I know, alas! how black is my heart—how blunted is all the womanly feeling I once possessed, like you. But you have been nurtured in the lap of luxury, while I, fed from infancy upon the offal of a slum, and taught to regard the world from a cynical point of view, have grown old in evil-doing, and am now a mere derelict in the stream of life. Long ago we met, and parted. I treated you, as I did others, as an enemy. We have now met again, and I, conscience-stricken and penitent, have come to atone for the past—to prove your friend, to beg forgiveness."

My wife shrugged her shoulders with a gesture of quick impatience.

"Ah! You don't believe I am in earnest," cried the unhappy woman. "Has it never occurred to you that I alone can free you from the bond that has held you aloof from your husband?"

"What do you mean?" cried Ella, with a puzzled expression.

"I mean," she answered, in a deep, earnest voice. "I mean that if you will make full and open confession to Geoffrey I will furnish you with proof positive of the identity of the murderer of Dudley Ogle. By this means only can you obtain freedom from your bondage of guilt."

"My freedom!" echoed my wife. She was pale as death; her hot, dry lips moved convulsively, and she glanced at me in feverish apprehension. "How can you give me my freedom?"

"By revealing the truth," Sonia answered. "When you have told Geoffrey all, then will I disclose the terrible secret that I have selfishly kept from you because I envied you your happiness."

The silence remained unbroken for some moments. Ella stood with her gloved hands clasped before her. The haughty demeanour of the daughter of the Romanoffs had entirely forsaken her; with head bent she stood immovable as a statue. Terror and despair showed themselves in her clear, bright eyes. It seemed as though she mistrusted this woman of evil repute, whose assertions half induced her to confess to me.

"Come," Sonia said, "speak, and freedom, love and happiness are yours."

Her breast, beneath its lace and flimsy muslin, heaved and fell. Her fingers hitched themselves nervously in the trimming of her gown. Then, at last, with sudden resolve, she turned, and with terror-stricken eyes fixed upon me, said in English, in low, faltering tone, —

"To confess to you, Geoffrey, will cause you to hate, ah! even to curse me. After to-day I fear we shall part never again to meet."

"No, no," I cried, advancing to take her soft hand in mine. "Tell me your secret. Then let us hear what Sonia has to reveal."

"Ah! mine is a wretched, horrible story of duplicity," my wife faltered, standing in an attitude of deep dejection. "Although I am a Grand Duchess, the bearer of an Imperial name, I can hope for neither pity nor mercy from you, nor from the world outside."

"Why?"

"Because I have foully deceived you. I am a spy!"

"A spy!" I gasped, amazed. "What do you mean?"

"Listen; I will tell you," she answered, in a hard, strained voice, swaying slowly forward and clutching at the table for support. "Three years ago, when my mother, the Grand Duchess Nicholas, was still alive, we were spending some months as usual at our winter villa that faced the Mediterranean at St Eugene, close to Algiers, and my mother engaged as *valet de chambre* an Englishman. Soon this man grew, I suppose, to admire me. He pestered me with hateful attentions, and at last had the audacity to declare his love. As may be readily imagined, I scornfully rejected him, treated him with contempt, and finding that he still continued his protestations, meeting me when I went for walks along the sea-road to Algiers, or under the palms and orange groves in the Jardin Marengo, I one day in a fit of ill-temper, disclosed to my mother the whole of the circumstances. The fellow was at once discharged, but before he left for Europe he wrote me a letter full of bitter reproach, and expressed his determination to some day wreak vengeance upon me, as well as upon a young Englishman whom he suspected that I loved. His suspicions, however, were entirely unfounded. I, known at home and throughout all our family by the pet name of 'Tcherno-okaya,' or 'Sparkling Eyes,' a nickname taken from our Russian poet Lermontoff, had met this young Englishman quite casually, when one day, while passing through the Kasbah, I was insulted by two half-drunken Arabs, and he escorted me home. Then, when we parted, he told me that he was staying at the Hôtel de la Régence, opposite the great white mosque, and gave me his name. It was Dudley Ogle."

Chapter Thirty Six
The Thrall

"Dudley Ogle!" I echoed in blank amazement. "Are you certain that the servant's suspicions were devoid of foundation?"

"Absolutely," she answered in quick breathlessness. "In those days I was supercilious and disdainful, being taught to regard my dignity as Grand Duchess with too great a conceit to make a *mésalliance*. My mother used constantly to urge that in the marriages contracted by members of our family love was not absolutely necessary—position was everything. Well, the months went by. We left Algiers, returned to St Petersburg, and soon afterwards my mother died, leaving me alone. I found myself possessor of great wealth, and when, after a period of mourning, I reappeared in society, I was courted and flattered by all sorts and conditions of men. In a year I grew tired of it all and longed to return to England, the land wherein I had spent many years of my youth; therefore I engaged a woman to pose as my mother, and dropping my title, went to London and lived there as Ella Laing. Then I met you," and she paused, looking earnestly into my face with her deep blue eyes. To me she had embodied everything that was fair, honourable, and pure, yet I had dreaded some sinister peril from an unknown source.

"And we loved each other," I said simply.

"Yes," she went on fervently. "But from the first I was fettered, being unable to act as my heart prompted. I loved you fondly, and knew you wished to make me your wife, yet I dared not to risk such a step without the permission of our House. I went to St Petersburg, explained who and what you were, and craved leave to marry you. A family council was held, but the suggestion was unanimously denounced as a piece of sentimental folly. Ah, shall I ever forget that night? I pleaded to them upon my knees to let me obtain happiness in your love, but they were inexorable and refused.

At length, when in a moment of despair I threatened that if shut out from love by the barrier of birth I would end my life, a suggestion was made—a horrible, infamous one, prompted by Makaroff, Minister of the Household. Yet I was ready to commit any act, to do anything in order to secure happiness with you. Permission was given me to marry you on condition that I entered the Secret Service as spy. I appealed personally to the Tzar, but in vain. You were in the Earl of Warnham's confidence, and it was seen that from you I could obtain information which would be of greatest utility to our Foreign Department."

"So you accepted," I said sternly.

"Yes. I accepted their abominable conditions because I loved you so well, Geoffrey," she said gloomily, her trembling hand upon my shoulder. "It was not my fault, indeed it wasn't. If I had known what was to follow I would have killed myself rather than bring about all the trouble and disaster for which I became responsible."

"No," I said, "don't speak like that."

"I would," she declared despairingly. "What followed was a dark, mysterious tragedy, while all the time I knew that you must suspect— that, after all, you might forsake me. Within a week after binding myself irrevocably to the Tzar's army of spies I made a discovery that held me appalled. I found that my master, the man to whose will I was compelled to submit, was none other than our discharged *valet de chambre*—the man who two years before had declared his love. At the time my mother had engaged him he was already in the Secret Service, and had no doubt kept watch upon us. He came to me at 'The Nook,' and, exulting in the fact that I had become his puppet, renewed his protestations of affection. When, frankly, I told him that I hated him and loved only you, he at once informed me, with a grin of satisfaction, that the department in St Petersburg found it compulsory to obtain possession of a copy of a secret convention at that moment being concluded between your country and Germany, and that I must get possession of it at any cost, through you. It was in order that I might betray you that the Imperial permission had been given to our marriage. In indignation I refused, whereupon he threatened to expose me to you as a Russian spy, and I saw only too clearly that any such revelation must end for ever our acquaintance. He cajoled, urged, threatened, and explained all the elaborate precautions that had been taken by two clerks in Russian pay at your Foreign Office in order that on a certain day you should carry the precious document in your pocket, and how he had prepared the dummy envelope sealed with your Minister's seal. At last—at last, after striving long and vainly against the performance of this ignominious action that I knew must reflect on your honesty, I was compelled to submit. Ah! you can never know what agony I suffered. I verily believe that in those few days the terrible vengeance of that scoundrel drove me insane. The hideous ghost of the past causes me to shudder whenever I think of it."

I echoed her sigh, but no word escaped me. Her revelations were astounding. I had never suspected her of being actually a spy, although the discovery of the stolen convention in her escritoire had lent colour to that view.

"I deceived you," she went on in a hard, monotonous voice. "But only because I loved you so fondly, and dreaded that this man, who had long ago vowed to wreck my life, would expose, and thus part us. Yet I could not bring myself to commit the theft. How could I place upon you—the man who was all in all to me—the stigma of having traitorously sold your country's secrets? The man who held me enslaved, and whose attentions I had spurned, exulted in his malevolent revenge. Once he offered, if I would renounce all thought of you and treat him with more cordiality, to commit the theft himself; but I refused, determined at all hazards to remain with you as long as possible. Once it was thought that the secret convention would be sent to Warnham Hall, and I was compelled to go down there to devise some means of obtaining it. I found Dudley staying in the village, and we returned to London together. The end must soon come, I knew. Therefore I lived on in daily terror of what must follow. At last the day dawned on which I had to meet you at the Foreign Office, and filch from you the bond of nations. After breakfast I stood out on the lawn by the sunny river's brink, contemplating suicide rather than your ruin, when there rowed up to the steps Dudley Ogle, who hailed me, inviting me to pull up to Windsor, and there lunch with him. At once I accepted, and after embarking, told him of my dilemma, and besought his assistance. As you know, he was a good amateur conjurer, and skilled in feats of sleight-of-hand. Without thought of the consequences, he resolved to commit the theft for my sake, and when I had fully explained all the facts and given him the dummy envelope that the cunning chief of the *Okhrannoë Otdelenïe* had prepared, he turned the boat and put me ashore at 'The Nook,' afterwards rowing rapidly down to Shepperton to change and go at once to London."

"He did this because he loved you?" I exclaimed sternly.

"No," she answered reassuringly. "Poor Dudley was simply my friend. He called on you and extracted the document from your pocket while you lunched together, because he saw in what a dilemma I was. He knew I loved you dearly, and never once spoke a single word of affection to me. That I swear before Heaven. What followed his visit to Downing Street I have only a hazy idea, so full of awful anxieties was that breathless day. From Waterloo Station he telegraphed to me that he had successfully secured the agreement and handed it to the chief of spies. The latter, who had been waiting in Parliament Street expecting me, seeing him, took in the situation at a glance, and approaching him, asked for the document, which he gave up. An hour afterwards, fearing that you might suspect me, I telegraphed to you at Shepperton to dine with us, well knowing that already the text of the convention was at that moment being transmitted to Petersburg, and that war was imminent. You came; you kissed me. I loved you dearer than life, yet dreaded the frightful consequences of the dastardly act I had instigated. Suddenly, while we were at dinner, and you were laughing, happy and unconscious of the conspiracy against the peace of Europe, a thought flashed across my mind. I well knew that an awful conflict of armed forces must accrue from my deep, despicable cunning, and it occurred to me, as I sat by your side, that I would, using the secret cipher I had been provided with, telegraph to St Petersburg in the name of the chief of spies, assuring our Foreign Department that a mistake had been made. I slipped out, and running down to the telegraph office just before it closed, sent a message to an unsuspicious-looking address, stating that the text of the convention already sent had been discovered to be that of a rejected draft, and not that of the actual defensive alliance which had received the signature of the Emperor William."

"Then it was actually this message of yours that prevented war?" I gasped, in profound astonishment.

"Yes," she answered. "Before receipt of my telegram all preparations were being made for the commencement of hostilities, but on its arrival the Tzar at once countermanded the mobilisation order, and Europe was thereby spared a terrible and bloody conflict. Ah! that was indeed a memorable night, brought to a conclusion by a dark and terrible tragedy."

Her astounding disclosures held me dumbfounded. I remembered vividly how, during our lunch at the Ship, Dudley had risen and gone out to the bar to speak to an acquaintance. It was at that moment, having stolen the document from me, he glanced at its register number and imitated it upon the dummy with which Ella had provided him.

"But how came you possessed of the original of the convention?" I asked.

"A week before I fled from you I received it by post anonymously," she replied. "When compelled by my enemy to leave you and return here to my true position, I unfortunately left it behind, and knew that, sooner or later, you must discover it. The man who, with the Tzar's authority, held me under the lash, still holds me, the plaything of his spite, and threatens that if I allow you to come here and occupy your rightful place as my husband, he will denounce me to the British Government as a spy. Hence I am still his puppet, still held by a bond of guilt that I dare not break asunder."

"Be patient," urged Sonia, in a deep, calm voice. "Be patient, and you shall yet be free."

"Ah! Geoffrey," sobbed my wife, her blanched, tearful face buried in her hands, "you can never, I fear, forgive. After all, notwithstanding the glamour that must surround me as Grand Duchess, I am but a mean, despicable woman who foully betrayed you, the man who loved me."

"You atoned for your crime by your successful effort to preserve the peace of Europe," I answered.

"Yes, yes," she cried, with a quiver in her voice there was no mistaking for any note save that of love; "but, alas! I am in the power of an unscrupulous knave who parted us because he saw me happy with you. Can you ever forgive me? Can you, now you know of my unworthiness, ever say that you love me as truly as you did in those bygone days at 'The Nook'? Speak! Tell me?"

"Yes," I answered, fervently pressing her closely in affectionate embrace. "I forgive you everything, darling. You sinned; but, held as you have been by the hateful conditions imposed upon you by a base, unprincipled villain, I cannot blame, but only pity you."

"Then you still love me, Geoffrey?" she cried, panting, gazing up into my face.

For answer I bent until my lips met hers in a long fond caress. In those moments of ecstasy I was conscious of having regained the idyllic happiness long lost. Even though her story was full of bitter and terrible sorrow, and rendered gloomy by the tragic death of her self-sacrificing friend, the truth nevertheless brought back to me the joys and pleasures of life that not long ago I believed had departed from me for ever.

Again and again our lips met with murmured words of tender passion — she declaring that her crime had been flagitious and unpardonable, yet assuring me of what I now felt convinced, that her love had been unwavering. If it were not that she had resolved to renounce her title and become my wife she would never have fallen beneath the vassalage of the infamous scoundrel who sought her social ruin.

Thus we stood together locked in each other's arms, exchanging once again vows of love eternal, while Sonia stood watching us, sad, silent and motionless, save for a deep sigh that once escaped her. She knew that supreme happiness had come to the woman she had once denounced as my bitterest foe.

Chapter Thirty Seven
Conclusion

It was four o'clock on the following afternoon. The black, iron-studded doors of the Bank of England were just closing. The beadle mopped his brow. The traffic around the Royal Exchange was becoming more congested, as it·generally does at that hour, and perspiring clerks hurrying along Threadneedle Street sought the shady side, for the sun was still powerful. So hot indeed was the season that general permission had been granted everywhere in the City to wear the jacket suit and straw headgear reminiscent of Margate, in place of the conventional silk hat and frock coat. Although in the West the houses were mostly closed, and thousands were absent in the country and by the sea, the great, turbulent, bustling crowd that constitutes business London showed no sign of inactivity or decrease as, accompanied by my wife and Sonia, I walked up Old Broad Street to that pile of offices known as Winchester House, through the swing doors of which passed a constant stream of hurrying clerks.

By the lift we ascended to the second floor, and then passed down a long corridor to a door on which was inscribed the name "Mr Andrew Beck." We entered a large office of business-like aspect, where some dozen clerks were busy writing, and were informed that their principal, although absent, would return in a few minutes, therefore we decided to wait, and were ushered into a comfortable private room, one door of which opened on to the corridor.

Scarcely had we been seated a few moments when the click of a latch-key was heard in the door, and my friend Beck entered. He was well-dressed as usual, with a green-tinted carnation in his button-hole, and a glossy hat with brim of the latest curl stuck a trifle rakishly upon his head. The instant he confronted us the light died out of his face.

He drew himself up with a quick look of suspicion, while from his lips there escaped a muttered imprecation. Without further ado he turned on his heel, as if preparing to make a hurried exit, but in a moment Sonia, detecting his intention, sprang towards the door and prevented him.

"Well?" he asked, with a sorry endeavour to remain cool, "why are you all here? This is an unexpected pleasure, I assure you."

It was Sonia who, standing before him with dark, flashing eyes, answered in a tone of fierce hatred and contempt, —

"I have come, Andrew, to present my congratulations upon your forthcoming marriage," she said, with her pronounced foreign accent.

"They could have been conveyed by a penny stamp," he retorted impatiently.

"You taunt me, do you?" she cried in a towering passion. "You, the cunning, cowardly spy whom I shielded because you professed love for me. Had I spoken long ago you would have met with your deserts, either at the hands of the Nihilists, or at those of justice. Although myself a criminal I yearned for love, and foolishly believing that you cared for me, preserved the secret of your guilt, allowing you to wreck the happiness of Geoffrey Deedes, the man who twice proved my friend, and of Elizaveta, the only honest woman who ever spoke kindly to me or endeavoured to induce me to reform. Because you were chief of the Tzar's spies and I was notorious, with plenty of money always at command, you imagined that you held me irrevocably. Well, for a time, you did. Your false protestations of affection caused me to refrain from exposing your base, cunning, heartless infamy. It was you, with your renegade underling Renouf, who contrived to get me introduced to Elizaveta in order to further your own ends; but it was you also, when fearing that I might make some ugly revelations, made unfounded allegations against me to General Sekerzhinski, and informed him of my whereabouts, so that I was compelled to fly from Pembroke Road and seek shelter where I could."

His eyes were fixed upon her with a look of fierce hatred, and he muttered some incoherent words between his teeth.

"Yes," she went on defiantly, "I know you are anxious to close my lips, because of the startling disclosures it is within my power to make. The Department in St Petersburg have in you a keen, cunning spy, but when it becomes known throughout England that Andrew Beck, the popular Member for West Rutlandshire, is in the pay of the Russian Government, do you anticipate that you will still occupy your seat in the House of Commons, or at the Committee you have so ingeniously obtained for the investigation of the strength of England's defences?"

He started. His face was ashen pale; his cigar dropped from his nerveless, trembling fingers.

"Geoffrey," she went on, "has already heard from Elizaveta how cleverly you tricked her, and with what dastard knavishness you compelled her to instigate the theft of the secret convention. She—"

"Then the world shall know that the Grand Duchess Elizaveta Nicolayevna is in the Secret Service!" he cried fiercely. "She has betrayed her country and her kinsman, the Emperor!"

Sonia, smiling in contempt, said,—

"The denunciation will be your own condemnation."

"Why? What have I to lose?" he asked indignantly. "Your life. The police have not yet forgotten the tragedy at 'The Nook.'"

He glared at her open-mouthed.

"Perhaps it may be well at this moment to recall some facts that you may have found convenient to forget," she went on ruthlessly, while I, standing beside Ella, drank in eagerly every word. "You will remember where you reduced the stolen document to cipher, imitating Dudley's handwriting on the telegraph forms. It was at my house. The envelope containing the agreement had been opened in the 'cabinet noir' at the Embassy, the intention being to replace it at the Foreign Office. But it was I who broke the seal. In your hurry you left the document behind, and even when you returned two hours later, your mind was so full of other things that you did not remember it; so I gummed down the cut edges, and sent it afterwards to Elizaveta. When you came the second time you had with you a pair of men's gloves. Whose they were I knew not, but you got me to sew inside the index-finger of the left hand a tiny, jagged splinter of glass, and upon that glass, when you thought I did not observe you, you smeared some of that fluid that Ruyandez, the Haytian merchant, had given me long ago. That poison I kept locked away in a small cabinet, but many months before I had shown it to you and explained that it was some of that used by the Obeah men, and so rapid was it in effect that one single drop would cause paralysis of the heart within five minutes without leaving any trace of poison. You obtained a key to that cabinet, for when I had gone from the room on that afternoon I watched you unlock it, take out the reed containing the decoction, and prepare the glove."

"Liar!" gasped Beck. "I didn't touch it."

"The glove," she continued, "belonged to Dudley Ogle. That day Elizaveta had told him that you, a member of the English Parliament, was the chief of Russian spies, and you feared lest he should expose you, as no doubt he would have done if you had not, with cowardly cunning, taken his life."

"Murderer!" cried Ella, amazed. "You—you killed him! Ah! I suspected it. Tell us, Sonia, how it was accomplished."

"The gloves this man brought to my house were a pair he had taken up by mistake when at Shepperton on the previous evening. For cool and desperate plotting, the manner in which he killed the man he feared was astounding, for, having introduced into the finger of the glove the tiny piece of glass, he, during that evening at 'The Nook,' took out his victim's gloves from his overcoat in the hall and replaced them by those prepared. When Dudley left to walk home he bade farewell to you, and at once proceeding to put on his gloves, received a scratch on the finger so slight as to be almost unnoticeable, yet within five minutes the effects of the poison had reached his heart, and he was beyond human aid."

"Amazing!" I cried, regarding my whilom friend with intense loathing as he stood before us, his face a ghastly hue.

"It's untrue! Who will believe such a woman?" he cried.

"Everyone will," Sonia retorted quickly. "See, here is the proof," and she drew from her pocket a well-worn suède glove of dark grey, which I recognised at once as being one of the kind always worn by Dudley. "The splinter of glass is still inside."

The man who had led the double life of spy and legislator, and who had amassed a great fortune in his speculations in African gold, stood livid, with terror-stricken eyes riveted upon the evidence of his crime, like one transfixed.

"The Tzar will have no further employment for a murderer," exclaimed Ella at last. "Neither will the House of Commons permit a spy to sit in its midst. When I consented to enter the Secret Service of His Majesty, it was with one object—to obtain permission to marry. This I have attained, and because of Geoffrey's generosity and free forgiveness I have now no further fear of the opinion of the world or of revelations by a man who is proved to be a murderer. At last I have secured freedom from your hateful tie."

"Then you intend to denounce me?" Beck cried, glancing round with a wild, hunted look.

"Twenty-four hours from now I shall place Lord Warnham in possession of the whole of these curious facts. If you are still upon English soil, you will be arrested for the murder of my friend," I answered calmly. "I see plainly how, while I left you alone with the dead man, you placed in his pocket the brass seal found upon him, and how cleverly you managed to introduce the bogus passport and evidences of forgery among his possessions. Yours was a devilish ingenuity, indeed."

"If I fly you will not follow?" he gasped eagerly.

"Wherever you may hide you will be followed by your guilt," I answered. "A murderer can hope for no forgiveness from his fellow-men."

With his chin sunk upon his breast, and his wild eyes downcast, he stood in silence, leaning heavily against the wall. Then, slowly, with a final look upon him, I passed out behind my wife and the pale-faced woman who had so clearly substantiated her terrible charge. The vengeance he had sought to bring upon Ella had fallen upon him and completely crushed him.

In the library at Berkeley Square on the following afternoon I explained the whole of the startling facts, to the wizened, ascetic old Earl, who sat speechless in amazement when he realised that Andrew Beck was actually a foreign spy. It was during the conversation that followed I learnt that the man who had been loved by Sonia was Cecil Bingham, the young country gentleman who, known to both, had sought to assist Ella in unearthing the identity of Dudley's murderer. Sonia had misjudged my wife entirely, for she had never denounced her to Cecil, and the latter, being at that moment a guest in the Earl's house, was sent for, and before us all the pair became reconciled.

Elizaveta Nicolayevna, or Ella, as I still call her, has now renounced her country, and become thoroughly English. A year ago Lord Warnham, assured of my wife's probity—for greatly to Monsieur Grodekoff's dismay, she had given some valuable information regarding the activity of the Russian Secret Service at Downing Street—appointed me to a responsible post at our Embassy in Paris, so that we now live together at the big white house in the Avenue des Champs Elysées, while Sonia and Cecil are also married and live quietly in a quaint old manor-house near Winchester.

It was only the other day, however, that we heard mention of Andrew Beck, the popular legislator who so mysteriously accepted stewardship of the Chiltern Hundreds. There was a paragraph in the newspapers stating that he had been found drowned in the Scheldt, near Antwerp, and foul play was suspected. Then Ella explained to me that the woman who had passed as her mother, Mrs Laing, was, she afterwards discovered, a well-known Nihilist, and it was in order to keep observation upon her that the detective Renouf had entered her service. This woman, whose real name was Sophie Grunsberg, was greatly incensed against Beck on account of certain false accusations he had made against members of the revolutionary organisation, and there was little doubt that he had fallen beneath their far-reaching vengeance.

Here, as I pen these last few lines of my strange story of England's peril, my own betrayal, and my wife's fond love, Ella, with sweet, glad smile moves forward to stroke my hair with soft, caressing hand. The odour of sampaguita pervades her chiffons, stirring within me memories of the past. We are together in the room I know so well, with its great windows overlooking the leafy Avenue. It is warm, the sun-shutters are closed, and from somewhere outside the gay air, "Si qu'on leur-z-y f'rait ça" is borne in upon the summer wind.

At last our days are full of passionate love and idyllic happiness. Verily there is great truth in those words of Holy Writ, "Whoso findeth a wife, findeth a good thing."